T0293505

ROUTLEDGE LIBRARY EDITIONS:
THE ECONOMICS AND BUSINESS OF
TECHNOLOGY

Volume 43

THE TELECOMMUNICATIONS REVOLUTION

THE TELECOMMUNICATIONS REVOLUTION

Past, Present, and Future

Edited by
HARVEY M. SAPOLSKY, RHONDA J. CRANE,
W. RUSSELL NEUMAN AND ELI M. NOAM

Routledge
Taylor & Francis Group

LONDON AND NEW YORK

First published in 1992 by Routledge

This edition first published in 2018
by Routledge
2 Park Square, Milton Park, Abingdon, Oxon OX14 4RN

and by Routledge
711 Third Avenue, New York, NY 10017

Routledge is an imprint of the Taylor & Francis Group, an informa business

British Library Cataloguing in Publication Data
A catalogue record for this book is available from the British Library

ISBN: 978-1-138-50336-6 (Set)
ISBN: 978-1-351-06690-7 (Set) (ebk)
ISBN: 978-0-8153-6058-2 (Volume 43) (hbk)
ISBN: 978-1-351-11570-4 (Volume 43) (ebk)

Publisher's Note
The publisher has gone to great lengths to ensure the quality of this reprint but points out that some imperfections in the original copies may be apparent.

Disclaimer
The publisher has made every effort to trace copyright holders and would welcome correspondence from those they have been unable to trace.

The Telecommunications Revolution

Past, Present, and Future

Edited by
Harvey M. Sapolsky
Rhonda J. Crane
W. Russell Neuman
and Eli M. Noam

London and New York

First published 1992
by Routledge
11 New Fetter Lane, London EC4P 4EE

Simultaneously published in the USA and Canada
by Routledge
a division of Routledge, Chapman and Hall, Inc.
29 West 35th Street, New York, NY 10001

Typeset by LaserScript, Mitcham, Surrey
Printed in Great Britain by Mackays of Chatham PLC, Kent

British Library Cataloguing in Publication Data

The Telecommunications Revolution: Past, Present and Future.
  1. Telecommunication
  I. Sapolsky, Harvey M., II. Crane, Rhonda J., III. Neuman, W. Russell,
  IV. Noam, Eli M.
  384

ISBN 0–415–06771–5

Library of Congress Cataloging in Publication Data

The Telecommunications Revolution: Past, Present, and Future/edited by
Harvey M. Sapolsky, Rhonda J. Crane, W. Russell Neuman, Eli M. Noam
  Includes bibliographical references and index.
  ISBN 0–415–06771–5
  1. Telecommunication policy. 2. Telecommunication – Deregulation.
  3. Telecommunication policy – United States. 4. Telecommunication –
  United States – Deregulation. I. Sapolsky, Harvey M., II. Crane, Rhonda J.,
  III. Neuman, W. Russell, IV. Noam, Eli M.
  HE7645.T46 1992
  384′.068–dc20   91-26477
                         CIP

To: Ithiel de Sola Pool

respected colleague, teacher, scholar, and friend

Contents

Contributors

Alan Altshuler is Professor of Public Policy and Director of the Taubman Center at the Kennedy School of Government, Harvard University.

Jean-Pierre Chamoux is Director of Regulatory Affairs in the Ministry of Posts, Telecommunications, and Space in Paris, France.

Peter F. Cowhey is Professor of Political Science at the University of California at San Diego.

Rhonda J. Crane is Director, Federal Government Affairs, AT&T and was recently Senior Advisor for Science and Technology, Office of the United States Trade Representative, Executive Office of the President.

William H. Dutton is Professor of Communication and Public Administration, the Annenberg School for Communication, the University of Southern California.

Geza Feketekuty is Senior Policy Advisor in the Office of the US Trade Representative, Executive Office of the President and resident scholar at the International Trade Commission.

Jill Hills is Professor of Social Science at the City University of London.

Charles Jonscher is Vice President of Booz Allen & Hamilton International and is based in London.

Kevin Morgan is a Lecturer, Department of City and Regional Planning, University of Wales, Cardiff.

W. Russell Neuman is Director of the Audience Research Program at the Media Laboratory, the Massachusetts Institute of Technology.

Karl-Heinz Neumann is Director of Policy at the Institute for Telecommunications Services of the Bundespost in (West) Germany.

Eli M. Noam is a Professor in the Graduate School of Business at Columbia University and Director of the Center for Telecommunications and Information Studies. Recently he was a member of the New York Public Service Commission of the State of New York.

Douglas C. Pitt is Professor of Administration at the Business School, University of Strathclyde in Glasgow, Scotland.

Michael E. Porter is Professor of Strategy at the Harvard Business School and a corporate consultant.

Kenneth Robinson is Special Assistant to the Chairman of the Federal Communications Commission and previously served in the National Telecommunications and Information Administration in the Department of Commerce.

Harvey M. Sapolsky is Professor of Public Policy and Organization and Director of both the Communications Forum and the Defense and Arms Control Studies Program at the Massachusetts Institute of Technology.

Alfred C. Sikes is currently Chairman of the Federal Communications Commission. Previously he was Assistant Secretary of Commerce and Administrator of the National Telecommunications and Information Administration.

Marvin A. Sirbu is Professor of Engineering and Public Policy at Carnegie-Mellon University in Pittsburgh.

Peter Temin is Professor of Economics at the Massachusetts Institute of Technology.

Lester C. Thurow is Dean of the Sloan School of Management at the Massachusetts Institute of Technology and a prominent commentator on economic trends and policies.

Tetsuro Tomita is Special Assistant to the Chairman of Fuji TV and was previously Vice Minister of the Ministry of Posts in the Government of Japan.

Eberhard Witte is Professor and Director of the Institute for Organization at the University of Munich and was the chairman of the commission that recommended changes in the structure of West German telecommunications.

Preface: Decentralization and deregulation on the march

Harvey M. Sapolsky

These are heady, confusing times in the telecommunications business. What until recently has been in most countries a very predictable, largely bureaucratic undertaking that provided basic telephone service and little else is being transformed nearly everywhere into a dynamic, mainly commercial enterprise that offers consumers a growing, some would say bewildering, number of sophisticated communications options. Privatization is reducing the scope of public administration in telecommunications. Competition rather than monopoly is increasingly the market norm. Telecommunication suppliers, managers, and regulators, whose comfort was guaranteed in past regimes, are groping desperately to find places in a rapidly evolving, very challenging system.

The demand for telecommunication services is expanding, but so too is the capacity to provide them. The pace of technological progress has been great, perhaps causing, certainly benefiting from the significant structural changes that have been occurring in the industry. On the horizon is the promise of even more progress as once intentionally separated technologies begin to blend together and find complementarity.

This book examines the origins and likely consequences of the great changes currently affecting telecommunications policy worldwide. A major focus of attention appropriately is the situation in the United States because it significantly influences policy elsewhere. Nevertheless, several studies of other leading industrial countries are included and a number of the essays seek explicitly to identify the political and policy differences that persist among these countries.

The book grew out of a symposium held to commemorate the many contributions of Ithiel de Sola Pool to the field of communications research. During the three decades that Ithiel was a member of the political science faculty at the Massachusetts Institute of Technology (MIT), he influenced the careers and work of hundreds of students and colleagues. Although most can recall some uniquely helpful suggestion that was offered while collaborating on a project or during a seminar discussion, all were inspired by Ithiel's ability to combine so effectively on an international scale a deep involvement in practical affairs with enduring scholarship. It is appropriate that this volume include essays by academics, officials, and executives from around the world.

Ithiel's interests were catholic. He made significant contributions to social science methodology (including pioneering work in content analysis, in structure of social networks, and in the computer simulation of political phenomena), to the understanding of social and political development in which, in Ithiel's view, communications played a central role, and to the effects of changing communications technologies on the exercise of liberty. He was a master builder of institutions – not least of which were MIT's Political Science Department, its Center for International Studies, and its Communications Policy Research Program and Communications Forum. And in his role of wise and demanding teacher, he never failed to motivate students, encouraging them to seek out new paths just as Ithiel did himself. Ithiel focused on telecommunications policy in his last decade, as found in his award-winning *Technologies of Freedom* which has gained ever increasing scholarly attention and admiration. This work tells us that, if we are to achieve the full benefits of liberty, we must think about the structure of the systems by which we communicate as much as we think about what we say.

Revolutionary is a descriptive over-used by social scientists to trumpet changes both small and large. Ithiel early claimed that developments in communications technologies would have revolutionary impact on many aspects of society. Once skeptical about Ithiel's tenaciously held pronouncement, Lester Thurow, the Dean of the MIT School of Management and author of our first chapter, is now almost a believer. Thurow thinks it is possible that the computer and associated technologies may deserve rank with the most profound inventions of modern times, but he wonders when their envisioned benefits will be fully realized. The office and the city, he argues, still function much the same way they did before billions were invested in advanced business communications. Most machines sit idle on office desks and the centers of cities remain crowded. Perhaps, he suggests, we need to rethink the uses of these technologies.

Some new thinking has been done, if not about the efficient application of communications technologies then about their regulation. Eli

Noam, a lawyer, an economist, a professor at Columbia University, and recently a member of the New York Public Service Commission, believes that the restructuring of communications is following a broader social pattern visible in several fields – the breakup of integrative networks. Large, sophisticated users find advantage in separating from public networks to establish their own. Noam argues we may need to build a global regulatory framework to reassert integrating values once so much the goal of communication expansion.

The origins of the regulatory changes that led to the restructuring of telecommunications in the United States is the subject of Alan Altshuler's chapter. Altshuler, a political scientist who directs the Taubman Center at Harvard University's Kennedy School of Government, traces the intellectual history of deregulation in the United States. He argues that the recent wave of deregulation marks an important and perhaps rare triumph of ideas in the policymaking process. Good fortune and persistence permitted the economists' concern for enhanced competition to overcome long dominant interests that wished to limit the free functioning of markets.

Peter Temin, a leading economic historian and the author of *The Fall of the Bell System*, elaborates on the deregulation theme by examining the famous Carterfone and MCI cases. An important issue in debates over regulation is whether or not regulation can keep pace with technological change. Temin maintains that regulation does not always lag technology; at times regulators may intentionally seek to stimulate technological change. He worries that excessive enthusiasm for technological change will not permit full consideration of the economic consequences of major innovations for industry and especially for market-leading firms.

In the hope to avoid random policy change, the United States government has periodically reviewed the nation's opportunities and needs in telecommunications. Kenneth Robinson, a senior civil servant who directed *NTIA Telecom 2000*, the most recent report on telecommunications, describes the purpose of the study and its major findings. *NTIA Telecom 2000* argued that the same technological, economic, and social forces that led to deregulation in the United States affect other nations and mandate removal of restrictions on competition for them as well. The report records the significant beneficial impacts telecommunications developments have on society, noting that these benefits will accumulate faster if markets for telecommunications goods and services are unfettered.

Agreeing on the desirability of increasing competition is not enough. Needed also is a clear understanding of how and when it is achieved. Michael Porter of the Harvard Business School examines the ways by which regulators have pursued the supposedly common goal of increasing competition in telecommunications. He notes their frequent failure to view competition as a dynamic process with the prevailing tendency being to draw narrow definitions of markets, to ignore the power of buyers, and to overestimate barriers to entry. A better approach, he suggests, is to view competition as companies do, as the elusive search for advantage in a strategically uncertain environment. Forced into this situation, some companies at least will innovate, providing consumers with the enormous benefits of increased choice.

The divestiture by AT&T of its local operating units, the recent major watershed in United States telecommunications policy, is the topic of the chapter by Kevin Morgan and Douglas Pitt, British researchers who are acute observers of the American scene. Morgan and Pitt use the term 'regulatory turbulence' to describe the disjointed, often conflicting policy mandates that the American political system offers its domestic communications industry. Competition for control among political authorities and jurisdictions yields incoherent guidance to an industry struggling to adjust to the vastly more competitive equipment and service markets that resulted from divestiture. The pushing and hauling among domestic interests, they argue, leaves the American industry vulnerable to competitive erosion from foreign rivals, many of which have the strong support of their governments in trade matters. Deregulation in one country, the thrust of US policy to date, it seems has serious consequences which Morgan and Pitt believe need a more unified, interventionist approach to telecommunications by government agencies to correct than the US political system is likely to muster.

William Dutton, a political scientist at the University of Southern California, places the complexities of telecommunications regulation in a theoretical context. Dutton suggests that an ecology of games perspective best explains the politics that underlie the regulation. The incoherence so visible in the practice is the product of different sets of interests seeking to fulfill independent and even unrelated agendas involving overlapping resources. One set worries about anti-trust matters, another about trade, still another rate and service regulation with interacting, but uncoordinated effects. The decentralized nature of the system and its incoherent goals stand in sharp contrast to that of other nations and not necessarily favorably.

The chaos of American policy debates notwithstanding, one issue – the deterioration in America's trade position – has gained extraordinary attention. Of course, solutions vary. Some wish management reforms. Others blame a decline in national research and education investments. Still others prefer a mercantilistic alternative if only to counter what they see as the similar policies of America's major trading partners. But Charles Jonscher, a London-based observer of the communications industry, views the American trade dilemma differently. It is the product, he argues, not of corporate inefficiency, government under-spending, or open markets, but rather of gluttony. Americans have had a party, a very big party, he says, with borrowed money. No one should fault Americans for wanting a party, Jonscher says, but only for avoiding the tab. Other countries, with a bit more self-discipline, he suggests, could benefit by moving toward the liberalization that characterizes American trade policy.

This liberalization can and will spread internationally, Alfred Sikes argues in the next chapter. Sikes, Assistant Secretary of Commerce in the Reagan Administration and now Chairman of the Federal Communications Commission, believes that deregulation in the United States is stimulating liberalizing reform in the telecommunications policies of other countries. He cites a number of initiatives taken and reports prepared by the leading industrialized nations favoring increased competition and open markets for telecommunications. These nations recognize that the opportunities provided by new communications technologies can be realized fully only when liberalization occurs. The policy changes are not without risks, he points out, especially in short-term trade balances, but they are the key to long-term productivity and prosperity.

As if to second these thoughts, Eberhard Witte and Karl-Heinz Neumann recount the German experience in telecommunications. Witte, a professor at the University of Munich, was the chair of a commission that reviewed the policy options for Germany. Although there are constitutional obstacles in Germany to the privatization of all telecommunications functions, the recommendation was for substantial institutional change to permit greater competition. Karl-Heinz Neumann of the Bundespost reports on progress toward that objective. The political consensus achieved by the Witte commission, he indicates, has led to a freeing of several important communications markets, but only with the establishment of certain regulatory controls and with the maintenance of the monopoly for the basic telephone network. Although these changes may not satisfy every advocate of competition, they do represent major liberalization steps in the German context.

Jean-Pierre Chamoux, Director of Regulation in the French Ministry of Posts, Telecommunications, and Space, outlines the reforms that over the past two decades have revitalized the telecommunications field in France. What was once one of Europe's most limited telephone systems has been transformed into its most pioneering. Especially affected have been new services which are mainly privatized and competitive. But as Chamoux points out, the basic telecommunication system remains publicly owned and thus subject to the vagaries of politics despite its recent modernization.

In telecommunications, world attention is focused increasingly on Japan which has taken a dominating lead in many user equipment markets and which has yet to exercise its full economic strength. Tetsuro Tomita describes the history of Japanese telecommunications policy including some pending reforms. It's a history that Tomita knows well for throughout his tenure as an official in the overseeing ministry he was an advocate for increased liberalization of Japanese markets and practices. From the Geisha house communications network which he sought to create in anticipation of the 1964 Olympics but which was only realized after the event, to the 1985 Telecommunications Business Law, Tomita pressed for reductions in monopoly powers assigned to the major national carriers. The success of these efforts has important implications for progress in both international trade and domestic Japanese services.

Jill Hills of London City University provides a comparative perspective on attempts at structural reform in telecommunications. In a comprehensive essay she traces the experience in the United States, Britain, and Japan. Policy options, Hills argues, are broadly limited by the opportunities afforded nations by their technological prowess and their international competitive positions, but within these bounds variations in traditions of business–government relations are largely determinant. But in each of these nations bureaucratic competition for jurisdiction is becoming a more important factor, she notes. As a result, there is an increasing politicization of telecommunications policymaking.

Delineation of the power struggle within telecommunications policymaking is the task Marvin Sirbu undertakes in the chapter that follows Hills'. Sirbu, a professor of engineering and public policy at Carnegie-Mellon University in Pittsburgh, describes a multidimensional battle for network control among users, suppliers, and carriers. Each of the contenders attempts to define network relationships for special advantage and seeks to promote technologies that reinforce their power relative to the others. The outcome, Sirbu foresees, raises again the concern expressed earlier by Noam for the loss of integration in a world of many networks.

Peter Cowhey, a political economist on the faculty of the University of California at San Diego, examines the trade implications of the evolving telecommunications regime. Although throughout the world liberalization is on the march, Cowhey notes that there is also increasing emphasis on verification of the promised results and protection of rights for users. Corporate alliances will develop across national boundaries, he believes, and these alliances will both desire and force the creation of an international regulatory system. In turn, international developments will mandate further alterations in domestic regulatory arrangements. There is, it seems, a circle to close. What begins in one country reverberates around the world, affecting the originating agent eventually.

Some of the consequences of a failure to bound international trade competition are revealed in Rhonda Crane's chapter. Crane, recently the Senior Advisor for Science and Technology and American Electronics Association Fellow in the Office of the US Trade Representative, reviews the history of color television standards and the current debate on policy for high definition television, which she describes as a major development with potential for wide impact on the future of the telecommunications industry. Winning the standard for the new television system will bring billions in manufacturing opportunities. She argues that without better coordination within government and better cooperation between government and business than so far has been demonstrated, the United States is likely to lose this contest and perhaps much more.

What is at stake are shares of the world information economy according to Geza Feketekuty, a policy authority on trade issues and currently on loan to the International Trade Commission from the Office of the US Trade Representative. The combination of computers and telecommunications technologies per- mits the global management of enterprise based on the rapid and long distance exchange of information. The international trade system is beginning to recognize this new reality and the opportunities it permits for increased consumer welfare. Negotiations to secure the benefits are underway although they will be complex because of the many issues involved.

Theory has become practice. Throughout the world, deregulation is now the policy guide in telecommunications. And with the triumph of deregulation, the challenge, as Russell Neuman, Director of the Audience Research Program at the Media Laboratory, MIT, points out in the Epilogue, becomes to develop new theories and to improve practice to cope with greater domestic and international competition, accelerated technological change, and expanded diversity and decentralization in telecommunication networks.

*   *   *

Several of those forever in Ithiel Pool's debt collaborated to make this volume possible. Ivan Shefrin, one of Ithiel's last students, suggested the theme and the format for the symposium at which several of the papers collected here were originally presented. Joining the program committee for the symposium were two of Ithiel's doctoral students, Rhonda Crane and Richard Solomon; an undergraduate thesis student, Carolyn Cook; Ithiel's son Adam; a research associate, David Allen; and three of Ithiel's faculty colleagues, Eugene Skolnikoff, Russell Neuman, and myself. Eli Noam, one of Ithiel's intellectual disciples, stepped forward from the symposium rostrum to aid in converting the proceedings into a book and in attracting new contributors. AT&T kindly provided a grant that facilitated MIT sponsorship of both the symposium and the book. It was, as I believe will be obvious from this volume, a collaboration that was both enjoyable and enlightening. We are grateful to the many who assisted us in this fitting tribute to a major communications visionary, but especially to Jean Pool whose interest in the project provided great encouragement.

Harvey M. Sapolsky
for the editors
Cambridge, Massachusetts

Chapter 1

Is telecommunications truly revolutionary?

Lester C. Thurow

More than a decade ago I heard Ithiel Pool say there was going to be a computer telecommunications revolution. I was skeptical. Now I am much less of a skeptic. Historically only two inventions have revolutionized our industrial world.

The train speeded up transportation from one point to another. I much remember a history book pointing out that Napoleon's army did not move any faster than Julius Caesar's army. Two thousand years, and armies moved exactly the same way with horses and carts moving as fast as human beings could walk. The internal combustion engine and the automobile are not that important. If they had not been invented, we would have had a lot more street railways, and perhaps not quite as much suburbanization, but the world would look approximately the same without the automobile as it looks with it.

The other major invention is electricity. It clearly revolutionized the world in all kinds of ways. It made night usable. I periodically climb mountains in the Himalayas and get to villages where there is still no electricity. To live in a world with absolutely no electricity, no batteries, no lights, is a very different experience from the life most of us are used to. Electricity essentially changed night into day and altered human habits in profound ways.

Is the computer telecommunications revolution equivalent to trains and electricity? We will not be sure until we look back on it, but I am more persuaded today that Ithiel Pool was on to something, and that this could be a third major revolution.

In business schools we talk about MIS (management information systems) and refer to telecommunications systems as if they were ways to bring information to managers for them to do a better job. I am convinced that what is going on is more fundamental in the sense that the telecommunications industry is becoming the production technology of many industries. Finance is a good example. Finance has become a technological enterprise. The financial institution that can bring information from Hong Kong to New York five seconds faster than some other group does not make part of the arbitrage profits – it makes all of the arbitrage profits.

Look at who the banks have been hiring recently. Salomon Brothers last year hired as many computer programmers and telecommunications experts as they did financial experts. A gentleman came into my office the other day and was absolutely convinced that the Japanese banks were going to drive every other bank in the world out of business because they were willing to put up satellites and build better telecommunications networks than the banks in Europe and the United States. They were going to be able to move information around the world faster and a few pennies cheaper per document than anybody else. They were going to turn finance into manufacturing. The one who can produce a product the cheapest and the fastest wins; and they were going to win because of their superior technology. He may be wrong about the Japanese advantage. At Citibank the person in charge of computer telecommunications has a budget of one billion dollars. One company one billion dollars to invest in telecommunications in one year.

Technology certainly changes the world capital markets. In one sense, Alan Greenspan, the Chairman of the Federal Reserve Board, and every other central banker in the world, has become technologically obsolete. Alan Greenspan is in charge of *the* American money supply. But in today's world, because of technology, there is no '*the* American money supply.' There is a world money supply. We can instantly borrow dollars or Euro dollars or Euro yen or Euro marks in London without ever being there. Those transactions do not have anything to do with any central banker in the world. I could buy and sell a house in Boston by using German marks. You could do a deal in the Bahamas without ever being in the Bahamas. We have major institutions like national central banks that are becoming obsolete.

Central banks can collectively control *the* world money supply – and there is a world money supply – but they cannot control it individually. The way we regulate, operate, and do our economics will have to be quite different because of the telecommunications revolution that has occurred.

After the Second World War, we had capital controls. They were difficult to enforce in the good old days, but today we could not make them work at all. How would you monitor financial transactions across national boundaries if they are done with personal computers (PCs)?

If you look at the Brady Commission's report on why the stock market fell in October 1987, it perfectly illustrates a group of human beings who are presumably intelligent, writing a report that is technologically obsolete. The Brady Commission wrote about the fall of the American stock market as if it was the only stock market in the world that fell. Almost no word about any other markets falling. They blamed the fall on telecommunications computer trading. Portfolio insurance and program trading supposedly brought the system down. The interesting point is that London was crashing for five hours before New York crashed and London does very little portfolio insurance or computer trading compared to New York. Stock markets have also managed to crash hundreds of times, hundreds of years before anybody invented this technology. The Mississippi Bubble, Tulip Mania, the South Sea Bubble, the Great Crash of 1929, all managed to occur without computers and telecommunications.

If one reflects on the Brady recommendations, how would you stop program trading? Suppose you wanted to stop it. How would you do that, in a technical sense? This is a little like stopping sex between consenting adults. Can one really stop people in the privacy of their own office from looking at their computers and using their telephone to trade stocks, bonds, and commodities around the world?

Computer telecommunications has effectively become the modern devil that is blamed for everything wrong. If a package does not get delivered to my house, what went wrong? Well, the computer did it. Exactly the same thing happening on the stock market. We needed a convenient scapegoat to blame for what went wrong, and computer telecommunications took the blame.

The telecommunications revolution has two important economic puzzles. It was widely predicted when the revolution began that computer telecommunications would decentralize economic activity because it would make it much cheaper to move information from one place to another. And you can find examples of decentralization, like Citibank processing all its credit cards in Sioux Falls, South Dakota rather than in New York City. But the aggregate data show precisely the opposite. We *are* piling up, in record amounts, in narrower geographic areas. Big central cities around the world are growing. If a city is a financial capital plus a government capital, probably 40 per cent of all the people in the entire country live there. This is true in South America, in Japan, in Britain. Where you would predict decentralization, the technology somehow seems to be contributing to centralization. It is clear that, in the aggregate – despite dramatic examples like Citibank out in Sioux Falls – something very different is happening.

The second puzzle concerns productivity. Computer telecommunications is a wonderful new technology, with wondrous capabilities. It should make productivity grow faster, which makes the standard of living grow faster. Thus this technology is going to pay off in a higher standard of living than we would otherwise have.

Again, the data belie these expectations. Precisely those industries that are most intensively using this technology have the worst productivity performance. In fact, the industries using it the most generally have negative productivity growth, like financial services. Financial services are certainly using telecommunications to move information around the world, to do new things such as computer accounting, to service customers with ATM machines, the robots of the financial world. But no matter how you measure productivity in financial services in the United States, it is falling. For every employee exiled from a little branch bank that no longer has any employees in it, banks are adding two employees in the telecommunications office to replace the one from the old-fashioned office.

Financial services in the United States have had negative productivity growth for the last ten years. Every year productivity is falling about 1 percent. Part of the explanation is reasonably clear. We find that maintenance expenses are soaring. The conventional computer system that a company might buy requires annual maintenance expenses that are half the original purchase price. It takes an enormous amount of labor and supplies to keep these systems running. The enormous labor force necessary to maintain the systems has more than offset the productivity gains.

This problem is not limited to finance. The worse the productivity performance the more that industry is using computer telecommunications systems. Is this just a temporary phenomenon – that it takes a while to get used to new technology so people can use it efficiently? Or is this something where the payoff ultimately comes much later when ways of doing business actually change? One could argue the issue both ways. One answer may be that Ithiel Pool was right: It is a real revolution, which means we have to do things differently as opposed to just automate the old.

Consider office automation. If you think about the model office, it is remarkably similar to the office that was invented in Florence during the

Renaissance. The way we shuffle paper around the system has not changed much in 500 years. And then we bring in office automation and we simply automate exactly the same paper shuffling that we were doing before we automated. That may very well be a way you cannot make the system pay off. When I walk into business firms in the United States, every desk has a computer terminal and a telecommunications system attached to it, and I would bet that 95 percent of them are seldom turned on.

Recently we have been putting about half of the total investment in the United States into computers and telecommunications. Putting half of the investment for an entire country into an area that does not pay off in productivity creates a major problem. At some point we will either have to do it differently or quit doing it at all. From an industrial point of view, that is going to be the key question over the next five or ten years.

Chapter 2

Beyond the Golden Age of the public network

Eli M. Noam

Telecommunications policy today is an environment in which there are many battle-hardened troops, but too few strategists. There is an abundance of activities, plans, facts, fights, but only a limited analytical apparatus. We are in short supply of the Ithiel de Sola Pools, just who we need the most to get us beyond the traditional concepts that have organized thinking in this field.

What are these concepts? I find four main ones that are the golden calves worshipped by professional associations and denominations. For technologists, the primary organizing concepts in telecommunications policy are economies of scale and their first cousin, standardization. Economists worship at the altar of competition – in this case genuflecting to the triad of structure, conduct, and performance. What is an increasing disenchantment with this view is represented more in academia than in the regulatory environment. Lawyers, third in this field, judge policy issues in terms of conflict of interest, which translates here into a potential for cross-subsidies. Structures that make such cross-subsidies theoretically possible must be avoided, hence the AT&T divestiture. Finally, many social scientists, as well as most politicians and journalists, organize reality in telecommunications policy around the concept of income distribution, that is, around the question of who pays more, who pays less.

All of these concepts have legitimacy but they have been carried by their proponents to the edge of explanatory power and then some. Used single-mindedly, these notions have degenerated to rallying slogans. Perhaps the greatest common failing is that they engage in what I would call supply-side telecommunications. That is, they look at the subject from the angle of production and producers: AT&T versus MCI, inter-exchange carriers versus local exchange companies, enhanced versus basic services providers, voice versus record, and so on.

It is not surprising that this should be the natural way to look at things. After all, regulators deal primarily with carriers, technologists with networks, economists with competitors, and journalists have a horse race angle to their coverage. But this supply-oriented perspective obscures its reverse. What we need to do is engage in what could be called a demand-side telecommunications analysis. What does this perspective mean? At its most basic, we should not think of telecommunications as a service produced by carriers but as an interaction of groups and subgroups in society, facilitated by service vendors that we call carriers. The supply structure, if left to its own devices, is a reflection of the underlying interaction of communication users with each other within an all-encompassing user coalition, which we call the public network, or in several smaller user groupings along other dimensions.

Thus, we should not see deregulation and divestiture as a policy of primarily liberalizing the entry of suppliers. Just as important, it is the liberalization of an exit by some partners from a previously existing sharing coalition. Telecommunications are only one instance for widespread ascendancy in recent years of centrifugalism in previously shared social arrangements. Wherever you look, people break up all kinds of networks of interaction and form new ones. Examples abound – the public school system, the mass transit system, public safety, dispute resolution, health provision, to name a few. The departure from the public school system, for example, cannot be explained primarily by the supply of new options or by new technology but rather by an increased demand to exit. In a similar sense, recent centrifugal development in independent electric power generation had very little to do with new technology.

Perhaps it is useful to ask ourselves why it seems that there is usually only one public telephone network in each country. It is not the interconnectedness of all participants or else we would have only one large bank for all financial transactions. Interaction does not usually require institutional integrations, and this was one of Adam Smith's major insights. To distinguish telecommunications from this observation by labeling it 'infrastructure' requires us to define that term, which is almost impossible to do.

No explanation is natural monopoly. Maybe it exists for a local exchange area, but the examples of the United States, Canada, Denmark, Finland, and several other countries show that this does not prove that a widespread horizontal integration of local exchange areas is required. And if it were, why do they miraculously have national frontiers? If we look at the birth of the monopoly system in the sixteenth and seventeenth centuries and the establishment of European postal monopolies, we see that the monopoly was unnaturally caused by politics of the revenue needs of the state, rather than by second-order conditions of production functions.

Perhaps the best way to look at the network is as a cost sharing arrangement among several users. If fixed costs are low, a new participant C can help A and B to lower the costs. This situation could be compared with the economics of swimming pools or national defense, both of which may be regarded as a public good. But although there is only one national defense system, there are many swimming pools – some of them public communals, others private communals, and still others exclusive ones.

There is a wide spectrum between the pure private good and the pure public good. We may want to share the pool with a few dozen families but not necessarily with thousands. A few might admit everyone; some maybe only admit one. The many cases in between include the telecommunications network. It is not a private good, yet it does not meet the two conditions for a public good, namely non-excludability and non-rival consumption. Indeed, non-excludability had to be established by law, and we call it universal service obligation.

What has been happening in recent years to telecommunications is what goes by the more dramatic label of 'divestiture.' Deregulation is merely a shift in the degree of intermediateness – of the intermediate position between public and private. The formation of such intermediate collective consumption and production arrangements is carefully analyzed by theorists of clubs. One can apply economic club theory to networks and show that different user groups tend to cluster together in associations according to dimensions of price, interactive density, and ease of internal decisionmaking, provided that they have mobility of choice. This can be called voting with one's telecommunications node. A reasonable assumption is that economically optimal association size will not encompass the entire population. Alfred Kahn used to put it as follows, 'People who don't have a telephone, I don't want to talk to.'

It is generally inefficient to attempt income transfers by integrating diverse groups and imposing varying cost shares according to some equity criteria. It is more efficient to allow homogeneous groups to form their own associations and then redistribute by imposing charges on some groups and distribute to others. The incentives to group formation can lead, where legally permitted to do so, to arrangements shared by alternative network associations. The process could be called the tragedy of the common network because it is not the failing of the traditional arrangement but, ironically, its success that undermines it. The success of communalism creates the forces of particularism. In the early stages, the first network participants affirmatively seek additional participants to share costs and enhance their reach. They try to prevent new arrangements, but in time they pay a price for it because democratizing participation leads to democratizing of the control of cost sharing in a way that is redistributory. And over time the redistributory burden grows.

Furthermore, in time, the volume of the first users, who ultimately become the largest users, has risen so high that they can account for much of the cost savings of sharing just among themselves. They therefore try to form alternative network associations for large parts of their communication needs – first in-house and later with their closest suppliers, customers, and market participants. An illustration of this is found in Wall Street's 1987 Black Monday, where one would expect an enormous increase in communications traffic but the public network in lower Manhattan and the financial district increased its usage by only 10 percent over normal.

In the United States, the Golden Age of the public network, in which substantial universal service coincided with group substantial monopoly, was as brief and romanticized as the cowboy era; it lasted about twenty years from 1950, but in the mid-1960s centrifugal forces began their assault. This time-span coincides with the beginning of computer data communications as a major form of usage. In Western Europe and Japan, universal service was behind that of the United States; but it was achieved in the last ten years or so and now centrifugal forces have begun to gather there too.

Where does this all lead? It leads to normalization – nothing dramatic. Normalization simply means that telecommunications network provision will resemble much of the rest of the economy. The network environment will be essentially a pluralistic network of user associations, a network of networks that are partly overlapping and partly specialized along various dimensions such as geography, price, size, performance, virtualness, value added, ownership status, access rights, kind of specialization, extent of internationalization, and so forth.

This is not to say that domestic economies of scale and scope will become irrelevant. There still will be broad-based public networks, powerfully integrated networks with broad-band capability. But just as important will be economies of group specialization, economies of clustering, and economies of trans-nationalism.

Where does such normalization lead future regulators? It would be naive to expect less regulatory tasks. To the contrary, many disputes become less intramural and more public in that they form the regulatory realm. The main regulatory tasks that normalization raises are as follows: protection of interconnection and protection of access; establishment of new mechanisms of redistribution; prevention of oligopolistic behavior and of cyclical instability; establishment of new global regulatory arrangements to match the global scope of networks. None of these tasks is beyond our grasp in relation to their complexity or political feasibility, but they require us to end the palpable nostalgia for the simplicity of the Golden Age, and to imagine a very different environment – one in which the public network is replaced by the pluralized network.

Chapter 3

The politics of deregulation

Alan Altshuler

The triumph of the regulatory reform movement in numerous policy fields has been one of the great watershed developments in recent American political history. It is also one of the clearest examples ever of the power of intellectual analysis to overturn a deeply entrenched political regime. What is most striking about this episode is that as recently as 1975, deregulation seemed to be an academic idea without a political constituency.

What I intend to do here is to trace the sources of this transformation in the political and regulatory arenas, and to hazard a few guesses as to where it may be headed. Is this likely to prove a fleeting episode or an enduring transformation of the political system? In its origins, economic regulation was sold as a means of constraining the predatory practices of monopolies. But from the outset, its focus was at least as much on regulating and restraining competition. As regulation gradually reached out beyond the railroad industry to other segments of the economy, the central rationale of regulation became predominantly one of concentrating on the evils of unrestrained competition in trying to constrain it.

The high tide of this anti-competitive sentiment, which was very strong before the 1930s, occurred during the Great Depression. Indeed, most of the regulatory statutes that have been deregulated in recent years are ones that were enacted during that period. Until about 1950, criticism of the regulatory regime was almost exclusively a province of the legal profession, and it was concerned mostly with the procedural rules of fairness. During the 1950s, beginning in the early part of that decade, a new pattern of behavioral analysis emerged, and it led to criticisms of regulation right across the board, that is, from one social science perspective after another.

Political scientists produced studies maintaining that regulatory agencies had been captured by those they were supposed to be regulating. Economists often associate this critique with George Stigler, an economist at the University of Chicago. What Stigler provided a couple of decades later was an economic explanation of why the phenomena that the political scientists had described in the 1950s occurred. Legal scholars joined in. For example, Louis Jaffe of the Harvard Law School wrote an article on why it is that regulators are pro-regulatory even more than they are pro-industry. That is, whenever regulations go wrong, the solution is more regulation to prop up a system, as opposed to thinking about any other ways to deal with it.

In the late 1950s, the economists entered the debate, led most notably by transportation analyses done by John Meyer, Merton Peck, and others. Their argument initially centered on transport regulation; it was similar to, though not as sophisticated as Michael Porter's case presented in this book. They contended that, with the growth of new transportation modes in the twentieth century, the transportation industries had become increasingly competitive and that the railroads' economic power no longer was a real source of monopoly or oligopolistic power. They argued that regulation for the purpose of managing this competition was counterproductive. Accordingly, the appropriate solution would be less regulation rather than more.

It is interesting to ponder why this critique arose at that time. If one were an intellectual historian, one would concentrate on things like the fact that America had had a couple of decades of prosperity by then, and so the tendencies of American economists to favor competition could emerge in a way that would not have been so easy to do in the 1930s. But that is not the complete explanation. Certainly another factor was that the railroads were collapsing economically, and what one had was an industry that had long been regulated as a monopoly dying of competition.

The problem of explaining how this phenomenon could have happened under a regime of regulation presented a fascinating intellectual challenge. The new criticism quickly swept the profession, achieved the status of orthodoxy within economics, and generated a modest political response. As early as 1962, President Kennedy sent a pro-competitive bill on surface transportation regulation to Congress. The bill never got out of committee in either house of Congress, and a pattern that persisted over the next fifteen years was thereby established; one of economics' orthodoxy being unable to elicit any effective political result. The fate of these bills re-enforced the political science critique of regulation in that the main protectors of the regulatory programs who were flushed out by these political initiatives proved to be the regulated parties themselves. It turned out that the protectors of regulation were not the consumers but the shippers – the producers of the services. Their ability to defend their captured regulatory programs appeared to be beyond challenge. The iron triangle of interest group, congressional committee, and bureaucratic agency seemed unbreakable.

The political environment was changing in ways that were assumed to demonstrate chinks in the capture theory, but these chinks did not, in the first instance, lead to less regulation; rather, they led to more regulation. The new American populism that burst forth in the 1960s placed a high priority on direct participatory democracy, on economic equality, on hostility to business and the profit motive, on suspicion of certain features of big government. I will not go into the movements: civil rights, anti-poverty, anti-war, environmental, consumer. Instead, I will focus on the main regulatory outcome during the late 1960s and early 1970s – the rise of the new social regulation. The wave of new regulatory programs was directed at health, safety, and environmental protection, and each program was associated with more, rather than less, regulation. One thing was clear about the new agencies that were created, however: They were not captured, at least not in the early years, and not by the companies they were supposed to be regulating. This gave rise within a few years to a rethinking within the academic world of the various possible outcomes of regulation.

Why did social regulation triumph during this period while the critique of economic regulation had such little impact? First, a majority of the public favored increased health, safety, and environmental protection. There was no comparable constituency for increased economic competition; it was hard to make the case that citizens had much stake in it. Second, the American economy was booming and inflation rates were low. It was the economy that had dominated the world for several decades after the Second World War; American political leaders did not seem to have much reason to worry if the new regulation imposed inefficiencies on the economy. These appeared to be inefficiencies that the nation could afford as a luxury, and politicians had to decide whether it was worth taking sizable political risks to rectify them.

There was not even a substantial business constituency in favor of reform. The businesses that had the most intense stakes in regulation were largely accommodated by the regulatory regime. For example, in interstate freight transportation, the largest shippers could escape the effects of regulation by utilizing private or contract trucking, which was virtually exempt from regulation. Agricultural shippers had also achieved an exemption. So those left in the cold were mainly consumers – small businesses and larger companies – for whom freight was a major cost item. If they occasionally thought about pressing for regulatory relief, the last thing that they considered feasible was a broadside attack on the entire regulatory regime itself. They would pursue specific types of relief.

A few pro-competitive stirrings were felt during this period, and these were most obvious in telecommunications, particularly with matters like the telephone terminal equipment decision in 1968 that allowed competitors to AT&T to sell such equipment, and the decision in 1971 allowing private line long-distance telephone services as a competitive area. But these were peripheral adjustments associated with even greater regulation of AT&T to prevent it from using predatory practices to eliminate incipient competition. The pattern of regulation continued to be one of preoccupation with the dysfunctions of competition rather than the benefits of competition.

What happened in the mid-1970s to change this pattern? The most dramatic change was clearly in the macroeconomy. Following the oil crisis of 1973, inflation emerged as public enemy number one in the United States. Policymakers were desperate for remedies and did not have many. They especially lacked remedies that did not create negative side effects. That is, you could impose wage/price controls or tighten the money supply, but such approaches had considerable costs. No one thought that regulatory reform offered any major anti-inflationary benefits, but the consensus among economists was that at least the anti-inflationary benefits would be real and would not harm the economy in other ways. Intense concern emerged about lagging productivity growth in the economy. Just a few years earlier the economy was so dynamic that any negative impact of regulation seemed trivial, but no longer. The potential benefits of regulatory reform in this way became significant. A whole generation of economists had been trained in the irrationality of anti-competitive economic regulation. Many of them had moved into key positions in government and were producing reports calling for less regulation. For years, they merely lacked a political constituency. Now an opportunity began to emerge.

Conservatives had mobilized a backlash to the social regulatory initiatives of a few years earlier. One of their chief targets, however, was excessive government regulation. When their leaders talked about regulation, they spoke mainly of the new social regulation, to them the most evil of the villains. But they also talked about the irrationality of economic regulation.

The consumer movement, which had not even existed in a serious way a dozen years earlier, was a major force, but it was coming on hard times in the mid-1970s. With the conservatives moving into high gear in the United States, the prospects for more social regulation were essentially nil. The consumer movement had always been in favor of more government, but in this political environment, regulatory reform looked like an attractive change of pace. But it was one that required a shift of alliances because in the 1960s the consumer movement in America had been allied with organized labor in pressing for social regulation. Shifting to an alliance with business and conservative organizations was not so easy, but the consumer leaders made the change. In this context some politicians, led initially by Senator Kennedy and later by President Ford, perceived an opportunity to gain political support from this constituency by pressing for less economic regulation.

First the politicians went after the airline industry, which had been widely regarded as a thoroughly competitive industry. Being a relatively small industry, it did not have an important political base. It was also one that charged prices that were highly visible to consumers because it dealt directly with the public. One interesting sidelight to this familiar story is that when Alfred Kahn came to the chairmanship of the Civil Aeronautics Board in 1977, he was committed to produce more efficient regulation of the sort that Michael Porter indicated is sensitive to corporate strategies. Within a year, though, he became convinced that efficient regulation was an oxymoron. It could not be done, he concluded. The only solution was to eliminate regulation in this industry, and he pursued that strategy successfully, quickly becoming the most popular bureaucrat in Washington.

What is astonishing is that the rising tide of pro-competitive sentiment soon became a tidal wave engulfing all three branches of government. A bit of luck was operating in the sense that the early stages of airline deregulation coincided with economic upturn, so it was possible to have reduced prices and increased profits at the same time. But it also became clear that deregulation had touched a responsive cord with constituencies stretching across the political spectrum (leaving out organized labor), and that it might offer lots of people in Washington a chance to make their marks on history. In this context, numerous agencies that had long been considered to be the most captured by client politics began to move vigorously in a different direction.

The telecommunications case seemed to be intrinsically a harder one, because telephone service looked at least like a natural monopoly, or had until recently. And so as technological change undermined the natural monopoly argument during the 1960s, 1970s, and into the 1980s, the FCC had to react. As was mentioned previously, it took tentative steps around 1970, but at the same time it was increasing its regulation of AT&T, which tried hard to reverse this trend with congressional action. The firm mounted a major campaign in 1976 and again in 1977, but failed. When the FCC pulled back from its commitment to competition in the mid-1970s, it was prodded by the courts in a pro-competitive direction.

Illustrative of this was the Execunet case, which was the first MCI effort to offer per call rather than private line competitive services with AT&T. The FCC rejected the service, but the Circuit Court of Appeals for the District of Columbia overruled them, saying for the first time that the Federal Communications Act did not authorize the FCC to propagate monopoly for monopoly's sake. The court maintained that it had to make a powerful case-by-case rationale if it was going to do so. This decision was upheld by the United States Supreme Court when it refused *certiorari* in 1979, and the FCC decided not to proceed further. In this situation, AT&T did not have much choice but to pursue wider authorization to compete, rather than try to suppress competition in its historic monopoly markets. Meanwhile it was encountering pro-competitive sentiment in the Antitrust Division of the Justice Department and in the Federal District Court, leading ultimately to the divestiture settle- ment of 1982. Remarkably, the thrust of pro-competitive sentiment, so different from the sentiments and theories that had dominated American politics in the 1930s, 1940s, and 1950s, had penetrated to the heart of what had seemed to be the most powerful and secure monopolistic area of regulation in America.

Clearly, the pace of technological innovation and its thrust in expanding the potential for competition gives no sign of abating in the foreseeable future. Indeed, naturally competitive possibilities seem to be cropping up all the time. The unlikely consensus among consumers, conservatives, and academics in their organized expressions in favor of competition wherever it can thrive, still seems rock solid despite the problems that emerged in the airline industry. As Alfred Kahn said, Congress did not repeal the antitrust laws when it deregulated the airlines. Hence some issues concerning the re-emerging concentration in the airline industry may be an antitrust problem rather than a regulatory one.

It is impossible to know what the consequences of a major economic downturn might be. However, it does seem inconceivable that the competitive genies that are out of the bottle can be put back in. The commitment to new pro-competitive initiatives might flag, but even that is far from clear. The current period, after all, is not like the 1920s, when the intellectual foundations for the anti-competitive regulatory acts of the 1930s were laid in the trade association movement and the activities of the Federal Trade Commission. Few economists would argue today, as they did in the 1930s, that in a new depression, suppressing competition would be a plausible path to a renewed prosperity.

In short, we have here a policy revolution that provides remarkable evidence of the power of ideas in American politics. This revolution attests to the system's capacity to reach at times for the broad public interest, at least as intellectuals understand it, rather than narrow, highly organized interests. Moreover, we have a policy revolution that seems likely to prove extremely durable.

Chapter 4

Did regulation keep pace with technology?

Peter Temin

I approach the question of whether or not regulation can keep pace with technology by relating two familiar stories. My justification for using these tales is that they were critically important in the development of modern telecommunications policy.[1] However, I begin by briefly considering the question: What standard are we to use in evaluating the behavior of a regulatory commission? It is not fair to use perfect hindsight in looking at this question because there is no reason why any contemporary should be able to understand the implications of a new technology. Instead, I propose to compare the regulator, the Federal Communications Commission (FCC), with the regulated, AT&T, in order to rank the regulator's actions in relation to the opinions of contemporary participant–observers in the regulatory process. Moreover, I wish to emphasize that new technology does not appear in isolation; its introduction is always mixed up with other issues. Paramount among them is the matter of price: What should customers be charged for a new – or possibly an old – service? Regulators and firms, I submit, have an easier time dealing with new technology than they have with establishing prices.

Soon after being appointed director of the FCC's Common Carrier Bureau in 1963, Bernard Strassburg instituted an inquiry into the use of computers in telecommunications. The Commission's attention had been called to this nascent issue by complaints from computer users who could not understand why the Bell System did not immediately reconfigure the entire telephone network to deal with their very particular needs. AT&T, taking an equally extreme position, did not want to bother with the myriad demands from these tiny – relative to the Bell System's national market – and obstreperous customers. The age of computers was just dawning; at that time only a few people were experimenting with new ways to use them in communications and even fewer were protesting to the agency about the Bell System's performance in this regard. But Strassburg moved out ahead of the specific complaints coming into the Commission in an attempt to formulate a general policy for the new technology. The problem Strassburg had to deal with derived from the 1956 Consent Decree. It made no sense to bar AT&T from supplying telephone terminal equipment for computer users. Under the terms of the decree, however, AT&T could supply this equipment only if it were regulated. But it also did not make sense to extend regulation to all terminal equipment. A computer with a modem connects to the telephone network. Should it therefore be regulated? Should all computers be regulated? IBM, just bringing out its 360 series of computers, was not amused by that prospect. But the FCC lacked a logical formula for defining the limits of the regulated monopoly.[2]

AT&T's opposition extended to the 'Carterfone,' even though the phone did not make an electrical connection with the telephone network. The sound of conversation from an ordinary telephone handset activated the switch of a radio which then communicated with the user of a mobile radio/telephone. The Carterfone thus allowed the mobile radio/telephone to be patched onto the Bell System Network, albeit not electronically.

AT&T, reaffirming its end-to-end responsibility for the network, refused to permit the innovation to be used. But Thomas Carter of Carter Electronics was not awed by the telephone giant. He sold his device to customers in defiance of AT&T's tariff, and when AT&T discontinued his customers' service, he filed a private antitrust suit against the company. The Court decided that regulation under the Communications Act and not prosecution under the Sherman Act was still controlling. It referred Carter's complaint to the FCC under the doctrine of primary jurisdiction.[3]

For Strassburg, in the midst of his computer inquiry, this was a marvelous opportunity to welcome a new technology. In addition, he could lend a hand to a small entrepreneur and make the giant Bell System more responsive to its clientele. AT&T argued to the Commission that the Carterfone should be proscribed because it was manufactured by an unstable firm, not useful, and could not be guaranteed to work properly, thus casting blame on the telephone company from customers who could not differentiate between the Carterfone and the Bell System. These tenuous arguments had eagerly been accepted by the FCC in the 1940s and 1950s, but Strassburg no longer found them appealing in the context of his computer inquiry. He required that AT&T explain exactly how its network would be damaged (not just how customers who used the Carterfone might be inconvenienced) before the agency would prohibit the device.

As this conflict between Bell and Strassburg was reaching its climax, AT&T's top management changed. H.I. Romnes, who represented the flowering of the Bell System's engineering tradition, became Chairman of AT&T's Board and its Chief Executive Officer in 1967. Shortly after taking office, Romnes expressed an expansive view of the use of computers in communication and of the impending Carterfone decision, anticipating abundant new opportunities in a telephone network with a wide variety of terminals at its ends. His concern, as he expressed it in 1967, was merely that the Bell System's 'prime responsibility for maintenance' of the network be preserved by 'suitable interfaces or buffer devices to keep the attached equipment from affecting other users of the network.' Subject to this safeguard, Romnes accepted Strassburg's initiative.[4]

He appointed an AT&T Tariff Review Committee in mid-1967 to devise alternative interconnection tariffs that would protect the system. The Tariff Review Committee operated in a crisis atmosphere. As engineers responsible for the network, its members were wary of change and of non-Bell outsiders. They advanced scraps of data, exposing minor hazards of interconnection as grounds for caution. They clothed their fear of the unknown in specific scenarios for disaster.[5] Cooler heads might well have recalled that the Bell System never had included all of the devices connected to the network and that there was a long history of terminal interconnection for those who wanted to see it.

The independent telephone companies, often quite small and primitive, could be thought of as early PBXs. Defense Department equipment on military bases was connected to the network under 'letters of military necessity' without protective devices. The sound in video equipment of the TV networks, increasingly large customers of the Bell System, generated signals sent directly over the network without evident difficulty. It was possible to argue that these were special cases in a controlled environment. But they represented extensive experience with terminal interconnection before the Carterfone – experience that was quite varied and apparently trouble-free.

The Committee, none the less, recommended tariffs allowing ancillary equipment – answering machines or computer modems – to be attached to the Bell System 'only in connection with special interface equipment provided, installed and maintained by the telephone company.' As Strassburg later acknowledged, the idea of a protective connecting arrangement grew out of 'the established regulatory culture.'[6] It embraced a natural division of responsibility between AT&T and its customers. If these devices were used, the telephone company would not need to tell its customers what they could or could not attach to the network. It would not have to monitor or control what other people were doing; its protective coupling device would simply screen out harmful signals. The Bell System would know what signals it was getting. The vendors of equipment would know the electrical characteristics of the network they were facing. AT&T would avoid all competitive and legal problems attendant on examining plans or equipment of its customers and competitors.[7]

In a decision of June 1968, the Commission rejected AT&T's existing tariff prohibiting the use of non-Bell equipment. The FCC did not deny that AT&T needed to regulate interconnection and to be responsible for network standards. But the Agency repudiated AT&T's customary argument on the grounds that they were imprecise in defining harm. The Commission invalidated AT&T's existing interconnection tariff and approved the use of the Carterfone.[8]

Romnes responded at a gathering of company executives on September 5, 1968. He introduced a small device labeled a protective coupling arrangement (or PCA) through which equipment owned and maintained by Bell's customers could be connected to the switched network. He proclaimed, 'We welcome competition,' and emphasized that 'our intent is to make interface as simple and inexpensive as possible.' In fact, he said, 'The more the merrier.'[9]

Romnes made it clear that he was promulgating a new strategy for the Bell System. He stressed the existence of a new era in telecommunications and a new openness in the network. AT&T had set the stage for an expansion in the use of increasingly sophisticated devices connected to the Bell System. It was starting to do for customer equipment what Strassburg was trying to do for computers: setting a general rule for new entrants. It is ironic that in antitrust suits against AT&T these tariffs would be assailed for being anti-competitive when they were the telephone company's initial opening toward competition.[10]

The protective couplings might not have been attacked so vociferously if AT&T had decided to offer them free to customers as a matter of right. The company decided instead to charge the owners of independent terminals for the PCAs through which they would be attached to the network. To do anything else, the Tariff Review Committee reasoned, would be to charge the general rate payers the cost of accommodating computer users and others who were experimenting with new kinds of equipment.

The Committee did not conceptualize the issue as one of protecting the ratepayer's network – in which case they might be expected to pay. Nor of course did the Committee conclude that what was involved was an effort to quiet the Bell System's fears – in which case AT&T should have eaten the cost itself. And even though Carter's initial legal action had been in the form of an antitrust complaint, the group does not seem even to consider the antitrust implications of the PCA charge. In light of the company's background and the amount of attention its every action attracted in Washington, this issue cried out for analysis before the fact.

Both the FCC and AT&T had risen to the challenge of new technology for terminal equipment. PCAs would be shown to be unnecessary in the following few years, and the FCC policy of customer-owned terminal registration would be designed to replace it. But one could not really ask for a clearer or faster regulatory response to a new technological opportunity.

Prices, however, were a different matter. The issue here was not regulation – the FCC did not concern itself with the price of PCAs – but rather with company policy. AT&T unfortunately decided to charge for PCAs on the narrowest of grounds. It did not stop to consider the antitrust implications, even though the 1956 Consent Decree was fresh in everyone's mind. Nor did the company turn a welcoming face toward the private individuals and firms attempting to introduce new terminal technologies.

This company policy is relevant to the question of regulatory pace. It shows that contemporaries could not see clearly the combined implications of a new technology and new prices. The new technology was introduced, but the company understood only some of its implications. The pricing problem was botched.

The results of this clumsiness were momentous. The PCA issue continued to bedevil AT&T throughout the 1970s, first in regulatory proceedings to eliminate PCAs and then in antitrust suits. It is too much to expect that the regulatory and antitrust pressure on AT&T would have gone away with this issue. But its absence would have reduced the force of other issues. AT&T's lawyers understood during the troubled 1970s that the company was fighting on too many fronts. The PCA issue was not connected in any legal sense to other issues; instead it created a context in which AT&T appeared as an opponent of progress and competition.

Pricing and technology also were intertwined in other matters before the FCC at the same time as *Carterfone*, albeit in different proportions.

Microwave Communications, Inc. (MCI) was even smaller than Carter Electronics; it had neither staff nor finances. It had applied to the FCC in 1963 for permission to build a private microwave line from St Louis to Chicago. It proposed a new use for a new technology. MCI clearly was too small to use this facility itself, as permitted by the FCC's *Above 890* decision, and so it proposed instead to sell capacity to others.

Bill McGowan, MCI's head, contended that MCI would exploit the new microwave technology; parallel to *Carterfone*, a small company was asking to introduce new technology into the network. MCI would tailor its services to the needs of customers and provide greater flexibility than AT&T. AT&T countered that MCI was simply cream-skimming.

MCI was cream-skimming in three different ways. It proposed to serve only one low-cost route, avoiding Bell's obligation to support the entire national network. MCI proposed also a bare-bones service; it would attract only the low-cost customers, that is, customers who did not care about the quality of service.[11] And MCI argued that it had lowered costs because it was exploiting the new microwave radio technology.

But MCI's construction advantage did not come from the new technology – AT&T had long used microwave radio itself. Instead, the smaller firm used lower quality construction and limited facilities in ways that the Bell System could not. The new firm's crews were nonunion; they were not always careful about obtaining building permits; they did not build carefully designed structures. In fact, MCI argued that its rural facilities did not even need restrooms – technicians could use the fields![12] The Communication Workers of America, state commissioners, and the FCC surely would not have allowed the Bell System to do any of this. To the extent that MCI's construction costs were below AT&T's for these reasons, the FCC was being asked to change the structure of the telecommunications industry for only a transitory gain.

The FCC ignored AT&T's protests and accepted at face value MCI's claim to be furnishing 'interplant and interoffice communications with unique and specialized characteristics.' On a four-to-three vote – with the Chairman voting against MCI – the FCC found AT&T's 'cream-skimming argument to be without merit.'[13]

The Commission regarded McGowan's tiny business as a fringe firm rather like Western Union. Strassburg in particular conceptualized the *MCI* proceeding as a very specific one, concerned with a small company and a single line. Nevertheless, the FCC's vote was close. It had required the enthusiasm of the head of the Common Carrier Bureau and of several pro-competition commissioners to get it through. One of these commissioners, Kenneth Cox, found his views so close to McGowan's that he left the Commission to work for MCI shortly after the vote. With only a hair less support, one imagines, McGowan might never have got his fledgling enterprise off the ground.

With this decision to hand, though, MCI's boss quickly advanced on a broad front. He was not about to conduct an academic experiment for Strassburg, to proceed at a stately pace while generating the data needed to evaluate the effect of the Commission's decision on this one specific route. Instead, his affiliated MCI companies immediately flooded the FCC with applications for permission to construct microwave systems for hire all over the country. By mid-1970, the Commission was facing almost 2000 such requests, most of them coming from MCI companies and another firm, Datran, that aspired to construct a digital data network.

In an unusual move, the FCC decided that it was unable to deal with this aftermath of its *MCI* decision on a case-by-case basis. The Commission took the initiative in setting out the general issues to be decided. Having dealt with MCI's initial application on highly individual grounds, it then recognized MCI as the forerunner of a class of applicants and approved the applications from the class as a whole, under the title of *Specialized Common Carriers*.[14]

The arguments by the applicants were roughly the same as those originally presented by MCI. They would provide a wider range of services than AT&T, and they would open up new markets with new low-cost technology, thereby meeting the criterion of public good.

This argument of course raised the question: Why was not AT&T serving these new markets? AT&T was not lowering its prices enough to expand its private line customer base because that would impact its existing revenue base. To some extent, it was burdened by historical costs and to some extent it was acting like any monopolist faced with a technological change. But even had AT&T wanted to, it was quite clear from the FCC's earlier TELPAK investigations that the Commission would not have allowed AT&T to lower all private line rates. And reducing rates on some routes would have raised the problem of discrimination that the FCC had been unable to resolve in its TELPAK investigations. The *Specialized Common Carriers* decision appears to have been a way for the FCC to allow lower prices for the use of new microwave technology without allowing AT&T to discriminate between different users.

The FCC's procedure, designed to avoid a particular regulatory pothole, brought a rush of new carriers into the market and into the political arena. *Specialized Common Carriers* fundamentally changed the way in which telecommunications services were to be supplied, a radical change that seemed not to have been intended by most of the FCC Commissioners. Intended or not, the decision decisively increased competition in the industry. Insensitive to this larger implication, the agency noted that licensing these other carriers would virtually compel their interconnection with the Bell System; the new carriers clearly needed local distribution facilities that they could not supply. The FCC thus acknowledged that the next assault on AT&T's position would be against its monopoly in the provision of service at the local level.[15]

Still the FCC refused to recognize any danger to AT&T from such interconnections. It predicted that the total effect of competition would be slight and that the Bell revenues would not be endangered. Echoing numbers used in *Above 890*, the Commission claimed that only AT&T's private line business, 3 percent of its revenue, would be at risk. Competition from specialized common carriers, the staff asserted, 'can be expected to have some beneficial results without adverse impact on service by established carriers.'[16] There would be no danger of cream-skimming and no threat to the existing rate structure.

This, of course, was nonsense. The danger was apparent to AT&T at the time, but the company's arguments were seen as self-serving (which they were) and therefore incorrect (which they were not). Here the FCC moved in the spirit of *Carterfone*. It quickly changed the regulatory rules to take account of a new technology. But, unlike *Carterfone*, the question in *MCI* and *Specialized Common Carriers* only appeared to be primarily one of technology. It was in fact one of price. The FCC was too fast to take account of only apparent gains.

MCI went on to challenge AT&T at increasingly high levels. Competitive pressure spread from private lines to the switched network. The forum for discussion and possible decision spread from the FCC to the courts and Congress. Independent of the wisdom of the FCC's decision in *Specialized Common Carriers*, AT&T had to live with it.

The pressure from interexchange competition was amplified by continuing controversies over PCAs and terminal equipment more generally. Rapid regulatory action had initiated an unstable process that soon began to outrun the FCC's planned pace and then went to a conclusion that was not foreseen by any regulator of the late 1960s who was considering whether Carter Electronics or MCI should be allowed into the telecommunications market.

AT&T, as in *Carterfone*, lagged behind the Commission. But since the FCC was in a great rush to exploit what only appeared to be a new technology, the company's resistance appeared insightful rather than recalcitrant. The FCC was balanced on a knife edge in *MCI*. The issue could easily have gone either way, with dramatic implications for the history of telecommunications. But as it turned out, the problem in *MCI* and *Specialized Common Carriers* was not one of regulatory lag; it was one of regulatory lead.

One or two examples do not make a rule. History only illuminates the possibilities in diverse circumstances. And these familiar stories show that regulatory commissions need not lag in their taste for new technologies. In fact, the danger may well be an excess of enthusiasm. AT&T was the laggard in the introduction of new technology, at least in terminal equipment; the FCC was the proverbial fool rushing in with microwave radio. There is no clear preference for private or public action.

NOTES

1 This material is taken from my book, *The Fall of the Bell System: A Study in Prices and Politics* (New York: Cambridge University Press, 1987), where further documentation – particularly to company sources – can be found.
2 FCC, *Notice of Inquiry*, FCC Docket 16979, 'Computer Inquiry,' adopted November 9, 1966, 7 FCC 2d 11; FCC, *Report and Further Notice of Inquiry*, FCC Docket 16979, adopted May 1, 1969, 17 FCC 2d 587 at 591.
3 *Carter v. AT&T*, 250 F. Supp. 188, 192 (N.D. Tex. 1966), *aff'd*, 365 F. 2d 486 (5th Cir. 1966), *cert. denied*, 385 U.S. 1008 (1967).
4 H.I. Romnes, 'Dynamic Communications for Modern Industry,' speech before the American Petroleum Institute, Chicago, Illinois, November 13, 1967; Alvin von Auw, *Heritage & Destiny: Reflections on the Bell System in Transition* (New York: Praeger Publishers, 1983), p. 137.
5 For example, the central office might not respond to the initiation of a call if the impedance across the line was too high; the call might be charged to a wrong number on multi-party lines; a wrong number might be reached; all digits might not be registered; the connection might be dropped in the middle if the station opened the line for more than half a second or if it sent a 2600 Hertz tone through the line. Edward M. Goldstein, talk presented to Tariff Review Committee, 'Effects on Switching, Signaling & Charging,' April 10, 1968; *US v. AT&T*, CA No. 74-1698 (D.D.C.), Defendant's Exhibit D-7-1, V.N. Vaughan notes.
6 'Illustrative General Exchange Tariff Covering the Provision of Interfaces

for COAM Devices,' draft, presented at the Tariff Review Committee meeting, April 10, 1968; *US v. AT&T*, CA No. 74-1698 (D.D.C.), Bernard Strassburg, testimony, October 14, 1981, Tr. 17243.

7 *US v. AT&T*, CA No. 74-1698 (D.D.C.), Defendant's Exhibit D-T-2, Edward M. Goldstein, testimony, July 8, 1981, pp. 30–31.

8 FCC, *Decision*, FCC Docket 16942, 'Carterfone,' adopted June 26, 1968, 13 FCC 2d 420.

9 H.I. Romnes, 'Connecting with the Telephone Network,' talk on videocassette tape, September 5, 1968.

10 The FCC allowed AT&T's revised tariffs permitting interconnection through a PCA to become effective on January 1, 1969, but noted that it was unable at the time to evaluate the revised tariff fully. The Commission noted that the tariff went beyond its *Carterfone* decision and acknowledged that the question of whether a customer should be able to provide his own network control signaling unit was an open one. FCC, *Memorandum and Order*, re 'AT&T "Foreign Attachment" Tariff Revisions,' December 24, 1968, 15 FCC 2d 605.

11 Larry Kahaner, *On the Line* (New York: Warner Books, 1986), pp. 27, 85–9.

12 MCI's offering of two kilohertz channels is a case in point. The Bell System used four kilohertz voice grade channels as its unit; it had abandoned two kilohertz as substandard. MCI was allowing customers to subdivide these channels in pursuit of lower prices. The service, of course, would be of lower quality, of such low quality that it is not clear that any two kilohertz channels were used. FCC, *Decision*, FCC Docket Nos 16509–519, 'Applications of MCI for Construction Permits,' adopted August 13, 1969, 18 FCC 2d 953.

13 *Initial Decision of Hearing Examiner Herbert Sharfman*, FCC Docket Nos 16509–519, October 17, 1967, 18 FCC 2d 979 at 1006.

14 FCC, *First Report and Order*, FCC Docket 18920, 'Specialized Common Carriers,' June 3, 1971, 29 FCC 2d 870. *Specialized Common Carriers* was 'rulemaking' rather than 'adjudication.' Strassburg's views prevailed none the less. See *US v. AT&T*, CA No. 74-1698 (D.D.C.), Defendant's Exhibit D-7-266; Bernard Strassburg, 'Case Study of Policy-Making by Federal Communications Commission re Competition in Intercity Common Carrier Communications,' Draft, January 14, 1977.

15 FCC, *Further Notice of Inquiry and Proposed Rulemaking*, FCC Docket 18920, June 21, 1971, 30 FCC 2d 288.

16 FCC, *First Report and Order*, FCC Docket 18920, June 3, 1971, 29 FCC 2d 870 at 878–85.

Chapter 5

The significance of Telecom 2000

Kenneth Robinson

American communications policy, traditionally the prerogative of a small number of Washington, DC-based authorities, became more central to public policy debate in the early 1980s, for three reasons. First, the Bell System breakup, announced in January 1982 and implemented two years later, impressed on the public the fact that communications policy really matters. For the first time, most people were compelled to make choices about a utility service that previously had been taken for granted. Some $148 billion in net current assets and over 1 per cent of the United States civilian workforce was reorganized pursuant to a court order. In 1984, the first year following AT&T's divestiture of nearly three-quarters of its assets, serious long-distance service fulfillment problems arose. The transaction had traumatic effects, chiefly for the former Bell System workers, but also for much of the public. The predictable consequences of decisions reached by a small number of government officials were visited on the general public, and that in turn sparked greater interest in communications policy.

The second reason that communications policy came into public scrutiny is that the Bell System breakup coincided with a fundamental overhauling of long-established telephone industry pricing and cost-allocation schemes. The Federal Communications Commission (FCC), in its *Access Charges* action and related decisions sought to reduce greatly the cross-subsidy burdens previously placed on long-distance services – or, more accurately, the users of long-distance services – by shifting those burdens to local telephone subscribers, denominated as the 'cost causers.' As in most other countries, the United States previously had followed the practice of generously assigning telephone plant and operating costs to toll services. The purpose was to achieve subsidies of local prices, especially for politically sensitive local residential services. An effect was that long-distance prices artificially ballooned and local charges were shoved well below so-called 'true costs.' Perhaps because one of the FCC's principal constituencies was comprised of large users of overpriced long-distance services, but also for sincere 'pro-efficiency' purposes, a regime of 'customer access-line' (later renamed 'end user') charges was instituted. At the same time, divested Bell operating companies were seeking large local price increases. This major change in pricing and subsidy allocation policies, plus industry proposals for much higher local service charges, disturbed many citizens, state regulators, and members of Congress. The effect was to impress upon the general public the reality that telecommunications policy really matters.

The third aspect of communications policy that drew public notice was the matter of growing trade deficits and apparent loss of competitiveness in telecommunications or, more broadly, the 'information economy.' Throughout the late 1970s and early 1980s, as major, labor-intensive industries – textiles, footwear, steel, and automobiles – came under severe import pressures, the American political leadership responded chiefly by stressing the redemption of a high technology tomorrow. 'Information' and 'knowledge-intensive' enterprises were to be the key. Convenient economic rationales including the 'law of comparative advantage' gained new prominence. Again coincident with the disruptions and public dismay engendered by the Bell System breakup and the FCC's pricing changes, however, escalating trade deficits arose in precisely those high-technology sectors that were supposed to be the country's economic salvation. American jobs were 'out-sourced,' and alternative, high-technology opportunities did not quickly materialize. The public learned, as one critic commented wryly, that 'we can't all be astronauts.' One immediate consequence was to pay increased attention to overseas communications policies, and especially market access conditions. For a majority of Americans and American politicians assumed that if the country was losing the battle for worldwide technology and commercial hegemony, it could only be because other countries' trade policies and practices were unfair.

Against this background, in October 1988 the National Telecommunications and Information Administration (NTIA) released its *NTIA Telecom 2000* report. Some 672 pages in length and consisting of two parts – first, a broad overview of communications and, second, seventeen sector studies covering everything from consumer electronics to program production and movies – the report purported to establish the policies the United States government should pursue, and the programs it and the private sector should implement, to ensure that national economic, government, and social needs will be met in the year 2000 and beyond.

The idea of publishing such a *magnum opus* on communications had arisen a year earlier, in conjunction with the planned revision of a 1985 report entitled *NTIA Competition Benefits Report*. That document, comparable in many respects to the second part of the *NTIA Telecom 2000* report, had been prepared on the eve of a series of NTIA-led European 'market access and fact-finding' (MAFF) talks aimed at expanding communications equipment, services, and related exports. The assumption in 1985 had been that, given the public dismay regarding deregulation then prevailing in the United States, European politicians (and, to some extent, Japanese authorities as well) would be even less willing to embrace the kind of market-opening regulatory reform proposals United States companies were seeking, unless there were a modest policy backfire demonstrating that, press reports to the contrary notwithstanding, in American communications, all was not lost.

The *NTIA Competition Benefits Report* proved something of a minor best-seller, especially abroad, with a total of about 9,000 copies distributed. Its overriding message might be labeled the 'technological imperative.' That is, through adroit manipulation of data, coupled with a candor unusual for government documents, the report showed that the government had resisted most of the pro-competitive market developments driven by technological, commercial, and demographic changes in the 1970s, yet had proven unable to staunch the flow. It preached the message that, sooner or later – and probably sooner – foreign administrations would confront precisely the same disruptive pressures in communications, and that the more prudent course was to accommodate change now, rather than attempt to mount what would inevitably prove an unsuccessful effort to maintain the status quo.

Because the 1985 report had been tied closely to specific communications and information industry sector developments, and had focused on economic matters, it commanded little popular readership. In 1987, however, the decision was made to see if a publication endeavoring to relate communications developments and objectives to a broad range of national issues – education, health care delivery, rural development, and the like – could be prepared: in effect, a document aimed at popularizing telecommunications policy.

Comprehensive federal communications policy reviews are not new. Historically, they have occurred about every twenty years this century.

The first such significant report was issued in 1912 following the *Titanic* disaster. A factor that contributed to the magnitude of that tragedy, which cost 1513 lives, was the *Titanic*'s inability to summon help as other ships in the area had their radios turned off. As the official Department of Commerce history notes, 'The disaster caused Congress to strengthen legislation requiring passenger steamers to have radio apparatus. It also alerted Congress to the imminent importance of wireless communications.'

Some twenty years thereafter, the US House of Representatives' Committee on Interstate and Foreign Commerce commissioned a special review of communications policy. That effort, conducted under the leadership of a government communications expert, William Splawn, produced the Splawn Report which, in turn, was in large part the basis for the Communications Act of 1934.

Twenty years later, the Truman Administration commissioned its own review of communications policies. That effort concentrated on two matters: overall radio frequency management and government communications policymaking organization. It concluded that the United States had to do a better job managing use of the radio spectrum; it also recommended elevating communications policymaking responsibilities (and helped to bring about the position of Special Assistant to the President for Telecommunications, which was to evolve eventually into the Office of Telecommunications Policy in the Executive Office of the President under President Nixon).

Twenty years after the Truman effort, there was yet another comprehensive review of telecommunications policy. Under-Secretary of State Eugene Rostow headed the study for the Johnson Administration. The Rostow Task Force report was important as it institutionalized and legitimized competition in communications markets. It also advanced proposals – the so-called 'open skies' policy favoring free entry into domestic communications satellite services, for example – that were implemented by the FCC in the early 1970s.

Executive Order 12046, which established NTIA, directs the agency to make recommendations regarding long-run trends affecting the country's communications economy and the national welfare. To meet that responsibility, NTIA in 1987 undertook to develop a long-range communications policy planning report. An array of special staff studies of individual telecommunications and information markets and issues was commissioned, and extensive discussions with business, government, academic, and other experts were held. Many of the recommendations contained in the *NTIA Telecom 2000* report should be familiar.

First, the report stresses the virtues of limited government, and maximum possible reliance on competitive private enterprise. Second, it emphasizes the importance of maximum possible individual freedom and choice. In our domestic communications and information services markets, the report urges continued reliance on competition to the maximum extent possible. With respect to the US government, the message continues to be that less is more.

Other parts of the report go beyond the narrow focus of previous telecommunications policy reports. For instance, *NTIA Telecom 2000* reviews the problems of simply transferring pro-competitive, deregulatory United States policies from the domestic to the international communications arena.

On the domestic side, deregulation usually leads to a marketplace solution. Some argue that the resulting market may be insufficiently competitive, and that competition cannot be counted on to function as an adequate surrogate for what regulation might accomplish. But domestic deregulation usually does result in a dispersion of decisionmaking authority. Instead of having five members of the FCC in Washington making most of the decisions, many more people in the private sector make the judgments.

That does not always happen internationally, however, when the United States tries to deregulate unilaterally. Internationally, deregulation can result in simply strengthening the hand of foreign, government-sanctioned monopolies. Instead of a marketplace decision, one runs the risk of a decision being made by another government entity or group of entities – namely, foreign communications administrations. Consequently, the *NTIA Telecom 2000* report reviews the limitations on deregulatory policies resulting from the fact that, although America's is a competitive, largely market-driven communications economy, most of the rest of the world's is not.

Another aspect of the report that is distinctive is the scope of the analysis. Most previous reviews of communications policy have been rather narrow. What they have said is, 'Do thus and such, and you will affect the following communications sectors in these ways.' What *NTIA Telecom 2000* says, however, is, 'Do this or don't do this and you'll affect telecommunications, and you'll also probably affect the following additional things.' It demonstrates how communications policy choices will affect a broad range of other things such as educational opportunities, the competitiveness of American industry, population distribution and rural opportunities, and the quality of national life. This broader assessment reflects the deep involvement of communications and information services throughout the American economy and society – something which is shown in the statistics that are included in the report.

Communications and information services, as a percentage of the Gross National Product (GNP), have roughly doubled to about 6 percent in the last twenty years. The pace is accelerating. Recently, we are seeing an annual increase of over a half percent of GNP – a tremendous amount of new economic activity given America's nearly $5 trillion economy.

Twenty years ago, a communications policymaker could look out and say that there was a high probability that a decision would have a major effect on the communications market; there was only some vague notion that there might be wider implications. Today, with an economy that depends on these electronic tools, the likelihood that communications policies will have major effects that will ripple throughout society is much greater. That phenomenon will become even more apparent as we approach the turn of the century.

This circumstance alters the traditional benefit–risk equation. It increases the odds that a communications policy decision will yield major benefits. Conversely, it heightens the risks. Because if we make the wrong choices, it is not simply a question of affecting a communications industry adversely. One also incurs the risk that the country will be seriously harmed. *NTIA Telecom 2000* makes four major points. First, it notes that this is a sector that matters; it matters intrinsically because it represents over 6 percent of our Gross National Product, and it also matters as what economists call a 'production factor.' That is always such an obvious point to people who work in communications and information, but it is not something that many policymakers, much less the public, necessarily recognize.

If one looks at the total business investment in durables in 1988, for instance, one sees that about 24 percent of it went into communications, information, or related electronics-based products. Presumably that large investment, which is about eight times what it was ten years ago, reflects how much commerce and industry value this sector's economic contribution. And, of course, there are the absolute numbers. AT&T, for instance, has forecast that there will be at least a $1 trillion information economy worldwide by 1992.

Another message of *Telecom 2000* is that, all other things being equal, the less regulated a given communications market is, the faster it will grow. And, the faster the economy that it serves will grow as well. Hence, benefits of liberalization are discussed in terms of economic growth. A few years ago, the Organization for Economic Cooperation

and Development (OECD) started comparing the rate of telecommunications revenue growth and overall economic growth in various
countries. Many factors affect how fast a country's economy and its
telecommunications market grow. But if one looks at the numbers, what
is clear is that the more competitive a telecommunications sector is, the
faster it appears to grow. And, the faster telecommunications grows, the
faster the overall economy tends to grow.

In the general oversight part of *Telecom 2000*, three countries are
picked as examples: Britain, Japan, and Canada. Each has conducted a
public debate about competition in communications. Britain and Japan
decided to liberalize; in Canada, however, the government was more
cautious.

What do the figures show? In Britain, where competition has been
allowed in just about every part of the communications market including
local exchange (something that not even the United States has been
prepared to allow), between 1986 and 1987 telecommunications
revenues grew at an annual rate of 12.4 percent, and the British economy
expanded at a rate of 5.2 percent, the fastest of any OECD country. In
Japan, where competition has been legally authorized, but truly
effective competition is still to come, the telecommunications market
grew by about 5.1 percent during 1986 and 1987, while the Japanese
economy grew by about 4.3 percent.

In Canada, in contrast, where competition is much more limited,
revenue growth trends seem to be steadily downward. During the
relevant period, communications revenues increased by only about 2
percent, and the overall Canadian economy by 4.1 percent. Canada thus
has the distinction of being the only OECD member where the telecommunications sector is currently growing substantially slower than
the economy as a whole. (During the same period in the United States,
we had telecommunications sector growth of 8.4 percent a year and
GNP growth of 3.2 percent.)

The third major point made in *Telecom 2000* was the conclusion that
telecommunications markets today are becoming deregulated due to
what governments do and to changes in technology. In 1970, sales of
telecommunications equipment in the United States and the purchases
by the regulated phone companies, for example, closely matched. In
1985, however, United States regulated common carriers providing
public network services accounted for only about 59 percent of
equipment demand – about $13.6 billion out of a total of about $22.9
billion. In 1990, the regulated carriers are expected to account for about
55 percent of total demand of $30.6 billion. This means that regulated

companies over five years accounted for 4 percent less of a market that expanded 34 per cent. Moreover, NTIA estimates call for the regulated companies – or, more accurately, the regulated parts of the communications economy – to continue to lose about 1 percent of market share annually, as the market grows about 7 percent yearly over the next decade or so.

This is not necessarily only an American phenomenon. A Frost & Sullivan marketing survey indicated, for instance, that in 1984 European public carriers bought 63 percent of all the fiber optics and associated equipment sold in Europe, but only 32 percent in 1988.

What we are seeing is an application of the rule that the less regulated a sector, the faster it will grow. Private systems are less regulated, so they appear to be growing faster than the public systems that are more regulated. Also, there is a steady reduction in the amount of economic activity that the regulatory authorities directly control. In that sense, what seems to be happening in telecommunications is not much different from what happened in the banking and securities trading business, where a great deal of economic activity gravitated to those parts of the field that were only nominally subject to regulation, if at all.

A fourth point made by the *NTIA Telecom 2000* report concerns the potential contribution that electronic tools can make both to business and society. Once in a while somebody writes a *Fortune* or *Harvard Business Review* article suggesting that all the investment in communications and computers over the past decade has not yet produced commensurate productivity or profit gains. And then there is a counter-article that argues that the critic has not interpreted the data correctly or has overlooked some major gain.

Assume that there have been gains, and, by the same token, assume that most of those gains have been made by the business community and not necessarily by the average consumer. That circumstance should alter rapidly over the balance of the century. It will alter because of the advent of a computer-literate generation and because older persons are increasing their facility with communications and computers as their job responsibilities require it. And it will alter because most major retailing operations in the country – everything from gasoline stations to grocery stores to discount chains – have installed the computer and communications hardware sufficient to sustain a much more information services intensive tomorrow. Furthermore, it will alter as more and more government services delivery programs – from library services to Social Security payments – become computer and communications dependent.

Every major country appears to be according a great deal of attention to communications and communications policymaking. This reflects a consensus regarding the importance of these electronic leverage technologies and it indicates an understanding of the benefits these services can yield. In effect, most developed nations and many newly industrialized ones have targeted this sector for special attention, which frequently results in government-funded research and development, export subsidies, and an effort to protect home industries. Many countries are, at the same time, stepping up their efforts to turn international forums on satellite, spectrum allocation, and standards development into extensions of the underlying national policy. Although the United States government is prepared to represent American national interests at such meetings, much still needs to be done.

Over the next few years, there are likely to emerge major communications, information, and electronics-based equipment sales opportunities. Unfortunately, no US-based companies appear well-positioned to capitalize on these opportunities, or particularly interested in pursuing them. Among the likely foreign sales gains are:

- *Telephone handsets* With an average useful life not exceeding seven years, much of the customer premises terminal equipment sold to subscribers in the immediate aftermath of the Bell System breakup is likely to be replaced over the next two to three years. About one-third of the installed base, or about 85 million units, should be sold. At an average installed price of $50, handset sales alone should top $4.25 billion; almost all of these products, however, will be imported from abroad.
- *Television sets* During the past decade, color television set sales peaked at 788,000 units in 1980, and black-and-white sets in 1981, when 260,000 units were sold. After declining through 1985, TV set sales are now picking up. The number of United States households (currently about 96 million) is growing at a rate nearly double the rate of popu- lation growth (as the average household is smaller, and the number of single-person households is rising as well). Assuming an average useful life of about 10 years, we should see, in 1990–1, TV set sales again peak. Estimates are that about 900,000 color sets at an average price of about $400 will be sold that year. Foreign-based firms should thus reap at least $2.5 billion from set sales in 1991 alone (assuming no significant change in current dealer markups, or further expansion by foreign-based manufacturers into distribution and retailing). Profits for manufacturers, however, should improve

markedly; current sales prices are not projected to rise significantly but are based on economies of scope and scale that have not yet been achieved, particularly with Taiwan and South Korean producers. Once sales volumes match those producers' projected levels, the profits earned should be substantially greater than today.

- *Home computers*   At least 21 million home computers (defined by the industry as units costing $3,000 or less) should be sold in the United States through 1992. As many of these units are produced in Asia, or comprised chiefly of Asian components, subassemblies, and assemblies, the United States trade deficit with Japan in computers alone, for example, should rise from the current $4 billion to about $6 billion yearly, or more. At the same time, stronger competition in Europe from indigenous European manufacturers should reduce the surplus that we currently enjoy.

- *Information terminals*   France's Alcatel and Matra have projected United States sales of between 30 to 50 million 'Minitel'-like units in the United States over the next five to seven years, with demand depen- dent in part on actions taken by the Bell companies and the AT&T consent decree court. A study has reportedly been conducted on the feasibility of producing the terminals using the former ITT telephone equipment plant in Corinth, Mississippi, although the portable Minitel units that will be sold in France for Fr. 5,000 will likely be manufactured there. France Telecom currently purchases Minitel terminals for about $190 apiece. If sold at a comparable price here, potential sales would be about $9.5 billion. No US-based computer terminal or other producer evidently has indicated an interest in serving this market.

The former head of what is now the world's largest corporation, Dr Hisashi Shinto of Nippon Telegraph & Telephone, provides a good concluding line. In any number of speeches he suggests that, in communications, we are at the same stage we were in electricity when we learned it could be used to do more than just provide illumination.

As a nation, the United States may have learned over the past decades that it is important to get a better handle on developments in the communications and information field, and to organize ourselves better to facilitate progress. At the same time, much of the traditional bias implicit in federal and state communications policy remains. For the most part, government has concentrated on preventing real or imagined harms. The assumption appears to have been that if government deals with the harms, good things can take care of themselves. Meanwhile, our manufacturing base has been eroded, there has been demonstrable slippage on the research and development fronts, and in certain key respects we stand at risk of becoming a technological colony, chiefly of Japan.

For the prudent person, the events over the past few years ought to suggest that the government no longer should just worry about keeping bad things from happening. It should try to figure out how to make good things happen as well.

The *NTIA Telecom 2000* report is aimed at making good things happen, to the ultimate benefit of our country. But its fundamental message regarding the importance of communications and the contribution this sector can make to economic and societal progress is also universal. Whether it will have the sort of felicitous, affirmative effect that was intended, is an open question. As one of its authors, I hope it will.

Chapter 6

On thinking about deregulation and competition

Michael E. Porter

The first problem in thinking about regulatory reform is to know what this term means. The central issue of regulatory reform used to be whether or not we should deregulate. Today, the meaning of regulatory reform has become much more clouded: The question of whether one should re-regulate comes up as often as whether one should deregulate further.

In the telecommunications industry, however, the debate still centers on how regulations should proceed from here. By focusing on the part of the telecommunications industry that I know best, the interLATA interexchange market, I will try to review the important issues that every regulator must confront when contemplating how to reform regulation.

My perspective is that of a person who works primarily on problems of company strategy. Although my roots are in industrial economics, the perspective of an economist on competition and my perspective as a person who works with companies on strategy are different enough to affect the view of regulatory policy and reform.

I find there are three problems that obscure how regulators and other observers evaluate the rationale for reform of telecommunications regulation. First, the model of competition is often inadequate; second, most regulators have a flawed conception of company strategy, radically different from the one held in industry; third, regulators have the wrong priorities when they assess the benefits of deregulation. I will briefly touch on each of these three areas and use the interLATA market as a case study for how these problems have colored the debate about the future reform of regulation in that market.

With regard to models of competition, discussions of regulatory reform among policymakers often draw on a model of competition that has a long tradition in economics. The model rests on two variables. The first, seller concentration, takes into account the number of competitors and their degree of concentration. By this measure of competition, the interLATA interexchange market is highly concentrated in comparison with the average of all industries. The second variable, barriers to entry, is not universally accepted as a part of the model of competitiveness. For instance, some economists do not believe that there are any barriers to entry. Those who believe in barriers to entry, as I do, tend to view them in relation to the cost of replicating the position of industry leaders; thus, they are generally concerned with economies of scale, learning curve effects, and those sorts of things. Again, if we regard the interLATA market in this way, the barriers to entry appear to be high. The cost of replicating AT&T's position would be very large – in the billions of dollars.

As a consequence of adopting this model, policymakers spend an inordinate amount of time trying to define the industry. This is because seller concentration and, by inference, competition are a function of where the industry's boundaries are drawn.

From my viewpoint as someone working in company strategy, this image of competition is much too narrow. Seller concentration and barriers to entry are significant, but only part of the story – and in telecommunications only a small part of the story. Another model of competition is what I call the industry structure model. The idea is that the competition is broader than mere rivalry and barriers to entry. There are instead five major forces of competition: those two plus the bargaining power of buyers, the bargaining power of suppliers, and the threat of substitute products and services. These five forces determine demand and supply elasticity facing firms in an industry.

If we look at the interLATA interexchange market through this new lens, we reach a strikingly different conclusion than if we limit our view to the traditional lens of seller concentration and barriers to entry: The interLATA market is an intensely rivalrous industry. Why? Because the forces that drive rivalry in an industry are much more numerous than seller concentration alone. One important industry characteristic is its tendency toward intense rivalry. In this industry there are enormous fixed costs as a proportion of value added. There is also significant excess capacity. Moreover, we find high barriers to ever retiring capacity from the market – that is, high barriers to exit, to use terminology starting to become more common.

So we find competitors with high stakes in the market, with conflicting goals, and with tremendous cost pressure to cut price and/or add service to fill up capacity. Not surprisingly, they are locked in a vigorous struggle. The competition is enhanced by the fact that networks are competing. Companies with networks having varying technological capabilities can be readily redeployed to offer different kinds of services. Thus rivalry, far from being low as would be predicted in a highly concentrated industry, is actually intense and likely to remain so for the foreseeable future.

As for buyers, this industry traditionally neglects them, assuming that they are powerless. In a regulated world, they were. But in the deregulated industry, buyers are enormously powerful, very price sensitive, and quite sophisticated. Thousands of consultants advise companies on how to lower the telecommunications costs by buying better. Even grandma in Peoria can easily and cheaply switch from one provider of services to another with simply a phone call or a letter. Some shared tenant services merge the bargaining power of even relatively small business customers. The reasons why the buyers are sophisticated, why they care about this product, why they can buy efficiently, why PBX, the machines of the future, are going to enable them automatically to route these cost services are firmly embedded in the logic of the buyers' businesses. That is not going to change.

As for barriers to entry, it is difficult to replicate AT&T's position, but one does not have to do that. In this industry there are many less expensive ways of getting into the industry, including leasing excess transmission capacity and building regional facilities. Large amounts of excess transmission capacity will be the rule, which means potential entrants with access to customers will be able to lease this capacity from hungry providers who have no other use for it. Even replicating AT&T's national network is within the reach of several corporations. The capital spending budgets per year required to build a national fiber network are not out of line with what a Fortune 100 company would spend on capital investment. Barriers to entry are therefore not invincible. To the contrary, they are relatively low in some segments, and hence a company can slowly build a broader position.

Effective substitutions are taking place – the most significant being that the buyer backward-integrates, providing his own telecommunications capacity or at least a piece of the overall capacity. This is likely to happen more and more, and not simply for reasons of cost, but so that the buyers can obtain improved service and responsiveness in their telecommunications networks.

If, then, you take an old, narrow view of industry structure based on seller concentration and barriers to entry to replicate AT&T, you end up wringing your hands about regulatory reform. But if you look through the new and broader lens of the determinants of industry competition, the conclusion is resounding: Get on with deregulation. What are we worrying about? We have an industry structure that fundamentally supports active competition.

I mentioned earlier that the second problem with regulatory reform is how regulators think about strategy. Economists have not been very interested in strategy until lately. Their usual position is that the environment has driven strategy; that is, companies have maximized within constraints set by the environment. There is not much that a company can do; it is a passive actor in the environment. Most writers have also viewed strategy narrowly and assumed that it was heavily driven by costs. Further, the test of strategic position has been correspondingly narrow, measured primarily by market share. One's strategic position is fully reflected in one's market share. Again, industry definition becomes crucial. What the relevant market is, is of central importance. This conception of strategy by regulators is abetted by the fact that in regulated industries, companies tend to adopt homogeneous strategies. When many variables are regulated, companies do not have many degrees of freedom. They all follow the same strategy. So regulators start believing that all companies are alike, and they all approach the competition in the same way.

If we review the business strategy literature and analyze the experience of other companies, however, we discover that unregulated industries are heterogeneous. The essential issue in strategy is competitive advantage. How can one company gain a sustainable advantage over another? Competitive advantage is rich in character. It involves not only cost, but also what I call differentiation, or the ability to provide superior service and value and command a price premium.

In creating strategy, firms also have myriad possibilities for choosing competitive scope, or the breadth of their strategic target; for example, whether to stay in a niche or whether to offer a full line of services, or create an arrangement in between the extremes. It is clear from the research on strategy that high share does not equal highest profit. It is also clear from the research on strategy that high share does not equal lowest cost or even competitive advantage.

The airline industry provides an example. United Airlines has had the highest share, but they are nowhere near the lowest cost producer. Nor does United have the best quality product. United has a poor strategy and is being punished for it in the marketplace. American Airlines and Delta, with lower market shares, are the differentiated competitors and earn much higher returns. Continental is the low cost producer.

Relating this to the interLATA market, once again the old view of strategy and how it is measured turns us to handwringing: AT&T is dominant, and we should worry. With a broader conception of strategy, however, we find that AT&T's market share is not a good indicator of its competitive advantage. Indeed, Sprint's commercial, which showed that over a Sprint circuit you could hear a pin drop, went straight for AT&T's jugular. It showed that AT&T's service quality and the quality of transmission are not an advantage, nor is its breadth of services.

What about cost? AT&T has a big depreciated network, but AT&T's competitors have brand new, low cost capacity coming on stream. AT&T is racing to catch up and eventually will have the same kind of capacity itself, in which it will have to invest current dollars as well. So here is an industry where the leader, AT&T, does not have a compelling competitive advantage, but is indeed struggling to maintain its position.

My conclusion, already obvious, is that we should get on with deregulation. The price cap concept is unnecessary. Either it will not make any difference or it will turn into a great morass of trying to calculate things that are impossible to calculate – for example, the costs of an individual service where you compete network to network. There is the risk that we will find ourselves in an expensive mess where only the lawyers will be the winners.

As for the benefits of deregulation, many regulators think of them primarily in terms of prices. The perspective is of static efficiency and price–cost margins. Will AT&T rip off poor grandma on the farm? Much evidence in economics, however, suggests that these are not the first order of problems in thinking about deregulation.

There are essentially two main benefits of deregulation. The first is of strategic heterogeneity. Deregulation allows firms to choose different strategies, to offer different bundles of service, to have different mixes of cost and differentiation. That kind of variety is enormously beneficial from an economic standpoint. The second and even more important benefit of deregulation is in promoting dynamic efficiency of progressiveness or innovativeness. Research compellingly indicates that innovation is what really matters, not the price–cost margin. And yet, we concentrate on the price–cost margin and ignore how regulatory changes might affect innovation. Given the breathtaking technological changes in this industry, the real action is obviously in innovation; and so regulators must figure out how to ensure that innovation takes place.

What general conclusions can we draw? The issues I have raised are endemic to all regulation. They exist in electric power, energy, airlines, and a host of other sectors. The tendency is strong to view competition narrowly and inadequately when we assess how to deregulate, and whether and how to continue doing so. Regulators should use the same competitive model as other companies do, and should have a realistic view of competition as other industries do. By taking accurate readings of the health of competition, regulators can encourage and celebrate strategic heterogeneity. They must allow companies to take different approaches and not create policies that force them to adopt the same strategy. Finally, regulators need to think first and foremost about how they might affect innovativeness and technological progress.

As one who works with companies on strategy, I have found that it is easy to underestimate the time it takes for regulated entities to adjust their behavior to reflect competition. Having worked with many regulated entities as they entered a new era of competition, I know that the barriers to adjustment are enormous. They involve an entire generation of management brought up with different rules who are terribly uncomfortable with the new rules. Such problems add years to making strategic adjustments, and hence the behavior of companies will lag behind reality for a while. In such a setting, where behavior lags behind reality, we cannot afford to use these old-fashioned measures of competition and market power. Regulatory reform must be guided by the new realities, not the comfortable, understandable old ones.

Chapter 7

Viewing divestment from afar

Douglas C. Pitt and Kevin Morgan

No country has gone so far, or so quickly, in restructuring its telecommunications sector as has the United States. Indeed, the recent history of
telecommunications policy in the United States is at once awe-inspiring,
on account of the scale of the changes wrought by divestiture, and
bewildering, because the divestiture agreement was contested before the
ink was dry. These developments should not be treated as purely
domestic issues since their effects are being felt, albeit unevenly,
throughout the world. Although many countries have embarked on
regulatory reform, we argue here that the United States experience is
unique. This is because the US has witnessed not so much regulatory
reform as regulatory turbulence, and this can be attributed to the
coexistence of competing centers of regulatory power, itself the product
of an inordinately diffuse policymaking structure – what we call its open
network policy regime. We use the term 'regulatory turbulence' to refer
not just to the celebrated turf fights within government, but to a situation
in which radically different regulatory signals are being transmitted to
the domestic telecommunications community.

In this chapter we examine the political dilemmas facing United
States policy at home, where the main challenge is to devise a coherent
and sustainable telecommunications policy, and abroad, where the
United States faces the formidable political challenge of creating a level
playing field in the international telecommunications arena. We focus
first on domestic policy in the post-divestiture era and, second, on
United States efforts to overcome regulatory asymmetry in the world
market.

Instead of subsuming all regulatory change under the banner of
deregulation, it may be more helpful to speak of parallel regimes of
regulation at the federal level, the traditional regime of the FCC, and the
new Court regime of Judge Greene. Conflict between these two regimes

was not envisaged by the authors of the original divestiture script, that is, the Department of Justice and AT&T. If anything, the Department of Justice saw divestiture as the ultimate form of deregulation in that it would be a substitute for traditional regulation. For the Department of Justice the quintessential purpose of the divestiture was to draw a bright line between the monopoly and competitive segments of the telecommunications industry by vesting each in separately owned companies. In this scenario the *Modification of Final Judgment* (MFJ) should have removed 'the structural problems that have given rise to the controversies between the United States and AT&T over the last three decades.'[1]

As we know, the actual divestiture signally failed to deliver any such line. That it failed to do so provides a graphic illustration of the scope for policy mutation and this, in turn, speaks much about the fragmented policymaking process. One of the main reasons why the Department of Justice's vision failed to materialize was that the original agreement that it struck with AT&T made dubious assumptions about the post-divestiture behavior of parties that had not been privy to the agreement. Quite simply, these other parties refused to 'play the roles assigned to them.'[2] The main delinquents here were the Court and the Regional Bell Operating Companies (RBOCs). Concerned about the RBOCs' ability to sustain universal service, the Court tabled ten amendments to the original *Modified Final Judgment* (MFJ), the two most important being the decision to give the RBOCs the lucrative (and competitive) Yellow Pages business and the decision to waive the restrictions on the RBOCs upon a showing that they could not use their monopoly power to impede competition in the market(s) they sought to enter. Thus the MFJ had already breached the bright line about which the Department of Justice cared so much.

As regards the RBOCs, they were to confound all their critics. Animated by the desire to shed their pedestrian image, they exploited the Court's waiver mechanism to the full; so much so that even before the first triennial review of the MFJ, the Court had sanctioned well over 100 waiver requests, allowing the RBOCs into an array of businesses. Indeed, this waiver process encouraged the RBOCs to set their sights on markets that were forbidden to them under the terms of the MFJ, namely, interexchange, manufacturing, and information services. Before we examine this threat to the MFJ, it is worth elaborating on the respective regulatory policies of the FCC and the Court.

The centerpiece of the FCC's regulatory policies, all of which are geared to deregulation, is its *Computer III* decision, adopted in May

1986. Put simply, *Computer III* was a response to the problems associated with the FCC's previous *Computer II* ruling, which had distinguished between (regulated) basic and (unregulated) enhanced services. In an effort to ensure that carriers did not subsidize their unregulated ventures from regulated earnings, the FCC required structurally separate subsidiaries if carriers wished to offer enhanced services. However, in response to strong pressure from AT&T and the RBOCs, who argued that separate subsidiaries entailed excessive costs, the FCC dropped this requirement in favor of the nonstructural safeguards of *Computer III*.

Without a doubt the key regulatory mechanism in the FCC's current policy arsenal is Open Network Architecture (ONA). An extremely ambitious concept, ONA involves the overall design of a carrier's basic regulated network to permit all users, including competing enhanced service providers, to interconnect with basic network functions on an equal access basis. Although ONA is very much the jewel in the FCC's regulatory crown it is still at a primitive stage of development. Indeed, judging by the criticism that greeted the RBOCs' first ONA plans, this regulatory concept will need all the political support it can muster.

Among the main criticisms made were that the RBOCs have simply put an ONA gloss on features and functions that were already available; that they have not sufficiently unbundled these basic service elements; that ONA offerings vary from one RBOC to another; and that some of the RBOCs were engaging in strategic pricing of their ONA offerings.[3] Although disappointed by this adverse reaction, the FCC still approved the RBOCs' plans, albeit with certain caveats, like asking for more uniformity with respect to terminology, technical characteristics, and deployment of ONA services.

Phenomenally complex issues, and deeply antagonistic interests, are involved in this ONA challenge. For example, how far should local networks be unbundled when other forces, like ISDN, appear to be pushing in the direction of greater integration? Who will decide which tradeoffs are to be made between uniformity and diversity in ONA offerings across the country? Then there is the highly sensitive issue of regulatory jurisdiction as between federal and state authorities, the latter being deeply suspicious of the FCC's motives in this field. Indeed, the New York, Californian, and Michigan state commissions have jointly challenged the FCC's *Computer III* decision in the Court of Appeals, in which they assert state jurisdiction over intrastate ONA services, including the right to retain or remove structural separations on the RBOCs!

ONA is turning into a political challenge, not just for the RBOCs, who see it as a quid pro quo for getting into the forbidden information services market, but for the entire United States telecommunications system because no other country has placed such a high premium on the parts over the whole, on competition over coordination. ONA clearly raises a whole series of unanswered questions, and, in doing so, it creates a new wave of turbulence and uncertainty for government, industry, and users. If ONA is ever going to be successful, there will have to be a much greater degree of cooperation between federal and state authorities and between the RBOCs, enhanced service vendors, and users.[4]

The ONA cause has also suffered from the fact that the FCC lacks credibility as a regulatory enforcement agency because the Office of the Chairman became so politicized during the tenure of Mark Fowler, who was associated with a policy of deregulation at all costs. This credibility problem, which was severely exacerbated by the FCC's decision to repeal the fairness doctrine in broadcasting, helps to explain why potentially sound new policies, like the proposal to substitute price cap for rate of return regulation, command so little political support. Alongside the FCC the Court has emerged as a powerful new regulatory force. In several important rulings Judge Greene has earned himself a reputation as a robust and politically subtle jurist. Although opponents seek to disparage Greene as an inflexible regulatory czar, it is worth recalling that it was his decision to insert the famous section VIII(C) amendment into the divestiture agreement, without which the RBOCs would be operating under a much more draconian set of MFJ restrictions. This amendment covered the waiver mechanism to which we have already referred and allowed for the MFJ restrictions to be reviewed every three years by the Department of Justice and the Court.

The tension inherent in this system of parallel regulation first surfaced at the time of the triennial review. In its triennial report to the Court, the Department of Justice, which by this time had undergone a political metamorphosis, wanted to dismantle most of the MFJ restrictions. These, it argued, had been rendered futile by the growth of competition and the advance of technological alternatives. The Court, however, came to a radically different conclusion: In a major rebuff to the RBOC camp, Greene refused to make any fundamental change in the MFJ because, he argued, there was no evidence that the RBOCs' monopoly over the local network had been eroded since divestiture. Whereas the Department of Justice had expressed confidence in the FCC's regulatory capacity, Greene questioned its ability to control anti-competitive abuse, citing as evidence inadequate FCC resources and the weakening of regulatory safeguards, like the dropping of separate subsidiaries. The only concession to the RBOCs was Greene's decision to dilute the ban on information services by allowing the RBOCs to engage in the transmission (but not the content) side of information services. So while the FCC regime allows the RBOCs to participate fully in information, or enhanced services, the Court regime only allows them to play a gateway role.

Further conflict occurred when the Court delivered a ruling on the meaning of 'manufacture' in the divestiture agreement. AT&T had asked Greene to clarify what the term included, because a similar request to the Department of Justice had not been acted on in nearly two years. In the face of intense pressure from the RBOC camp, which wanted a narrow definition, Greene defined the term broadly, saying that the divestiture agreement intended 'to bar the Regional Companies from the entire manufacturing process, including design, development, and fabrication.'[5]

This manufacturing ruling was particularly notable for the way in which the Court assailed the Department of Justice and the FCC. Greene chided the former for its failure to enforce the ban, but he saved his main ire for Dennis Patrick, the FCC chairman, who, said Greene, 'took the unusual, if not unprecedented, step for the head of a federal regulatory agency, of exhorting those whom the agency regulates to refuse to comply with orders duly issued by this Court.'[6] Here Greene was counter-attacking. Earlier in the year Patrick had accused the Court of having abused its position and of having preempted the authority of Congress and the FCC, and he expressed surprise that the RBOCs were acquiescing in the 'ongoing administration of the MFJ.'[7] These are not harmless turf fights. What we have here is the spectacle of two centers of regulatory power locked in a fundamental conflict, each giving the industry radically different signals.

As things stand, government and industry are both internally divided over the future direction of domestic telecommunications policy. On one side a powerful anti-MFJ coalition has emerged, consisting of the RBOCs, the Department of Justice, the FCC, and the National Telecommunications and Information Administration (NTIA). The NTIA seems to have assumed the role of chief political choreographer in this coalition, partly because it is responsible for coordinating telecommunications policy in the Executive. Indeed, the NTIA was the first federal agency to question the wisdom of the divestiture agreement because it sees the MFJ as warehousing half the nation's telecommunications industry at a time when the United States position in high technology is under threat. This coalition has launched several legislative initiatives to get all or parts of the MFJ rescinded. For example, the so-called Dole Bill, which was an unsuccessful attempt to transfer control of the MFJ from the Court to the FCC, was actually prepared by the agencies mentioned above. One of the main reasons why the Dole Bill was stopped in its tracks was the enormously successful opposition campaign waged by the No-Name coalition. This coalition, a pro-MFJ lobbying force, was specifically set up to counter the Dole Bill, and it has stayed together to protect the integrity of the MFJ. The No-Name coalition represents the widest cross-section of corporate interests ever formed in the United States telecommunications sector, including strange bedfellows like AT&T and MCI, trade associations like ADAPSO, and user groups like the ICA. In many ways this is an unholy alliance, the one common denominator being a shared fear that the RBOCs represent a threat if the MFJ is ever rescinded. Not surprisingly this coalition preaches virtues of antitrust, its motto being 'Remember the Sherman Act.'

These contending interests are the main forces shaping United States regulatory policy. Resonant themes are being tapped on both sides. The pro-MFJ camp appeals to notions of fair competition, level playing fields, and to an antitrust tradition which the Reagan Administration tried its best to bury. The RBOC camp, on the other hand, appeals to notions of free competition and deregulation in an attempt to portray the MFJ as an obstacle to a better trade balance and a threat to intelligent (public) networks. The Reagan Administration tried, but failed, to resolve this contest in favor of the RBOCs. Its successor may find that the real challenge lies not just in composing a new telecommunications policy, but in getting the various branches of government to play the same tune.

If regulatory turbulence is the main feature of the domestic telecommunications environment, then regulatory asymmetry is what characterizes the international level. As the first country to dismantle its regulatory barriers to entry, the United States unwittingly exposed itself to what we might call the burden of deregulation in one country. Notwithstanding the benefits that have flowed from deregulation and divestiture, this experience has not been without its costs, many of which can be traced back to regulatory asymmetry (i.e., to the fact that the US was deregulating in a highly regulated, and therefore largely closed, world telecommunications market).

The conventional wisdom in Western Europe seems to be that deregulation and divestiture were the product of strategic decisions from governments bent on unleashing American firms onto the world market. However, there are two problems with this conception. On a factual level, deregulation and divestiture were prosecuted as matters of domestic policy with little or no reference to the international trade dimension. On a more theoretical level, such a contention exaggerates the degree to which concerted action is possible within government itself or between government and industry. Let us be clear: We are not suggesting that the United States government is not trying to play a more forceful role in support of its multinationals abroad, only that it faces great problems doing so given the extraordinarily diffuse United States political system. In short, the US capacity for cohesiveness is low, especially in telecommunications, where at least two dozen agencies could claim to be involved in the development and implementation of policy. However, we maintain that enormous efforts are underway to secure greater cohesiveness within government and between government and industry; in each case the aim is to export as much of the United States regulatory model as possible. It is in this way that the United States hopes to be able to remove, or at least ease, the burden of deregulation in one country.

The dangers of pursuing regulatory reform without any reference to the external trade dimension were evident at the time, and no one did more to draw attention to these dangers than Senator John Danforth. Backed by the equipment industry, Danforth bemoaned the fact that divestiture and deregulation had been driven by purely domestic considerations. In the context of introducing a new telecommunications bill (S. 2618), he said:

> In this interdependent world we cannot afford to make decisions in a vacuum. We cannot afford to let trade be the stepchild of domestic policy decisions. . . . In trade terms, the break-up of AT&T is more than just the unilateral elimination of a major barrier to imports. It also means that on January 1, 1984, we may have discarded the only trade concession that could ever be effective negotiating leverage for the US to gain reciprocal market access for our telecommunications exports. It is hard to imagine any other US concession providing as much incentive for foreign telecommunications manufacturers and their governments to really open up domestic markets.[8]

It was not that the Administration was wholly unaware of the potentially adverse trade effects of divestiture: It would be nearer the truth to say that it underestimated how quickly the trade deficit would subsequently mount, for two reasons. First, the Administration did not fully appreciate the negative effect on United States exports of a strong dollar. Second, it was too optimistic about the prospects for removing regulatory barriers to entry in overseas markets.

Whatever the precise reasons, the trade front has been a bounty for the prophets of doom. The telecommunications equipment trade balance has progressively deteriorated from a surplus in 1980 to a deficit of $2.7 billion in 1988, while in the same period the trade deficit increased from $36.2 billion to over $171 billion. Accustomed for so long to being the global leader in high technology industry (i.e., R&D-intensive sectors), the authorities were shaken by the fact that this high technology trade balance was also slipping badly.[9] We should not forget, however, that this dismal trade picture refers not to the declining fortunes of firms but, rather, to the decline of the United States as a place of production.[10] It seems that a significant part of the high technology trade imbalance can be attributed to American firms making greater use of their Southeast Asian subsidiaries, where labor costs are much lower than in the United States. Hence AT&T is one of the top 'Taiwanese' exporters in telecommunications and IBM is the largest 'Japanese' exporter in computers. The deepening trade deficit created a more fertile ideological climate for those who wished to fashion a domestic regulatory policy that was more compatible with United States trade interests. The NTIA has been the most vociferous advocate of such a change in policy, arguing that:

> the US today is engaged in the functional equivalent of economic warfare with certain of its traditional trading partners, particularly in the critical telecommunications and computer, or information industry sector. By virtue of self-inflicted wounds, Government actions proven imprudent in hindsight, and persistent foreign restrictions on US-based competition, there is a significant chance America's future in this 'sunrise,' high-tech sector will be eclipsed if current policies are not changed.[11]

If the trade deficit created a new climate, the event that persuaded the Administration to step up its offensive against foreign telecom regimes was the CGCT affair. AT&T had set a high premium on acquiring CGCT, a publicly owned French telecom firm, and it seemed well poised to do so because it had received reassuring signals to this effect from France Telecom. The contest turned into a major political dispute, though, when the Bonn government began lobbying in favor of Siemens, the German national champion. In an attempt to placate American and German feelings, the French government eventually decided to allow an Ericsson-dominated alliance to acquire CGCT in April 1987. The CGCT affair convinced the Administration that telecommunications had moved into the realm of high politics.

The CGCT affair had two other effects on the Administration. First, it encouraged the formation of the Breakfast Club, an informal gathering of the heads of all agencies with a major stake in telecommunications policy formation. This was yet another attempt to achieve greater interagency cohesiveness, the main aim of which was to try to present a common face to the external world on international policy issues. The fact that this club was thought to be necessary speaks volumes for the inefficacy of the Senior Interagency Group on International Communications and Information Policy (SIG), which was set up in 1984 with the aim of bringing greater coherence to United States policy formation in this area.

Second, the CGCT affair encouraged the FCC to try to expand its own authority in the field of international trade regulation. The FCC's ambitions in this field had been fueled by the new mood in Congress, which seemed to indicate growing support for sector-specific trade legislation like the Telecommunications Trade Act of 1985, which was introduced by Senator John Danforth.

It is worth dwelling on the FCC's initiative because it illustrates the potential for jurisdictional fights within the government and because it sheds light on how difficult it is for industry to agree to a common political platform. The clearest indication of the FCC's ambitions came in December 1986, when it voted to issue a notice of inquiry and proposed rulemaking with respect to what action it should take to persuade foreign governments to open their markets to United States firms.[12] Admitting that its authority in the trade arena was at best ambiguous, the FCC nevertheless suggested that it should develop an international model that would represent an ideal to be sought in international telecommunications and a benchmark against which national and international policies and practices may be compared. The Commission also invited comment as to whether it could or should vary access to the United States market for foreign firms depending on the degree to which their countries of origin were open to US firms. Among the proposed rule changes the FCC wanted to increase reporting requirements, the aim of which was to gain a better picture of foreign penetration of the United States equipment and services market, and this was eventually introduced in February 1988.

In all, forty-nine parties filed comments, and the vast majority of them objected to the FCC's proposal to restrict access to the United States market. The RBOCs, for example, saw the proposal as a threat to their freedom to procure equipment from wherever they wished, while companies with extensive overseas interests feared a protectionist backlash from foreign governments. Many other parties, prominent among which were federal agencies, claimed that the FCC did not (and should not) have the authority to take unilateral initiatives based on trade factors. What concerned the traditional trade players, like the United States Trade Representative (USTR), the State Department, and the Commerce Department, was that the FCC lacked the diplomatic skills necessary in international negotiations and that another player would make it more difficult to achieve interagency cohesiveness. The traditional trade players were also defending their political turf against the claims of an aspiring new player.

This was not the first time that the FCC had tried to create a more prominent role for itself in the international arena. For example, a major interagency dispute broke out in 1985, when the United States Administration decided to initiate a Market Access Fact Finding (MAFF) exercise, consisting of bilateral talks with countries whose telecom markets were thought to be closed to United States firms. Although the Department of Commerce led the first of these MAFF talks (with Germany in 1985), a battle arose between the FCC, Commerce, and USTR over which agency should assume the lead with other countries: The FCC insisted that its technical expertise made it the natural chairman; while Commerce, itself divided between the NTIA and the ITA, argued in favor of its wider expertise in trade negotiations. Instead of resolving the issue, however, an informal deal was struck whereby each agency assumed the lead role with different countries, for example, USTR with the European Community itself, NTIA with Spain and South Korea, ITA with Sweden and Italy, FCC with the UK and France.

This arrangement did nothing to resolve tensions in the system. Although these tensions undoubtedly reflect the jurisdictional wars so common in the American system, they reflect much more than this. At bottom these agencies have different political priorities and, as often as not, the main contrast is between the FCC and the State Department. With its narrow sectoral remit the FCC can afford to adopt a more aggressive line in international negotiations on telecommunications;

indeed, the FCC has been one of the main advocates of sectoral reciprocity in telecom trade talks, a concept to which the Reagan Administration was very much opposed. Being the principal foreign policy advisor to the President, the State Department occupies a radically different position, being obliged to take a far more panoramic view, and, not infrequently, the narrow material interest of the nation is subordinated to diplomatic or military exigencies. For example, State appears to have had a moderating influence on the Reagan Administration's attitude to telecom talks with Germany because it did not want to antagonize the Germans prior to sensitive negotiations in the North Atlantic Treaty Organization.

Not surprisingly, the telecommunications industry has been deeply critical of the fragmentation of political authority in this sector, a problem compounded by the lack of an institutional memory brought about because of the high turnover of expert staff within government. In such a fragmented political system there is a powerful incentive for corporations to forge coalitions through which to educate government as to the corporate agenda. Perhaps the most effective of the many coalitions in United States telecommunications is the US Council for International Business, which represents over 300 of the largest American-based corporations in and beyond telecommunications. The Council's telecommunications committee consists of companies that use, manufacture, and provide equipment and services. The leading firms on this committee are drawn from IBM, Citibank, Nynex, and GTE, each of which represents a specific segment of the telecommunications industry. The Council is the US affiliate of the International Chamber of Commerce and the Business and Industry Advisory Committee to the Organization for Economic Cooperation and Development (OECD). It can justly claim to have driven the telecom agendas of both these international organizations.

Because the Council's telecommunications committee is so broad-based, however, it has mirrored the conflicts in the wider United States telecommunications industry as to how best to respond to regulatory asymmetry. For example, there is a good deal of conflict about whether to proceed multilaterally or bilaterally through sector-specific initiatives like MAFF. This debate has divided the Council itself, especially between the equipment suppliers and the rest; the former favored sector-specific action in the Trade Bill, although many users and service vendors feared that their external interests would suffer if the equipment firms' interests were pushed too aggressively. The Council has played an important role in at least two ways: first, in bringing together the disparate segments of the industry so each has become more alive to the other's interests; second, in helping to forge a greater degree of cohesiveness between government and industry. The most tangible sign of this trend toward unity is the Telecommunications Trade Task Force that was formed under the auspices of the United States Chamber of Commerce near the end of 1987. The industry side of this task force is carefully balanced to reflect the main segments of the industry – users, equipment suppliers, and service providers – and the membership base includes individual companies (like AT&T, IBM, Nynex, Control Data) and trade associations (like ICA, ADAPSO, the United States Council for International Business). On the government side the main agencies involved are those with a major responsibility in the trade policy field, namely, USTR, Commerce, State, and the FCC.

The task force emerged at the time when the government was soliciting views from industry about what agenda should be adopted for the MAFF initiative. Since then its membership has grown quite significantly and it is now the chief forum for developing a common industry response to a wide range of telecommunications trade policy issues. The main aims of the task force are to obtain:

- market access on reasonable terms for telecommunications equipment providers and value-added and information service vendors;
- non-discriminatory access to and use of telecommunications transport services;
- freedom to choose customer premises equipment;
- safeguards to prevent anti-competitive behavior toward foreign providers by government-controlled monopolies;
- transparent and reasonable domestic regulations starting with the separation of regulatory and operational functions;
- unrestricted movement of information among countries and companies.

Along with these substantive aims – indeed, in order to achieve them – the task force sets a high premium on making the government's interagency policy process more coherent and consistent, thus reducing the scope for debilitating turf fights, and on forging a more structured relation between government and industry. If the most sophisticated thinking on regulatory asymmetry has been done in forums like the task force and the United States Council, however, the tide of events has often been driven by more elemental forces, such as the neomercantilist current in Congress, which has lobbied, in part successfully, for the Administration to adopt a much tougher trade policy stance. Some of the neomercantilist demands have been met, albeit in an attenuated fashion, by the passage of the Omnibus Trade and Competitiveness Act of 1988. In the emerging repertoire this new trade legislation is the most distinctive weapon, partly because of its provisions for unilateral action on the part of the United States. Thus in an effort to overcome regulatory asymmetry the nation has launched offensives on three distinct political fronts: the unilateral, the bilateral, and the multilateral, each of which merits attention.

As regards unilateral action, pride of place must go to the 1988 Trade Act, described by its sponsors as the most assertive trade legislation since 1945, and which America's trade partners consider to be the most protectionist. However, the Act is not protectionist in the classical sense of restraining imports; it aims, rather, to expand exports by forcing other countries to open their markets. In other words, the Trade Act is an attempt to systematize a policy hitherto pursued on a sporadic and *ad hoc* basis.[13] Although the Reagan Administration claimed to be resolutely opposed to any sector-specific trade measures, it eventually accepted the provisions designed to promote the telecommunications industry. Simply stated, the Act obliges the Administration to identify objectionable Acts, policies, or practices and requires these to be negotiated away under threat of sanctions: Special emphasis is accorded to countries with large trade surpluses and to issues like trade in telecommunications, intellectual property rights, and public procurement.

Under the terms of the Trade Act the USTR had five months after the date of enactment to identify priority foreign countries, that is, countries which were said to be denying mutually advantageous market opportunities to United States products and services. The first priority countries to be selected under the Trade Act were South Korea and the European Community, the rationale being their high volume of exports to the United States, their potential for United States sales, and their barriers to telecommunications trade. Arriving at this selection was not an easy task. In fact the USTR was inundated with recommendations for different priority countries by the agencies that constitute the interagency Trade Policy Review Group: among the countries cited were France, Germany, Spain, and Italy.

The USTR's decision to cite the European Community, rather than a particular member state, was a shrewd piece of diplomacy because the European Commission sees itself as the locus of authority for trade negotiations. Even so, some members of the Trade Policy Review Group are anxious for the Administration to keep the pressure on individual European countries, especially since the USTR review found that telecommunications trade barriers varied so much within the

Community, with Germany and France situated on the illiberal side of the spectrum as viewed through American eyes. All the ingredients are here for a telecommunications-related trade war between the United States and the European Community. The European Commission is deeply troubled by the Trade Act, particularly by the provisions which allow the United States to make unilateral decisions on what constitutes a trade barrier, and by the espousal of sectoral reciprocity in telecommunications, a concept which contravenes the GATT according to the Commission.

At bottom the Commission believes that the United States offensive against the Community is misdirected. It is at pains to stress that the Community's share of United States telecommunications imports has been on a declining curve and is of minor significance compared to the scale of imports from the Pacific Basin. On top of this the Commission argues that the United States has enjoyed a steadily growing telecommunications trade surplus with the Community, which stood at $320 million in 1986, a surplus that would be larger still if data processing equipment were added to the picture (and the Commission maintains that it should be included given the convergence between these sectors). In short the Commission feels that the United States is firing indiscriminately at its trading rivals when, in reality, the source of the trade problem is the Pacific Basin, and more fundamentally the chronic budget deficit.[14] As we see later, one paradoxical effect of the Trade Act has been to strengthen the hand of the neomercantilist lobby within the Community.

Because the Trade Act took some three years to get enacted, the Administration was forced by growing Congressional activism to take more immediate action on the telecom front, hence the Market Access Fact Finding (MAFF) exercise, which was launched in 1985. This is the bilateral front, where the US has tried to educate countries about the benefits of deregulation, to assess how much their markets are open to United States firms, and to pressure them to liberalize their telecom markets. What made bilateral action all the more appealing was the fact that telecommunications is not yet subject to the General Agreement on Trade and Tariffs (GATT), which meant that the payoff from multilateral action was too distant.

As we have seen, the first MAFF exercise was conducted with Germany in December 1985. The Germans agreed to these talks only after the United States had threatened to initiate Section 301 actions against the FRG on the grounds that the Bundespost was engaged in restrictive regulatory practices. The United States followed this in 1986 with MAFF talks with France, Spain, and Italy. Each of these member states has been advised by the Commission to refrain from further bilateral talks with the United States because trade negotiations must be handled at Community rather than member state level. As if to placate the Commission, the USTR has been careful with its political vocabulary: The MAFF exercise, it insisted, was all about 'talks' not 'negotiations.' But this distinction did nothing to allay the fears of the authorities in Brussels that the United States was using bilateral pressure to divide and rule the member states of the Community.

Fortunately for the United States, however, the Community is far from being a monolithic political bloc. On a spectrum of liberality the UK and the Netherlands are the most liberal and Germany, France, and Spain are the least liberal in terms of their telecommunications regimes. Because the UK is closer to the United States than it is to Germany as regards regulatory ideology, it was only a matter of time before they reached a bilateral agreement, which they duly did in 1988 with respect to international value-added networks (IVANs). The most notable feature of this deal was the fact that it took nearly two years to get it signed: One of the main reasons for this inordinate delay was the inability of the government agencies to agree among themselves, particularly in regard to what many of them saw as the FCC's uncompromising demands on international leased lines, demands which the UK government was reluctant to accept. The FCC's stance infuriated the United States Council; the latter felt that even without the FCC's demand the IVAN pact with the UK represented a very good deal for the United States. In other words an interagency turf fight had had a deleterious effect on United States interests. However, the United States is not about to give up on its bilateral offensive, especially since it is beginning to yield tangible results in Europe and Japan.

Last but not least is the multilateral arena, where the United States is engaged in much longer term initiatives. Because the United States is intent on prying open telecommunications markets worldwide, it is necessarily involved in the task of reforming (or perhaps even by-passing) the international institutions that have regulated these markets. For the United States this is especially the case with the International Telecommunications Union (ITU), the main regulatory and standards-setting body. Quite simply, the United States sees the ITU as a major obstacle to its deregulatory goals because it believes the ITU is overly influenced by public monopolies. Hence one of the main aims of the United States is to try to get the telecommunications sector subjected to the GATT process; from a United States standpoint this would force the telecommunications debate 'into a broader, and perhaps more congenial, policy milieu.'[15]

The United States has worked long and hard to get the public telephone monopolies covered by the GATT Government Procurement Code, which provides for a non-discriminatory tendering process for government purchases. The United States has also tried to improve the situation with respect to non-tariff technical barriers to trade because the GATT Standards Code does not cover network equipment. Finally, the United States is the major driving force behind the attempt to develop a GATT framework for telecommunications services in the Uruguay Round of trade negotiations. In the absence of a GATT framework some of the main multilateral battles have occurred in the ITU, especially in the run up to the ITU's World Administrative Telegraph and Telephone Conference (WATTC), which met in December 1988 to try to define the regulatory regime for new telecommunications services. The main conflict here was between those countries (like France) which wanted to extend the hand of regulation and those (like the United States and the UK) which wanted as few regulations as possible. While the outcome was sufficiently ambiguous for each country to carry on as before, WATTC demonstrated two things: First, the United States vision of regulatory reform was still being highly contested; second, the multilateral road was as laborious as ever.

To the extent that the United States travels down this multilateral road, therefore, it will be more than ever anxious to get the issues debated in liberal trade forums, like the GATT, rather than in the more technical and illiberal ITU type of forum. Even so, it is highly unlikely that the ITU apparatus will be bypassed in the event of a GATT-based telecommunications trade agreement. Rather, the likelihood is that there will be a growing overlap of jurisdictional boundaries, a situation which is bound to spawn continuous turf fights between the two organizations and their respective allies.

In an attempt to ease the burden of deregulation in one country, the United States has taken it for granted that the GATT is ineffective. It has thus pursued unilateral, bilateral, and multilateral action at the same time. This scatter-gun approach seemed the only way to deliver the goods – in this case the opening of foreign telecommunications markets. But some of these initiatives appear to be politically inconsistent with one another, especially between the unilateral and multilateral levels. For example, if the United States wishes to strengthen the multilateral trading system – and its enthusiasm for the Uruguay Round suggests that it does – then, logically, it must accept multilateral surveillance of its own actions. Logic, however, is a poor guide in the tempestuous waters of international trade politics. The United States conundrum may be summed as follows: 'Logic dictates that the United States has to change its own (trade) legislation. Political realities mean that the prospects of this are, unfortunately, remote.'[16]

Quite apart from their lack of consistency some of these initiatives appear to be having counter-productive effects. For instance, the unilateral provisions in the Trade Act seem to have strengthened the hand of neomercantilist elements in the European Community. This was all too clear when the Commission announced its directive on public procurement in October 1988, which covers the purchasing activities of entities providing water, energy, transport, and telecommunications services. The directive says that member states can reject any bid if the value of at least half the products and services comes from outside the Community. Even if a bid meets the 50 percent requirement, bids by European companies will be preferred as long as they are deemed to be equivalent and not more than 3 percent higher in price.[17] In other words, the directive embodied a much tougher line on trade than had been expected, and this was attributed to the hawkish United States Trade Act.

A trade war serves the interest of neither the United States nor Europe, yet early skirmishes have already begun. Telecommunications may well be at the forefront because it is a sector where the United States has chosen to seek bilateral reciprocity, as determined by the United States, rather than the GATT concept of multilaterally agreed non-discriminatory reciprocity. More generally the United States seems to be moving closer to the concept of managed trade, as is the Community. In short, there is little to choose between the ways in which United States and European trade policies have evolved: Both have adopted discrimination as a norm.[18] Much will depend on how the Community implements its 1992 proposals for a single European market. If the United States feels that a Fortress Europe is emerging (i.e., external barriers go up while internal barriers come down), European firms can ready themselves for a terrible backlash in the United States market.

In this chapter we have examined some of the political dilemmas of America's open network policy regime at home and abroad. One of the main conclusions is that deregulation does not necessarily involve less government intervention: At the federal level the role of government is changing rather than diminishing. For example, while the traditional regulatory role of the FCC is being scaled down, the rise of the

Court-based regime signals a form of reregulation. Although deregulation and divestiture have delivered real benefits – especially for the business user community – these policy changes carry costs as well, on the trade front especially. There is also the intangible cost of regulatory turbulence, which renders corporate planning more difficult than it would otherwise be.

The diffuse, pluralistic nature of the United States political system has many strengths – it is a bulwark against centralization and it offers great scope for policy experimentation, to name but two. Recently, however, the opportunity costs of this system have become more prominent. At a time when other countries are upgrading their telecom infrastructures and streamlining their regulatory processes, the United States regulatory system is inordinately time-consuming, in part because it affords firms unrivalled opportunities to contest regulatory decisions. The regime of parallel regulation at the federal level compounds this problem because the FCC and the Court have been emitting radically different signals to the industry.

The opportunity costs of such turf wars may have been easier to bear when the United States rode high in world markets, but that time has passed. Its extraordinarily diffuse political system means that America has a low capacity for political cohesiveness within government and between government and industry. Compared to the more centralized systems of Japan and France, which have strong government–industry interfaces, the United States system may find it more difficult to develop infrastructural technologies, like ISDN and High Definition Television (HDTV), which have high up-front costs and involve a degree of collaboration unprecedented in the past. This dilemma is now a resonant issue in the United States; indeed, it has induced elements in government and industry to press for new public–private partnerships to exploit ISDN and HDTV.[19] These initiatives are a modest attempt to overcome the opportunity costs of America's open network policy regime, associated as it is with regulatory turbulence and political fragmentation.

At the international level the government has been forced to become more, not less, interventionist, especially in the areas of standards-setting, communications trade policy, and market access. This is motivated by a renewed determination to create a level playing field – to remove the regulatory asymmetries in the global telecommunications market. However, this is going to be an arduous task, not least because it touches the sensitive issue of national sovereignty. Although the United States has made some progress in concerting itself here, its unilateralist actions on the trade front may prove to be counterproductive. As we have seen, the passage of the Trade Act fortified mercantilist elements in the European Community.

At domestic and international levels, then, it is naive to think that deregulation will remove telecommunications from the political arena. If anything, the reverse is true, namely that telecommunications issues are becoming the stuff of high politics at home and abroad. Time alone will tell whether America's open network policy regime, in which political power and regulatory authority are highly fragmented, is the most optimal system to carry the United States into the new era of international competition in telecommunications.

NOTES

1 Department of Justice, *Competitive Impact Statement* (Federal Register, Vol. 47, No. 32, February 10, 1982), p. 7177.
2 Peter Temin, *The Fall of the Bell System* (Cambridge, Cambridge University Press, 1987), p. 341.
3 See Kevin Morgan and Douglas Pitt, 'Coping With Turbulence: Corporate Strategy, Regulatory Politics and Telematics in Post-Divestiture America,' in Nick Garnham (ed.), *Proceedings of the Communications Policy Research Conference* (London, Communications Policy Research Conference, 1989).
4 Eli Noam, *Filing and Review of ONA Plans* (FCC Docket No. 88-2), 1988.
5 Judge Harold Greene, *USA v. Western Electric Company: Civil Action No. 82-0192, Opinion* (December 3, 1987).
6 *ibid.*, pp. 11–12.
7 Carol Wilson, 'Patrick Challenges RHCs To Question Greene's Authority,' *Telephony* (October 19, 1987), p. 8.
8 John Danforth, *Congressional Record* (Vol. 130, No. 53, May 1, 1984), p. 1.
9 Quick, Finan & Associates, *The US Trade Position in High Technology: Report to the Joint Economic Committee of the US Congress* (Washington, DC, Quick, Finan & Associates, 1986).
10 Richard Lipsey and Irving Kravis, 'The Competitiveness and Comparative Advantage of US Multinationals' (Banca Nazionale del Lavoro, 1987), pp. 147–65.
11 National Telecommunications and Information Administration, *NTIA Trade Report: Assessing the Effects of Changing the AT&T Antitrust Consent Decree* (US Department of Commerce, 1987), p. 54.
12 Federal Communications Commission, *Regulatory Policies and International Telecommunications* (FCC Docket No. 86-494, 1986).
13 Peter Montagnon, 'Row Over The Bill,' *Financial Times* (April 28, 1988).
14 Alan Cawson *et al.*, *Hostile Brothers: Competition and Closure in the European Electronics Industry* (Oxford, Oxford University Press, 1990).
15 Jonathan Aronson and Peter Cowhey, *When Countries Talk* (Cambridge, Ballinger, 1988).

16 *Financial Times*, 'The US in the Dock' (February 14, 1989).
17 Jennifer Schenker, 'Hard Line By EEC Telecom Trade,' *Communications Week International* (October 24, 1988).
18 David Henderson, '1992: The External Trade Dimension,' *The Group of Thirty* (London, private communication, 1990).
19 See National Institute of Standards and Technology, *Methods For Achieving A Unified ISDN in North America* (Washington, DC, 1988); and Kevin Morgan and Robin Mansell, 'The Coming Intelligent Network,' in Philip Cooke (ed.) *Regulation, Innovation and Spatial Development* (London, Unwin and Hyman, 1990).

Chapter 8

The ecology of games in telecommunications policy

William H. Dutton

In the 1980s, communications scholars began to pay more attention to the politics of communications policy, not surprising in light of the profound changes affecting broadcasting, cable, and telecommunications.[1] Why, for example, after over a decade of restrictive policy, did the British launch efforts to develop cable television systems? Britain, like France, Germany, and many other European nations, had previously restricted the development of cable to serve as relay systems, designed only to retransmit broadcast stations received over the air. Why the change? And how can we account for equally dramatic shifts in the telecommunications arena with the French P&T's development of cable television systems, the moves to privatize British Telecom and Nippon Telegraph and Telephone, and the divestiture of AT&T?

One approach to understanding the factors shaping these developments has been through research on the policymaking process in communications. Policy researchers have offered several explanations for policy change in communications. None, however, seems to incorporate the almost routine interactions between developments in communications and events outside the common purview of communications policy studies. In the United States, for example, efforts in the late 1970s and early 1980s to rewrite the Communications Act of 1934 were overwhelmed by antitrust policy – that is, the settlement of the Department of Justice's antitrust case against AT&T. In Britain the government's restrictive cable policy took a back seat once cable system development became identified with an information technology industrial policy (Dutton, 1987; Dutton and Blumler, 1988). Later, its effort to promote the development of private cable TV systems was nearly stillborn after the surprise announcement of a change in tax policy that disallowed capital allowances for investment in cable plants. In the European Community, the Commission's 1992 policy initiative in developing a common market for telecommunications was forced to respond to a wave of nationalism and democratic reforms throughout Eastern Europe, epitomized by the collapse of the Berlin Wall in 1989.

A central argument of this chapter is that prevailing explanations of policy change in communications fail to incorporate the role of such interactions across different domains of corporate and public affairs. Such interactions are treated as aberrations, or unique historical circumstances outside the reach of prevailing theories. It may be, however, that prevailing interpretations have fallen short of the mark because they are not anchored in an adequate model of the broader system of action governing the development of communications. I shall present the outlines of one candidate model of this broader system of action that is based on what Norton Long (1958) termed 'an ecology of games.'

I begin by describing the concept of an ecology of games. In doing so, I hope it becomes clear that this terminology is not being used to belittle the serious social, economic, and personal stakes at issue in the development of communications. Personal careers, corporate profits, national cultures, and the public's welfare are among the stakes in the games shaping communications. Once I have defined this idea more fully, I provide a more concrete, empirical grounding for it by describing the ecology of games shaping telecommunications policy in the United States. I then compare aspects of this ecology with the ecology of games surrounding communications policy in other nations, and I go on to show how the ecology of games can be linked to several factors, such as legal–institutional arrangements, in ways that explain the dynamics of a nation's communications policy. In the final section, I review strengths and weaknesses of this approach, not to validate an interpretation, but to suggest a line of inquiry that could be pursued in a variety of communication policy areas. The idea of an ecology of games, old as it is, provides a new way to think about the social and political shaping of world communications.

Most studies of the politics of communications policy stress the strength and interplay of organized groups and interests. So-called stakeholder analyses are common within industry as well as academe. At times, though, these analyses take on many aspects of traditional models of group politics – the billiard ball notions of the influence of pressure groups.[2] In the United States, depictions of interest group regimes in support of regulation and the role of large telecommunication users in promoting deregulation come close to these early models of group politics (Cowhey, 1988; Schiller, 1982). Ithiel Pool and his colleagues were among the first to challenge such billiard ball notions through empirical research on the role of interest groups in shaping Congressional behavior (Bauer *et al.*, 1963). Following the work of Pool and others, scholars of communications have offered a variety of more sophisticated, pluralist interpretations of the communications policy-making process; these scholars view policies as a compromise among complex and evolving coalitions of elites, including lay politicians, interest groups, and political parties (Dyson and Humphreys, 1986; Hills, 1987; McQuail and Siune, 1986).

In contrast to the pluralists, elite theorists have argued that the convergence of policy across several nations supports the notion that these changes are the consequence of the self-interested politics of transnational economic elites (e.g., Garnham, 1983). Elite theorists argue that information and communication technologies are driven more by military and industrial applications than by public communication needs, that public preferences are controlled through marketing techniques, and that while politicians and technocrats may participate in decisionmaking with respect to communications media, they are primarily responsive and accountable to the economic elite of a society (e.g., Garnham, 1983; Mosco, 1982; Schiller, 1981). These scholars build upon many ideas developed by such elite theorists as Floyd Hunter and C. Wright Mills, and they led to some of the same controversies with pluralists that emerged in the study of urban politics from the 1950s through the 1970s.

In the 1950s, Norton Long used the idea of an ecology of games to critique pluralist and elitist interpretations of local politics (Long, 1958).[3] According to Long, local events are seldom governed in the sense that either pluralists or elitists assume. Rather, the development of communities tends to unfold as a consequence of often unplanned and unanticipated interactions among relatively independent games. Individuals seldom make decisions about the larger community. Most often they make decisions as the occupant of a role, such as a real estate agent, council member, developer, or planning commissioner, in a certain game, such as a real estate game, a tax game, a construction game, or a zoning game, respectively. So the evolution of local communities might be viewed as the outcome of a history of separate but interdependent games.[4] The overall system of action within which groups and interests operate could be described as an ecology of games.

This idea is quite generalizable. The ecology of games notion implies that different actors and organizations within a territory are involved in games in which they play a certain role. For Long, territories were defined by local communities. But the territory of an ecology of games could be national or even global, which the arena for communications policy has indeed become. Games involve competition among players under a set of rules.[5] They 'provide a sense of purpose and a role,' 'a set of strategies and tactics' for the players (Long, 1958). Rules define how the players compete for the prizes of their game. Every game has its own prizes, but they might vary widely. In some games it may be profit; in others it may be virtue or recognition. Different games can also be interrelated by some players simultaneously participating in different games and some players transferring from one game to another. The outcome of one game might well affect the rules of play of another. Once we know someone is playing a game, we might be able to say something about their goals, the rules they play by, and the range of strategies and tactics they might exploit. In this sense, games structure the activity of their players.

The assumption that games provide a clear set of goals and objectives to players distinguishes this theoretical perspective from similar theories that stress the 'sequential, unfolding nature of activity' (Pfeffer, 1982). For example, Michael Cohen and others (1972) developed a 'garbage can model' of the behavior of 'organized anarchies,' like universities. This notion is similar to an ecology of games in that it emphasizes the fluidity of participation and the unfolding nature of activity. But it is also based on an assumption that the preferences of participants are problematic, which is quite at odds with an ecology of games because games provide their participants with goals and a sense of purpose.

Long was not the only political scientist to employ the concept of games. The most prevalent use has been in game theory, a well developed area of formal, positive theory, although it has found limited application to empirical studies of policymaking. (For a classic overview of game theory by contemporaries of Long, see Luce and Raiffa (1957).) But the notion of games has been used outside of formal theory as well.

One way is as an analogy to certain features of political behavior. In this vein, one of the most parsimonious ones was drawn by the political scientist, E.E. Schattschneider (1960), who compared politics to a fight:

Every fight consists of two parts: (1) the few individuals who are actively engaged at the center and (2) the audience that is irresistibly

attracted to the scene. . . . The outcome of every conflict is determined by the extent to which the audience becomes involved in it
(Schattschneider, 1960: 2).

Many political conflicts can be likened to a game in which there are no
limits on the number of players on each team and spectators can at any
time choose to join in the game. Contestants with a decided lead might
well try to maintain the status quo by keeping their side intact and the
spectators in the stands. In contrast, contestants about to lose a contest
might change the odds by dividing their opponents or drawing
spectators into the game. In politics, these strategies can be pursued by
defining the issues at stake. By determining what the conflict is about,
the key players can shape how individual players choose sides and the
number of spectators drawn into the conflict (Schattschneider, 1960).

The ecology of games is compatible with Schattschneider's analogy.
We might be able to describe the history of political conflicts surrounding communications; for example, we might identify the central
players or contestants and their attempts to shape the outcome of each
contest by defining the issues (i.e., using the politics of ideas) in order
to change the scope of the conflict (i.e., by incorporating or excluding
spectators) or to alter the nature of cleavages that determine how the
players choose sides.

A shortcoming with Schattschneider's analogy is that most conflicts
(even fights) are governed by rules that constrain the actions of players
and spectators. Nor is politics so simple as to be encompassed by a
single conflict. Likewise, the rules governing political conflict differ
across political systems, and also over time and within different institutional settings. Sometimes the rules and their application are unclear
or themselves a matter of controversy, requiring a mechanism, such as
an umpire, for interpreting the rules and their application. And the
outcome of games is not always zero-sum, like in a fight. For such
reasons, the more general concept of an ecology of games is attractive.
It suggests that different games can be played simultaneously, with each
player involved in more than one game. Each game can have a different
mix of players and spectators as well as its own rules and umpires.
Moreover, although different games, they might be interrelated.

Another use of the concept of games is found in the work of Michel
Crozier and Erhard Friedberg (1980: 56), which conceptualizes the
behavior of individuals as organized around games, and organizations as
collections of games. Policy outcomes, or other behavior of collectiv-
ities, is viewed by Crozier and Friedberg (1980: 57) as 'the result of a

series of games participated in by the various organizational actors,'
which I view as compatible with what Long (1958) would refer to as the
outcome of an ecology of games.

For over three decades Norton Long's concept of an ecology of
games has rarely found direct application, despite the fact that his ideas
are widely known. His 1958 article is widely reprinted and at one time
was a staple of many undergraduate and graduate courses in urban
politics and administration. Long himself did not develop the idea much
beyond his original article. It might be that behavioral research
paradigms of the 1960s did not prepare American social scientists to
work with this qualitative approach. Although even Crozier and
Friedberg (1980), European social scientists, do not use the concept of
an 'ecology of games,' their work is conceptually and methodologically
close to Long's. The idea of an ecology of games emerged from qualitative and historical case studies. Quantitative, behavioral research,
either experimental or survey based, did not form the foundation for an
ecology of games, since quantitative researchers could not readily
define the idea of an ecology of games in a way that was easily amenable
to measurement. (Similar problems have confronted efforts to apply
formal theories of games.) It is a sensitizing concept within a case study
mode of inquiry, which differs from a concept intended to be operation-
alized within a quantitative survey. In the 1990s, the social sciences are
more open to, and sophisticated in the use of, qualitative research.
Moreover, several theoretical streams of work, such as the new institutionalism (March and Olsen, 1984, 1989) and concrete theory (Lane,
1990), buttress the argument for a theoretical perspective that more
realistically captures the complexity of the policymaking process.
Maybe the 1990s are ripe to revisit the ecology of games and build upon
Long's notion (Dutton and Vedel, 1991).

It is possible to sketch the ecology of games surrounding communications policy in the United States and some of the principal ways it
differs from the ecology of games in other nations. This approach helps
make sense of the development of communications, provides a grammar
for discussing the development of telecommunications, and overcomes
some limitations of more conventional frameworks.

It is difficult to define the boundaries of any game as well as any
ecology of games. To build on the metaphor of an ecology, it should take
place within a territory. Analytically, a territory might be defined
geographically and functionally as the development of world communications. However, I will focus on a more limited territory, the development of telecommunications in the United States. The environment of

this ecology of games entails other functional areas of communications, such as publishing, broadcasting, and cable television, but it is not limited to communications-related activities. For example, developments in regulatory policy within other industries influenced the communications field. And all these ecologies can be viewed to exist within an international environment.

The history of telecommunications in the United States provides a rich source from which to extract a few examples of how developments reflect many features of an ecology of games. This history is, of course, too complex and controversial to characterize in a brief essay. But simply by looking at some of the most well documented developments within this history through a different lens, I can illustrate it as the outcome of interactions among separate but interdependent games. It also suggests certain features that might be characteristically American about this ecology of games.

Since the Second World War, numerous games shaped United States telecommunications. Among the most prominent, prior to divestiture, were public utility, boundary drawing, and antitrust games. The public utility game was organized around the provision of efficient telephone services to residential, business, and government customers in a universal and equitable fashion in return for monopoly revenues to the private telephone companies. The telephone companies, groups representing business and residential users, the Federal Communications Commission (FCC), and state public utility commissions, were some of the key players negotiating over regulatory policies, such as rate-of-return pricing. The rules of this game were established by the Communications Act and state legislation as interpreted by their respective regulatory agencies.

The play of this public utility game was importantly influenced by a boundary drawing game, which pitted the telephone companies against new telecommunications equipment and service providers, with the FCC serving as umpire. This game involved conflicts over the definition of basic telecommunications services and facilities. The Carterfone decision in 1968 and the computer inquiries were moves within this game. *Computer Inquiry I* (1965–9), *Computer Inquiry II* (1976–80), and *Computer Inquiry III* (1985–) have focused on defining the boundary between unregulated computing and regulated telecommunications services.

Outside of the communications arena *per se*, an antitrust game became significant to telecommunications beginning in 1949, when the Department of Justice brought an action against AT&T. Its rules were established by antitrust (not communications) law, but its outcome dramatically shaped communications policy. In 1956, a consent decree restricted AT&T to providing regulated telecommunications services. And the *Modified Final Judgment* of 1982 – which resulted from an action brought by the Justice Department in 1974 to modify a 1954 Final Judgment to the Department of Justice action begun in 1949 – stipulated the divestiture of the operating companies from AT&T, which restructured the American telecommunications industry. The Justice Department's role in this game was to block illegal efforts by AT&T to eliminate competition through cross-subsidies, discriminatory pricing, or other strategies. Given different players, objectives, and rules, it is not surprising that the antitrust and public utility games were at odds. They were by no means independent since AT&T was a key player in both games and the outcome of each affected the play of the other. But the actions of the key players within Justice and the court appear to have been governed almost exclusively by the goals and rules of the anti-trust game.

The ecology of games shaping telecommunications is clearly not this simple. Many other games were also quite significant prior to and following divestiture. Table 8.1 identifies some of the most salient ones, grouping them by type and indicating some of the key players, goals, and strategies associated with each. Taken together, they indeed compose a complex ecology.

At least three kinds of games seem to have animated the development of telecommunications in the United States (Table 8.1). At the center appear to be several that essentially entail competition among businesses for markets, like the competition between long-distance telephone companies. Marvin Sirbu's chapter (16) identifies a struggle for ownership and control over telecommunications networks that is different from the competition between MCI, Sprint, and AT&T for telephone customers, but the struggle fits well in this general category. Competition among electronic equipment manufacturers for sales to telephone companies is clearly in this set. Competition between telephone companies and cable operators also falls into this category and links this ecology of games to that surrounding cable communications. These business competition games take place under a set of rules largely determined by telecommunications policies established by state and federal government officials. The FCC and the courts largely perform a role as umpire, and the umpires can exercise discretion, but that is all part of how these games are played.

Another kind of game – policy games – involves competition among players attempting to influence public policies, from struggles over the rewrite of the Communications Act to conflicts over pricing policy to debates over antitrust law. These games are distinct from business competition games in several respects. First, they are largely fought over the rules that are to govern competition among businesses, including rules that might permit a business to establish a monopoly and avoid competition. Second, the government becomes a player, not just an umpire, with various governmental agencies competing to influence policy in that agency's view of the public interest. (Of course, governments can compete with businesses in telecommunications and other areas, such as when a state owns a telecommunications network, or when a municipality owns a cable TV system; however, a clear feature of the United States ecology of games is that this is the exception rather than the rule.) Third, this kind of game has a greater potential for conflicts to engage various spectators as players because it involves public agencies. Also, the prizes in policy games are more diverse, ranging across any number of motives leading actors to become involved with policy.

A third kind of game concerns metapolicy, that is, struggles over the political and administrative principles that govern policy games. In telecommunications, one metapolicy game involves the ongoing struggle over the first amendment and its application to communications. As Ithiel Pool (1983) pointed out in *Technologies of Freedom*, change in the Court's interpretation of the first amendment could directly affect the outcome of nearly every aspect of telecommunications. If cable companies, or for that matter telephone companies, become first amendment publishers, many of the rules now governing business competition in telecommunications would be problematic. A less salient game involves principles surrounding privacy and its application, as derived from interpretations of the first and fourth amendments.

These games differ from policy games in that they involve many who are not directly involved as players in policy or business competition games. The rules governing metapolicy games are key features of the larger political system, such as the separation of powers and role of the courts in the United States. As an aside, it is worth noting that critical scholars have long held that national economic and political systems have a systematic affect on policymaking. It may be that many structural considerations, so central to critical scholars, can be linked to the idea of an ecology of games, given the importance of national and international

Table 8.1 Games shaping the development of telecommunications in the United States

Types & examples of games	Key players	Selected goals and purposes	Selected strategies
Metapolicy games			
1st Amendment	A faction within cable industry, cities	Restrict franchising authority of cities	Define cable operator as 1st Amendment publisher
Regulatory theory	Economists, regulators, policy scientists	Define prevailing theory of regulation	Academic and business recognition
Partisan politics	Democrats vs Republicans Neo-conservatives vs Liberals	Pass partisan agenda	Legislation, campaigns & elections
Policy games			
Public utility	RBOCs, Common Carrier Bureau of FCC, State PUCs, business & residential users	Universal & equitable services	Regulation of monopoly suppliers
Boundary drawing	Telephone companies & industry associations, large users, providers of computing & information services	Gain new markets	Broaden (narrow) definition of basic services
Antitrust	Department of Justice, AT&T	Win settlement; prevent illegal business practices	Bring to trial/settle
Interagency politics	FCC, NTIA, State Department, House & Senate Committees	Maintain and enhance status of agency	Insure that agencies' policies appear to work
Federalism	Federal, State & local regulators	Legitimize jurisdiction over communication industries and services	Lobbying, oversight of other regulatory agencies

Business competition games

		Profit, market share	
Long-distance service	Long-distance companies (AT&T, MCI, Sprint...)		Qualitative improvements through modernization, cream-skimming on limited routes with used equipment, and nonunion labor
Local service	RBOCs, State PUCs, Residential & business users	Minimize cost of services; equitable and universal access	Rate-of-return pricing Cost averaging
Network control	International Communication Association, Large users, Local exchange carriers, Interexchange carriers	Control provision and operation of network services	Support network architectures biased toward individual interests
Terminal equipment sales	Westinghouse, Siemens, and other equipment manufacturers & retailers	Capture market for customer's networks (e.g. RBOCs & larger users)	Develop technology in support of networking strategy
Cable/Telco	Cable and telephone industry associations	Capture market for video services to households	Encourage policies in support of your technology. Maintain or erode policy and technological barriers to telephone entry
R & D	Bell Labs, Bellcore, other centers of R&D	Technological innovation, i.e. patents, royalties, licenses, recognition	Promote trials & experiments, pricing policies that encourage long-term investment (e.g. price caps vs rate-of-return)

economic systems in establishing the rules governing games, if not the games themselves, as well as their relative status.

Other metapolicy games have influenced telecommunications. One was a regulatory theory game that witnessed academic, industry, and government economists and policy analysts in a struggle to define prevailing regulatory philosophies. A central cleavage of this game developed between the proponents of marketplace competition versus the defenders of regulation, of which the former gained an upper hand in academic and policy circles (Derthick and Quirk, 1985). This game was being played alongside industry-specific conflicts over regulation of trucking, airlines, and other industries. Their outcomes, despite the differences in players, have been relevant to telecommunications.

It is possible to move beyond these three general types of games. For example, there are what might be called bureaucratic games. These are singled out as a separate class because they also are governed by different rules, sometimes unique to the corporate and governmental organizations in which they are played out. Also, they are played within organizations, which are assumed to act as single entities in the other games. For example, AT&T might be viewed as a single actor within the antitrust game that pitted it against the Department of Justice. But the moves of each player can also be viewed as the outcome of games played within each organization.

Within the former Bell system, there was a struggle over strategic planning that shaped AT&T's actions in the case. Given a declining rate of growth in ordinary telephone services, AT&T faced some of the same concerns over developing new markets that the European PTTs were facing. AT&T's problems were compounded by the inflation of the 1970s because the company was a major lender, financing telecommunications equipment that was repaid through rentals; indeed, Peter Drucker (1984) has argued that inflation placed major strains on AT&T prior to divestiture. The outcome of this conflict placed executives at the top of AT&T who were prepared to move the corporation into new markets, particularly into new information technologies and into the international arena. Within Justice, the decision to bring its suit to trial after holding off for six years might be viewed as the outcome of bureaucratic games that placed 'true believers' in positions of authority within the agency (Drucker, 1984: 11).

More generally, there have been a variety of bureaucratic games within the agencies participating in communications policy. This conflict has primarily concerned members of the FCC, the National Telecommunications and Information Administration (NTIA), and

House and Senate committees, as each has sought to establish, defend, and implement its own stamp on public policy. And interagency jurisdictional and administrative turf battles have generated some of the more enduring struggles in communications, including a continuing federalism game creating conflicts between federal and state agencies over the nature of overlapping authority in regulating telecommunications. The federalism game has been more salient for cable TV than for telecommunications, but it is relevant to both arenas.

I have not exhausted the games that might be identified, such as those including international players or the ones involving AT&T and the aerospace industry over the development of satellite communications facilities – which proved significant to the evolution of competing communications networks. Nevertheless, the point should be clear that the interaction of several different kinds of games shaped the development of telecommunications. They have unique sets of players, goals, strategies, and rules. Once this is recognized it is also clear that most considerations of telecommunications policy focus only on one or a few games that compose a much larger ecology.

Having such a framework to describe the larger system of action in which these games are played can help to anticipate as well as understand the actions of individual players, which are often rational from the perspective of a particular game, even though the interaction of decisions made within the context of different games may lead to dysfunctional consequences. Within the context of an antitrust game, judicial decisions might have been quite rational, while in the context of international trade in electronic equipment, it appears irrational, especially from an American perspective. In a similar sense, the actions of individual players may be more or less complex and more or less contradictory, depending on the set of games that they are simultaneously playing. Consider the differences in complexity surrounding the goals and strategies of a player in few games within this ecology (e.g., Judge Harold Greene) in contrast to a player in many games (e.g., AT&T).

I have argued that the development of communications is often affected by the outcome of games outside the communications arena *per se*. But the opposite is also true: The ecology of communications has impacts outside of its immediate territory. In the United States, telecommunications developments influenced at least three major areas, including national defense, international trade, and industrial and economic development (Drucker, 1984; Torerro, 1985). With regard to national defense, the Department of Defense had to adapt its communication systems to the post-divestiture environment. In the trade area, there has been a growing recognition that divestiture changed the rules of the game in international trade in telecommunications; for example, it created incentives for the Regional Bell Operating Companies to shop abroad for equipment. And divestiture has had implications for vital aspects of industrial and economic development, including the resources devoted to R&D in information and communications technology (Noll, 1987).

The ecology of games surrounding telecommunications in the United States differs markedly from that in Japan and most western European nations. First, in the United States, the most significant games tend to be those that define the rules of the game – what I have labeled as metapolicy. Conflicts over the First Amendment and its application to communication exemplify this type of game, which has implications for the play of most other games in communications. Antitrust policy is another – a game about the rules of the games that govern business competition. In Japan and western Europe, the most central games seemed to have revolved around more programmatic policy goals. For example, in France, Japan, and Britain, a well defined industrial policy, focused on information and communications technology, took precedence over the rules of business competition, which were compromised and adapted to address industrial policy objectives.

The second way in which the United States ecology of games in telecommunications differs from other nations is that business competition seems to be more central to the American ecology of games. This might be less so in Japan, and it is clearly less in most western European nations. Consider how much cleavages over communication policy are often deepest between business rivals (e.g., telephone versus cable companies) in the United States. Debate between the telephone and cable industries often seems to cut deeper than any bureaucratic, ideological, or partisan divisions. In France, for example, partisan cleavages are more clearly reflected in divisions over communications policy. Even in Japan, where competition between business adversaries is fierce, the major cleavages tend to be between the Ministry of International Trade and Industry and its allies and the Ministry of Posts and Telecommunications and its allies. Business competition has closer ties to political–administrative divisions.

Some games appear almost inconsequential to telecommunications policy in the United States but quite central in other nations. For example, a governmental budgeting game has been of much consequence to the public PTTs of most Western European nations. Competition among government agencies for funds has often resulted in governments drawing from PTT revenues to support the general fund, much like American local governments have used cable franchise fees to support the general fund, but at a much larger scale and in a far more flexible manner. In France, for instance, the play of this game was partly responsible for the French P&T's willingness to pull back on some of its more ambitious cabling plans; the Socialist government increased the amount it drew from the P&T to support the general revenue, thereby squeezing the resources it had thought were available to finance cable system development (Vedel and Dutton, 1990). Likewise, an international broadcasting game has been central to telecommunications policy in Canada as well as in France and other European countries for decades, but almost irrelevant to the American ecology of games until foreign firms purchased the lion's share of major Hollywood film studios in the late 1980s. The French P&T gained support for its cabling plan in part because cable offered a mechanism for gaining more control over the proportion of French programming that would be aired, compared to the alternative of relying on satellite distribution of programming.

Partisan political games have also been surprisingly less important in the United States than in Europe. As is often said, deregulation began under Jimmy Carter. Although the Reagan Administration made deregulation a priority of its conservative agenda, the rise of neoconservative politicians within the Republican and Democratic parties may have muted partisan debate between a Republican FCC and a Democratic Congress. Outside the United States partisan politics has been more closely tied to communications policy. In Britain the Conservative party's support for privatization of British Telecom and private cable systems was opposed by Labour. In France partisan politics has long been tied to communications policy, particularly in broadcasting but also in telecommunications.

Of most importance, an industrial policy game has been pivotal to shaping the development of telecommunications in Western Europe and Japan, but not in the United States. Communications and information technology were defined as strategic industries for revitalizing the economies of Japan, Britain, France, and West Germany, among others. During the late 1970s and early 1980s, each of these nations invested public funds in efforts to develop new telecommunication infrastructures and services as one aspect of an information technology-led industrial policy (Dutton *et al.*, 1987).

During the same period, the United States developed no comparable industrial policy; to the contrary, it focused on the rules of the game, rather than vice versa. Only in the late 1980s, with increasing awareness of the industrial and trade implications of a successful introduction of high definition television, did discussions of industrial policy emerge as a legitimate focus for debate, if only for a brief period of time. Even then public support for the electronics industry was only contemplated as programmatic support for national defense, rather than as an aspect of an industrial policy. This is not new for the United States. Fred Weingarten (1987) has noted that 'approximately 80 per cent of federally funded R&D in computers and communications is paid for by the Department of Defense,' which he takes to mean that 'national security is the dominant motive for Federal support' (Weingarten, 1987; Office of Technology Assessment, 1985).

The perspective of an ecology of games provides a framework for examining various factors that might affect the strength and interplay of the groups and interests shaping policy change in communications. One is a set of market factors, anchored in demand for services and the ability of industries to meet marketplace expectations. Given the centrality of business competition to the American ecology of telecommunications, its unfolding has been importantly shaped by consumer demands and the ability of competing businesses to meet them. For example, the absence of a mass market for newer information services and AT&T's inability to quickly succeed in the information technology area affected the strength and interplay of actors in ways not anticipated prior to divestiture.

Another set of factors shaping the American ecology of telecommunications is an array of legal–institutional arrangements, such as the governmental structures surrounding the regulation of communications industries. Legal–institutional arrangements define many of the players as well as the most critical rules in national ecologies. Business competition is central to a large portion of games in the United States largely because of the political–administrative traditions surrounding the private ownership of communications infrastructures. Likewise, the role and scope of the FCC gives the American ecology a unique makeup. The status of NTIA within the Department of Commerce distinguishes the US from other nations, such as France and Japan, that have major ministries responsible for communications. And the federalist structure of the United States has made state and local officials more significant actors in the national politics of cable and telecommunications matters than they are in many other nations, such as Britain, where local authorities have virtually no involvement.

Finally, a set of symbolic factors affects the strength and interplay of groups. Studies of the politics of regulation in the United States have argued that the deregulation of telecommunications has been driven by the persuasiveness of pro-competitive economic arguments, which have overcome the interest group regimes supporting government protected monopolies (Wilson, 1980; Derthick and Quirk, 1985; Altshuler, 1988). Derthick and Quirk (1985) refer to the important role of pro-competitive arguments in what they called the 'politics of ideas,' a theme closely related to what Murray Edelman (1971) discussed as 'symbolic politics,' which I would define as 'systematic efforts aimed at giving a symbolic character to objects or acts as a means for achieving political aims and objectives' (Dutton and Blumler, 1988). For example, images and symbols can be linked to objects or events such as technologies or policies that evoke positive or negative responses. They do so by referencing symbols that have specific meanings in a culture.

The politics of ideas clearly affected the ecology of games surrounding telecommunications. One of the most fundamental symbolic shifts was the idea that communications and information technologies were ushering in new businesses and industries – the so-called information economy. In Japan, Western Europe, and the United States this recognition had important consequences. It broadened the scope of the telecommunications games. Economic and industrial elites, at one time spectators, began to enter as key players in conflicts over telecommunications policy. They now saw telecommunications less as a public utility and more as a new area for business investment and a strategic resource for the efficient development and operation of other industries on a global scale, including travel, banking, finance, and insurance, increasingly dependent on telecommunications. 'Ma Bell', a benign public utility, began to be perceived as another large corporation subject to the same distrust shown others in corporate America – a 'dinosaur' that would slow innovation and crush its competitors.

A second symbolic shift was a growing awareness of the convergence of communication technologies. As the technological distinctions between print, common carrier, cable, broadcasting, and computing industries became blurred, players in any one of these areas began to see personal stakes in the outcome of games being played within the other industries. A related idea was that technological change in communications undermined the rationale for AT&T's monopoly over various telecommunications services, particularly terminal equipment and long-distance services. This belief introduced changes in the rulings of the FCC and launched efforts by Congress to rewrite the Communications

Act. More importantly, perhaps, it broadened the scope of conflicts over the regulation of AT&T by making antitrust claims against the corporation more salient within the FCC. In the end, however, the rules governing telecommunications policy and business competition were most dramatically reshaped by divestiture and the *Modified Final Judgment*, the outcome of a game played outside of the communications policy arena.

Another aspect of the politics of ideas has been a growing consensus on the economic rationality of competition in the marketplace over regulation in the public interest. Several analyses of regulatory policy have focused on the emergence of this consensus in favor of competition (e.g., Wilson, 1980; Derthick and Quirk, 1985). Others have labeled this as an antitrust ideology (e.g., Pool, 1983: 1132; Drucker, 1984). Regardless, this shift in regulatory ideology could be applied to telecommunications largely because of these earlier changes in how telecommunications was perceived.

I have argued that an ecology of games provides a theoretical perspective for discussing the strength and interplay of groups and interests shaping communications. Also the exact nature of this ecology of games is likely to evolve over time and differ across social, political, and economic systems in response to differences in three sets of factors discussed above, which I have labeled as market, legal–institutional, and symbolic factors.

From this perspective, the politics of communications is complex but neither random or chaotic. The notion of an ecology of games offers a framework for thinking about this extremely complex system of inter-actions shaping the development of communications. It highlights the role played by those who shape the rules of the game, such as the courts in the United States. And it emphasizes the potential for unanticipated, unplanned developments, while raising doubts about perspectives on the politics of communications policy that post a more governed, isolated, and predictable system of action. In fact, it helps explain why prediction is likely to elude those in the policy sciences who seek to attain it.

The ecology of games has other advantages as an approach to research. It helps identify the cross-pressures facing key players, who are often involved in more than one game. It provides an interpretation of the broader system of action in which the development of communi-cations takes place. Most conventional interpretations underplay the role of unplanned, unanticipated interactions between various organized interests, which have decidedly influenced the development of communications. For example, in Britain, France, and the United States, cable and telecommunications policies have been affected by decisions in other policy areas. The most obvious area was industrial policy, which is a major driving force in each country, although at different times and in different ways.

Nevertheless, conventional interpretations view communications policymaking as a self-contained system of action. Instead, it may be more useful to recognize that it is being formulated and implemented in parallel with other policies. Many players in one policy area are simultaneously in others. The outcome of the political process in one arena often shapes play within another. Nothing is new about these interactions; however, our theories tend to ignore them. Personality, historical circumstance, and the proverbial 'environment' are used to cover gaping holes in our theoretical frameworks. From an ecology of games perspective, such interactions are an explicit and central feature of the policy process and a key force behind policy change. This may be the central advantage of this perspective compared to other theoretical frameworks, such as interest group, pluralist, or systems theory – it focuses attention on different phenomena.

I have found the ecology of games to be a useful approach to the study of a variety of developments in communications (e.g., Dutton and Makinen, 1987; Dutton and Guthrie, 1989; Vedel and Dutton, 1990). However, my use of this approach has generated several charges from other social scientists.

One criticism is that the ecology of games is only a metaphor. Like many other theoretical perspectives, such as systems theory or pluralist theory, it is a rich metaphor, but it is more than that. It has all the elements of a theoretical concept in qualitative research. In many respects, it is a sensitizing concept – one that helps make sense of a wide array of concrete observations at the empirical level. Severyn Bruyn's discussion of participant–observer research defines what he calls a 'sensitizing concept,' by which he refers to a 'term coined by Herbert Blumer some years ago to indicate those kinds of terms which give a sense of reference, a general orientation, rather than a precise definition, to a phenomenon under study' (Bruyn, 1966: 32). The ecology of games is more of a sensitizing concept within a participant–observer, case-study mode of inquiry than an ideal type or a theoretical construct relevant to quantitative research. I have not focused on developing more precise operational definitions, because I believe this would over-simplify the concept. It is nevertheless a useful theoretical construct within a case-study mode of inquiry that summarizes empirical obser-vations within one case that can be validated to the degree that other social scientists discover similar patterns of behavior in other case studies.

In this regard, the ecology of games shares much in common with a class of contemporary approaches to the empirical study of politics, which Ruth Lane has labeled 'concrete theory' (Lane, 1990). The ecology of games, like other approaches to concrete theory, moves away from behaviorally deterministic models as well as overly simplistic models of economic rationality to develop more realistic perspectives on the actual behavior of elites pursuing multiple objectives in complex organizational settings. Although concrete theories look closely at the environment of decisionmakers, the ecology of games provides an approach for directly incorporating events outside a particular policy sector, like communications (Dutton and Vedel, 1991).

Also the notion of games evokes the criticism that the phenomena are not taken seriously; that is, games are played for amusement. Norton Long (1958), when addressing the same criticism, argued that games are a serious business. E.E. Schattschneider's analogy to a fight as one type of game illustrates that the stakes can be great. The concept is not used to trivialize the process or outcome of the politics shaping communications or brand them as entertaining. More often than not, the games of political life are not amusing.

A related criticism takes off from the use of an ecological metaphor – an implicit suggestion that somehow, as an ecology, the outcome is likely to be functional within a broader social ecology (Long, 1958). This assumption not only takes the biological analogy too literally, but also overstates the sustainability of natural ecologies. The long-range functional utility of this process is uncertain. Given that no political system as a whole is in any sense governing the policy process – at least from an ecology of games perspective – it is as likely to be dysfunctional as it is to be functional to some players, if not the broader society affected by the development of telecommunications. Of course, after the fact, it is always possible to develop an argument that any outcome was functional in some way. But the value of an ecology of games perspective does not hinge on any claims about its functionality.

In fact, it is well within the scope of this approach to ask: How functional is the US ecology of games in telecommunications policy? In the area of telecommunications policy, for example, have the industrial, economic, cultural, and social implications of the American ecology of games been as functional, in many respects, as that shaping communications in several other nations, particularly Japan? In the US, as argued above, communications policy is generally subordinated to anti-trust and other rules of the game governing business competition. In Japan, national policy objectives are more likely to be balanced with policies surrounding anti trust and business competition. A Japanese concern over 'excessive competition,' which seldom worries the American policy community, reflects this orientation. Two general factors might cause telecommunications policy to be subordinated within the American ecology of games. One is symbolic – the dominance of a limited vision of telecommunications as primarily a means for other industries, particularly the large users of communications, to gain a competitive advantage over their rivals (Dutton and Vedel, 1991). Another is legal–institutional – the absence of a Cabinet or department level executive agency responsible for communications. It is not surprising that telecommunications policy in the US is driven by anti-trust concerns and the needs of large business users given that NTIA is simply an agency within the Department of Commerce.

In Japan, friction between the Ministry of International Trade and Industry, which represents large users and equipment manufacturers, and the Ministry of Posts and Telecommunications, which is more responsive to the interests of broadcasters and NTT, reflects conflicts of interest between these groups. These conflicts must be continually negotiated and compromised. In the US, telecommunications policy has been subordinated to the rules of the game in business competition. Even if the telecommunications industry in Japan has not surpassed the US, the tremendous gains made by Japanese relative to US companies over the last decade should cause the US policy community also to question the functionality of this American ecology of games in telecommunications policy.

An ecology of games is a heuristically valuable sensitizing concept, which offers a new approach to the study of communications policy. It directs attention to the objectives, strategies, and rules shaping the behavior of individual decisionmakers as a means to explain collective outcomes. It incorporates factors outside of the communications policy sector *per se* into explanations of policy change. It is suggestive of cross-national variations in the politics of communications and the role that market, legal–institutional, and symbolic factors play in shaping the ecology of games within nations. Finally, it incorporates the notion that to some degree the outcomes of politics on the development of technology and, therefore, its role in society are less determinate, less governed, and more unpredictable than suggested by many other contemporary perspectives, whether elite, critical, or pluralist. As a consequence, the players and spectators have some liberty to shape their fate as they influence the games in world telecommunications policy.

NOTES

1 This essay is based on research supported by grants from the US France Cooperative Science Program of the National Science Foundation (INT-8414059), the National Center for Scientific Research in France, and Fujitsu America, Incorporated. The author gratefully acknowledges the comments of Russ Neuman, Harvey Sapolsky, William Loges, Michael Noll, David Hopelain, David Bogen, and particularly Thierry Vedel on an earlier draft.
2 The major scholars of group theory published key works in the early 1950s (e.g., Truman, 1951; Latham, 1952).
3 While I have borrowed the concept of an ecology of games from Norton Long (1958), he would not necessarily agree with my interpretation and elaboration of his ideas, nor the way I have generalized them to describe the development of communications. Long (1987) believes that an ecology needs to be confined to a well defined geographical territory – his examples are all local (Long 1958). I argue that his idea is adaptable to national, even global arenas. Despite differences in such assumptions, I have found his ideas useful to the interpretation of cable and telecommunications developments in local as well as global arenas (e.g., Dutton and Makinen, 1985, 1987; Dutton, 1987; Dutton and Guthrie, 1989; Dutton and Vedel, 1991; Vedel and Dutton, 1990).
4 Other theoretical perspectives on urban and neighborhood development are based on similar models in which development patterns are the product of the interaction of more localized or segmented decisions (Fumitoshi Kato (1988)).
5 I am not using game as synonymous with 'strategy' as is often done in the implementation literature; for example, see Bardach (1977) and Mintzberg (1983). Some, for instance, speak of the games people play in organizations to block or delay the implementation of an information system (Grover *et al.*, 1988). These are valid uses of the term, but quite different from the way I use it here.

REFERENCES

Altshuler, Alan (1988) MIT Symposium on World Telecommunications Policy, pp. 18–36.
Bardach, E. (1977) *The Implementation Game*, Cambridge, MA: MIT Press.
Bauer, R.A., Pool, Ithiel de Sola, and Dexter, Lewis A. (1963) *American Business and Public Policy*, New York: Atherton.
Bruyn, Severyn T. (1966) *The Human Perspective in Sociology: The Methodology of Participant Observation*, Englewood Cliffs, NJ: Prentice-Hall, Inc.
Cohen, Michael D., March, James G., and Olsen, John P. (1972) 'A garbage can model of organizational choice,' *Administrative Science Quarterly* 17: 1–25.

Cowhey, Peter (1988) MIT Symposium on World Telecommunications Policy, pp. 210–22.

Crozier, Michel and Friedberg, Erhard (1980) *Actors & Systems*, Chicago, IL: University of Chicago Press.

Dahl, Robert A. (1961) *Who Governs?*, New Haven: Yale University Press.

Derthick, Martha and Quirk, Paul J. (1985) *The Politics of Deregulation*, Washington DC: The Brookings Institution.

Drucker, Peter (1984) 'Beyond the Bell breakup,' *The Public Interest* 77: 3–27.

Dutton, William H. (1987) 'The politics of cable policy in Britain.' Paper presented at the Annual Meeting of the American Political Science Association, Chicago, IL: September, 1987.

Dutton, William H. and Blumler, Jay G. (1988) 'The faltering development of cable television in Britain,' *International Political Science Review* 9 (4): 299–303.

Dutton, William H. and Guthrie, Kendall (1989) 'Santa Monica's public electronic network: The political ecology of a teledemocracy experiment.' Paper presented at the 1989 Annual Meeting of the American Political Science Association, Atlanta, Georgia, August 31 to September 3, 1989.

Dutton, William H. and Makinen, Helena (1985) 'Urban telecommunications as an ecology of games.' Paper presented at IRIS 1985 and the 1985 meeting of Management Information Systems, Pacific Area Community (MISPAC) Seminar, Tokyo, Japan, July 3–14.

Dutton, William H. and Makinen, Helena (1987) 'The development of telecommunications: The outcome of an ecology of games,' *Information and Management* 13 (5): 255–64.

Dutton, William H. and Vedel, Thierry (1991) 'Revisiting the ecology of games.' Unpublished working paper. Los Angeles, CA: Annenberg School, USC.

Dutton, William H., Blumler, Jay G., and Kraemer, Kenneth L. (eds) (1987) *Wired Cities: Shaping the Future of Communications*, Boston: G.K. Hall.

Dyson, Kenneth and Humphreys, Peter (eds) (1986) 'The politics of the communications revolution,' *West European Politics* 9 (4): 1–224.

Edelman, Murray (1971) *Politics as Symbolic Action: Mass Arousal and Quiescence*, Chicago, IL: Markham Publishing Company.

Garnham, Nicholas (1983) 'Public service versus the market,' *Screen* 24 (1): 6–27.

Grover, Varun, Lederer, Albert L., and Sabherwal, Rajiv (1988) 'Recognizing the politics of MIS,' *Information and Management* 14 (3): 145–56.

Hills, Jill (1987) 'Is liberalization the answer?' Paper presented at the 1987 Annual Meeting of the American Political Science Association, The Palmer House, Washington DC, September 3–6.

Kato, Fumitoshi (1988) Personal correspondence, summarizing 'Spatial patterns and their generation rules.' Master's Thesis.

Lane, Ruth (1990) 'Concrete theory: An emerging political method,' *American Political Science Review* 84 (3): 927–40.

Latham, Earl (1952) *The Group Basis of Politics*, New York: Cornell University Press.

Long, Norton E. (1958) 'The local community as an ecology of games,' *The American Journal of Sociology* 64: 251–61.

Long, Norton E. (1987) Personal correspondence.

88   William H. Dutton

Luce, R. Duncan and Raiffa, Howard (1957) *Games and Decisions: Intro-
  duction and Critical Survey*, New York: John Wiley.
McQuail, Dennis and Siune, Karen (eds) (1986) *New Media Politics: Compara-
  tive Perspectives in Western Europe*, London: Sage Publications.
March, James G. and Olson, Johan P. (1984) 'The institutionalism,' *American
  Political Science Review* 78 (3): 734–49.
March, James G. and Olson, Johan P. (1989) *Rediscovering Institutions*, New
  York: The Free Press.
Milbrath, Lester W. (1960) 'Lobbying as a communication process,' *Public
  Opinion Quarterly* 24: 32–53.
Mintzberg, H. (1983) *Power In and Around Organizations*, Englewood Cliffs,
  NJ: Prentice-Hall.
Mosco, Vincent (1982) *Pushbutton Fantasies*, Norwood, NJ: Ablex.
Noll, A. Michael (1987) 'The effects of divestiture on telecommunication
  research,' *Journal of Communications* (Winter), 73–80.
Office of Technology Assessment, US Congress (1985) Information Tech-
  nology R&D: Critical Trends and Issues. 99th Congress, 1st Session.
  Washington DC.
Pfeffer, Jeffrey (1982) *Organizations and Organization Theory*, Boston:
  Pitman.
Pool, Ithiel de Sola (1983) *Technologies of Freedom* Cambridge, MA: Harvard
  University Press.
Schattschneider, E.E. (1960) *The Semi-Sovereign People*, New York: Holt,
  Rinehart & Winston.
Schiller, Dan (1982) *Telematics and Government*, Norwood, NJ: Ablex.
Schiller, Herbert (1981) *Who Knows?* Norwood, NJ: Ablex.
Sirbu, Marvin (1988) MIT Symposium on World Telecommunications Policy,
  pp. 90–113.
Torerro, Edward A. (ed.) (1985) 'Hello again: The future of communications,'
  IEEE Spectrum 22 (1): 44–114.
Truman, David B. (1951) *The Governmental Process*, New York: Alfred A.
  Knopf.
Vedel, Thierry and Dutton, William H. (1990) 'New media politics: Shaping
  cable television policy in France,' *Media, Culture and Society* (SAGE,
  London) 12: 491–524.
Weingarten, Frederick W. (1987) 'The new R&D push in communications
  technology,' in William H. Dutton, Jay G. Blumler, and Kenneth L. Kraemer
  (eds) *Wired Cities*, Boston, MA: G.K. Hall.
Wilson, James Q. (1980) *The Politics of Regulation*, New York: Basic Books,
  pp. 357–94.

Chapter 9

The economics of international competition

Charles Jonscher

Ithiel Pool had a keen interest in the subject of American global competitiveness and the way in which it interacts with international telecommunications policy – as he had, indeed, in all matters of international telecommunications policy. He may not have expressed the concern as one of America's competitiveness because he was more interested in maximizing social policy and not in how well one country is doing against another. I do not think that he would have been particularly taken by the question of whether America, Japan, or Germany happened to be doing best or worst in the telecommunications market, but he would certainly have been interested in whether the policy in international markets for telecommunications is moving in a direction that maximizes world wealth and consumer benefits.

Maybe the other reason why Ithiel Pool would not have focused on 'restoring American competitiveness' is that he may have had a strong intuition (he had extremely good intuitions on all matters of economic policy) that there is not a problem of restoring America's competitiveness because America is very competitive. I attended a recent meeting in Europe where economists researching this question for the OECD presented data showing, for example, that productivity per unit labor input of Japan versus the United States, and Japan's index of productivity compared with the United States', rose from 31 percent in the 1960s, one-third of the productivity, to 67 percent today. So Japan doubled its productivity in comparison with that of the United States in those twenty years, but it is still only two-thirds of that of the United States.

That might strike one as unexpected in the light of what is said about extremely efficient Japanese factories, but it is confirmed by macroeconomic data. The GNP per capita of the United States in 1988 is $21,000, and Japan's is $22,000; by that measure Japan has overtaken the United States. But it is important to bear in mind that the $22,000 figure is based on an exchange rate in which purchasing power parity is far from being achieved. So the $22,000 the Japanese are earning is not buying them as much as the $21,000 that Americans are earning per head. There is still roughly a two-thirds differential; all the major European economies also fall considerably short of the United States, although they are doing slightly better with respect to growth rates.

If the American economy is more productive on average, who really has the best factories? It is true that some of the highly automated Japanese factories in the most efficient sectors of the Japanese economy are doing spectacularly well – better than any in North America or Europe. Taken as an average, however, the American economy is producing more goods per head than any other major economy in the world; so why is there a staggering trade deficit? The deficit is what creates the impression of non-competitiveness, and in turn leads to enormous pressures for protectionism in telecommunications and other areas in order to ensure that the United States can export more goods and services.

I shall review some basic economics to show the direct link between this phenomenon and the United States federal deficit. The equation is as follows: worldwide consumption and production of goods are close to equal; that is, more or less everything that is produced is consumed. There are adjustment factors for investment and changes in business inventories, but they do not amount to enough to affect the numbers I consider here. So, worldwide, consumption and production of goods are of similar magnitude. In any one country, though, they can differ. At present the United States is consuming considerably more than it is producing – to the tune of $150 or $200 billion per year in trade deficit. That is what a trade deficit is: more goods coming into the country than going out.

If the United States is consuming more than it is producing, what should we call that? We could call it a party. Why is there an excess of consumption over production? For that we have to look at one other accounting identity: borrowing equals lending. Again, everything that is borrowed by one person is lent by another. There is again an adjustment factor which is that governments can actually produce money rather than lend it. They can either print money or issue bonds to finance their part of the borrowing–lending equation. As a Secretary of the US Treasury put it, 'I make money the old fashioned way; I print it.'

To be fair, he does not print much of it. The American budget deficit is almost exclusively funded by bonds, which are debt, and the

American people as private citizens and businesses have traditionally kept the lending–borrowing equation in balance. The US government deficit is financing the party. Who buys the bonds? Foreigners. The private economy is keeping its borrowing–lending and savings–investment equations in balance.

The federal government is, however, spending $150 to $200 billion extra per year. This expenditure is being financed by foreigners, not just with money but with goods. The way they finance it is to ship goods into this country to the tune of $150 to $200 billion per year and in return they receive IOUs, which one day they will claim.

So long as the federal deficit continues in this fashion, unless there is a massive adjustment in the internal savings-to-investment ratio (i.e., unless Americans start buying government bonds, in which case interest rates would shoot up and we would probably have a recession), then foreigners will be financing the deficit. The Japanese and the Europeans are happy to produce goods and services in greater amounts than they consume them in order to export them to the United States, and hence pick up more IOUs. But that situation will generate tensions in individual sectors, such as are now boiling up in the telecommunications sector.

In relation to the telecommunications industry, one must have sympathy with the argument that America has liberalized its market in terms of access to foreign supply much more than almost any other country in the world. But so long as there is a deficit, there will be a trade imbalance somewhere: if not in telecommunications, then in steel, or machinery, or textiles, or somewhere. With regard to telecommunications there is a hope that countries around the world are gradually discovering that the traditional approach they took to procurement, when pushed to excessive extremes, has resulted in unnecessarily inefficient and subsidized telecommunications industries within their own shores. According to the old Adam Smith argument we have heard for 200 years, we all would benefit from the liberalization of markets.

Liberalization of procurement policies is being closely linked to liberalization in internal competition policies on the provisions of networks, value-added service, and terminal equipment, although there is no absolutely logical link. You could liberalize procurement of the PTT while still making it a monopoly. Even so, there tends to be a strong coupling between the two.

I have carried out research that bears on how liberalization of network infrastructure, terminal equipment, and value-added services has been faring and what its impacts have been. Two colleagues,

Michael Tyler and Thomas Watts, and I have conducted a comparative study of telecommunications liberalization in the United States, the United Kingdom, and Japan. We examined closely the impact of liberalization on interests within these countries.

Ideally, we would like to have analyzed the social and economic effects of liberalization policies in those three countries, but we concluded before we even started that it would be too big a task. Determining the economic outcome of telecommunications liberalization with any degree of quantitative rigor is a mammoth task, so we did not attempt it. Instead, we investigated the impact on intermediate variables such as the range, quality, and price of telecommunications goods and services. We did not attempt to see how these variables in turn fed through to economic benefits, although we may yet try to do so.

Our results indicated that there are no simple answers. If Ithiel Pool himself were conducting such a study, he would contend that it is extremely unlikely to come up with a simple, single answer, and we certainly did not find one. By and large, the range and quality of telecommunications services available to consumers rose in the three countries at the time of the transition to telecommunications competition. Moreover, the prices came down. Not all of them, however; nor did all people benefit. Another recent study that I completed with colleagues in Hong Kong is an attempt to apply the techniques of benefit–cost analysis to the question of whether there should be one or two local telecommunications carriers. An interesting circumstance of this study was that whereas a competitive telecommunications network policy had been introduced in the United Kingdom, the United States, and Japan, this was the first time a government actually wanted a quantitative benefit–cost analysis of the situation. How much of the analysis they use in their decision may be unknown, but at least they commissioned it and are using it as an input to the policymaking.

What we did in Hong Kong was to look at the major single cost and the major single benefit. The major single cost was undoubtedly duplication of engineering and operational resources through running two networks rather than one. On the benefit side, the situation was more subtle and complex. Our evaluation of benefits used a method to forecast the likely tariff reductions that would arise following the introduction of competition. We kept in mind the extent to which competitive pressure would be brought to bear on the main telecommunications carrier in areas where the competitor was coming in. To elaborate on this study, in evaluating the cost side we listed all the cost elements required to create a second telecommunications network that would be competing with the main one. For each cost element (e.g., maintenance, cabling, duct work, switching exchange, gateway to the international exchange) we investigated what percentage of that cost was a wasteful duplication, in the sense that to do it in the main network would have cost less, and to what extent it was simply the same as the cost of doing it in the main network. The result was that we arrived at a measure of the economies of scale and of the excess engineering and operational costs.

On the benefit side, we took the revenue of the main telecommunications carrier, the Hong Kong Telephone Company, and divided it into components, including international, residential, leased line, data services, business telephony services, and residential telephony services. Then we forecasted the cost and benefits over a twenty-year period and determined what proportion of that revenue stream was subject to competitive pressure. For instance, inland residential telephony would not be subject to competitive pressure because this telecommunications service would not serve the residential market; but certain kinds of business services would be, international services would be, and so forth.

For the element that would be subject to competition, we showed illustrative price reductions; for example, we used the numbers 10 percent and 15 percent as typical of experience internationally. A methodology was applied to convert from user benefits to real economic resource benefits; I will not elaborate on that here.

The results of the exercise provide a cost–benefit balance for a number of different stages of liberalization, ranging from allowing the local network to become competitive to allowing all local and international services to become competitive. I hope that the study will generate discussion of methodologies for approaching this issue in other parts of the world. The findings themselves, whether the costs happen to exceed the benefits, will be particular to Hong Kong, but one could insert numbers for other countries into the same methodology and turn out results.

Insofar as exercises like this help governments reach a rational conclusion on how to open up or not open up their telecommunications infrastructure, the result will be a gradual change toward the homogenization of world markets rather than having some countries being wildly competitive while others are completely monopolistic. In turn this may make a small contribution to solving trade balance issues.

Chapter 10

The economics of international telecommunications

Alfred C. Sikes

Over the past few years, several important international trade relations have materialized, and we are continuing to see more of them. These relations have not necessarily been the result of traditional factors such as geography, comparative economic strengths, or common language. Instead, they have been an outgrowth of shared national perspectives, especially in understanding the value of information and information services.

Historically, domestic telecommunications markets were subject to several external constraints. In much of Europe, for instance, government-owned post and telecommunications entities effectively monopolized communications products and services. In the United States and Canada, the telephone companies were vertically integrated into all stages of production, equipment, local and long-distance services. These monopolistic companies, at least in part, sought to fulfill social objectives through their pricing policy. For the most part, legislators, regulators, and government officials were satisfied with the consequences.

The essence of regulated telecommunications operations in the United States and abroad was a government sanction that reinforced a regime of price discrimination, that is, selling the same product to different customers at different prices. This system was stable and sustainable only so long as customers lacked effective alternatives. But then the technological environment radically changed, at least in the United States. Moreover, previous barriers to competitive entry were lowered or removed altogether. That fundamental competitive change forced reforms and regulatory approaches in much of what the United States has experienced in its communications sector.

Japan was the first major country to undertake liberalization along the lines pioneered in the United States. New legislation was passed in 1984 that privatized a dominant firm, Nippon Telegraph and Telephone, and opened much of the domestic communications market to competition. Some attributed the changes undertaken by the Japanese government to United States trade pressures. Certainly some of the changes recently adopted by that nation are along the lines urged by the United States, such as liberalization of equipment rules and regulations that had restricted use of private lines. But much of the effort to liberalize communications was well underway in Japan before trade issues became a major component of our political agenda. While barriers to competitive communications developments have been lowered in many sectors, Japan's barriers are probably as high and as durable as they have ever been.

The next major move toward telecommunications liberalization took place in Britain. There, legislation to privatize British Telecom was introduced, passed, and several pro-competitive market opening initiatives followed. One can hardly say – and I do not know anybody who has said it – that liberalization in the United Kingdom was a result of United States trade pressures. Whether it was the result of a national view, the change was needed and would prove of great benefit to the country.

Other countries are studying or have followed with similar national initiatives. These include the Netherlands and our largest trading partner, Canada. But also in France, Germany, and other markets, telecommunications liberalizations have gained considerably more political support. In Germany that support is being converted into actual liberalization laws and regulations, and it is possible that the Germans might end up leading liberalization on the continent. But the conventional wisdom is that they will lag behind the more progressive nations.

Why is all of this occurring? One would have to assume that it is chiefly because nations saw communications policy changes as furthering their best interests. In short, national self-interest has been at work. It has been fueled in part by small, but growing groups of business, government, and academic leaders who have become convinced that the sword of closed protectionism once characteristic of telecommunications is undesirable given the dynamic technological changes in marketplace conditions.

Telecommunications used to consist chiefly of voice traffic, linking subscribers across town, or throughout a government or country, or occasionally internationally. These are small components of the gross national product: in the United States about two to three percent. Today we are all trying to contend with what someone once labeled 'the dazzling new electronic abundance.' We have girdled the world with high capacity satellites and fiber optic cables. We distribute not only traditional voice information but also an array of data, video, and other commercial information.

At the same time, telecommunications technology has exploded. Moreover, the industry has become much more critical in the world economy. The financial services, transportation, insurance, retailing, travel and tourism, and a whole array of other political industries, depend on the availability of effective and efficient telecommunications. In manufacturing, computer-aided design and manufacturing have become more and more the norm. Telecommunications in sum has become essential as a modern business tool. For this reason, tariffs, along with entrance barriers, are now crucially important. Subsidies that are too high, for example, can harm vital enterprises.

The share of the gross national product, at least in the United States, reflects this growing reliance on communications. At present, the industry constitutes about six percent of GNP, and that percentage has been increasing by more than one half percent annually. Indeed, telecommunications is one of the relatively few major industry sectors that has been steadily growing as a share of our GNP.

In the United States and abroad, marketplace forces are at work, and it is those forces, reinforced by national interest, that are pushing change. But there is still, unfortunately, stiff resistance in some quarters to accommodating the changes through the political process by altering the regulatory environment. In Italy, Korea, Switzerland, Australia, and some other countries, established communications administrations have enlisted local interest groups, including organized labor, in defense of the status quo. The point to bear in mind, however, is that such short-sighted efforts may place at risk the peaceful development of national economies and the emergence of a free international trade environment.

The domestic economic risks of rigid communications policies should be well known. Many of today's markets are global. That is true, for example, of automobiles, financial services, most business and consumer electronics, and aeronautics. Does it make sense for a country to tell its leading automobile or computer or electronics companies that they cannot have the sort of free, unimpeded access to telecommunications and information resources that their international trade rivals enjoy simply because those assets were not invented here? How can the Deutsche Bank, for example, hope to maintain its competitiveness vis-à-vis Japan, London, or United States-based banking organizations, when it may not have the same ability to exploit commercially advances in telecommunications technology?

The international trade risks also should be recognized. In the United States our communications markets are wide open. The manifest success that foreign-based companies have enjoyed in this country provides ample evidence of that fact. At the same time that our leading communications firms confront intensifying competition at home, however, their access to key markets overseas remains highly restrictive. Over time, the lack of competitive market access or effective commercial parity will have negative implications for United States firms. In recognition of those implications are continuing pressures to curtail foreign access to the United States communications market.

United States communications and trade policy leaders have been reassessing our past policies and our posture in this critical field. Options considered include the feasibility of establishing free trade alliances. Some have argued that United States market access should be conditioned on the availability of comparable market access overseas. Those arguments will gain in political currency, unless there is some change in market circumstances abroad.

For telecommunications policymakers overseas, several points should be clear. First, the domestic economic risks of failing to make pro-competitive regulatory changes are large today and should increase because telecommunications is becoming a more and more critical production component in global markets. They are getting increasingly rivalrous and competitive. Second, to the extent that liberalization is blocked or otherwise handicapped in succeeding, the result may be to heighten general international trade tensions. That could do genuine damage to the free trade foundation on which most developed countries' economies are more and more based. In conclusion, it is highly desirable as a matter of domestic and international policy that steps toward more open and freer telecommunications markets continue to accelerate.

Chapter 11

A history of recent German telecommunications policy

Eberhard Witte

The federal government of West Germany established a commission in 1985 to find ways of improving the telecommunications system by promoting technological innovations, developing international communications standards, and introducing competition in the telecommunications markets in West Germany and in Western Europe as a whole. Traditionally, the continental European PTT system has been a state monopoly, with one agency in charge of post and telecommunications. The mandate of this agency is to provide the market with universal services rather than favor the special demands of certain groups of customers or one company. Our commission, which consisted of politicians, industrialists, a labor union leader, scientists, lawyers, and a specialist in business administration (the author), created a proposal for restructuring the telecommunications system in the Federal Republic of Germany, a set of policies which, no doubt, will persist in the unification of Germany. The fundamental restriction on the commission was that the basic law of the Federal Republic of Germany, our constitution, should not be changed. (To make any change in our constitution requires two-thirds of the parliamentary majority.) Our constitution, drawn up in 1948, includes Article 87 stating that post and telecommunications is the responsibility of the federal government as a part of the federal administration. To change this part of the constitution in the short run is impossible; in the long run, I think it will change.

Telecommunications, as a part of the German PTT, the Bundespost, is headed by a minister who is responsible not only for the entire administration but for its day-to-day management. Two previous commissions in 1965 and 1971 had recommended that the ministry be separated from the day-to-day operations. But on both occasions the recommendations were not implemented because of opposition by the labor union. Therefore, our commission had to face considerable obstacles.

When we made our final report to Chancellor Kohl, he immediately decided to start the legislation process to bring our recommendations to a vote. Initially the recommendations did not argue for privatization; for, as I mentioned, to convert telecommunications into a joint state company like the German airline Lufthansa is possible only if Article 87 were changed. Only marginal areas, especially data processing, software, customer services, or equipment sales tend, as in the past, to be given to subsidiaries, which are limited companies. But ownership is not the only question with regard to liberalization. If our recommendations only lead to privatization and avoid monopoly, that would not necessarily be a better road. We have to establish competition in our telecommunications markets, and since our constitution does allow private competitors freedom in the marketplace, for the time being this is where short-term advances will be made.

The commission recommended that the market be completely liberalized for all terminal equipment, including even the telephone, which is currently under a monopoly. With the exception of the old telephone service, any private supplier should be permitted to offer all the other telecommunications services – an open market arrangement. This means that particularly small and medium-sized users who are not in a position to develop their own communications system could choose from an array of services offered by new private suppliers. Though no private suppliers presently exist, our hope is that, when they do, they will enter the market and offer new services.

Such services will not be subject to authorization by the government. At this point, our recommendations go still further than the liberal regulations of the United Kingdom and Japan, where the suppliers require government sanction. In the field of terminal devices and services, the aim is to have as much competition as possible to ensure that all customer needs are satisfied.

The installation and development of a telecommunications infra-structure covering the entire country will continue to be the responsi-bility of the public enterprise named Telekom. It will be required to ensure nationwide coverage of Germany and to charge every customer the same prices. The politicians on the commission insisted that we provide for uniform quality for all customers, that there be safeguards against emergencies and crises, and that the needs of our national defense system be met.

Accordingly, the state organization Telekom will continue to exercise a monopoly in regard to the telecommunications network. This arrangement is on condition that private service companies can lease transmission lines at competitive terms, however, which means prices for leased lines have to be affordable to a private supplier. Should this not prove to be the case after a trial period of three or four years, we recommended that the network be open to general competition.

The economic framework of the future will depend on the behavior of Telekom. If Telekom successfully develops the new infrastructure network (e.g., ISDN), gives leased lines to private competitors, and opens the market, it will remain as a monopoly. If not, the monopoly will be broken up.

The commission felt that the network monopoly should not apply to all means of transmission and recommended the following exceptions. First, data communication via satellite should be open to competition; in addition, foreign satellites should be used for data transmission between private customers. (This is a recommendation of the green book of the European Commission, and we followed it in our report.) Second, cellular radio telephones will be provided by private suppliers. Telekom and other private suppliers are in competition in mobile communications. Public pay phones also are not part of the monopoly. Rather, private companies may buy public pay phones from Telekom or install them by themselves. Telephone service as a transmission of the spoken language, what is called POTS in the United States, will likewise remain a state monopoly, but not the combined services.

We also recommended that new services including voice, text, picture, or data should be open to competition. (In the meantime, the law concerning the restructuring of Posts and Telecommunications passed German parliament.) We have to wait and see what new legislation passes through parliament to know the fate of this recommendation. Indeed, with increasing integration of telecommunications, the voice will no longer occupy the special place it used to hold. Anyone who wants to reduce the state monopoly could achieve this with the introduction of new telecommunications services, which also includes voice.

The implicit premise underlying our recommendations is that innovation can and will break monopoly. The restructuring of the telecommunications sector is not seen as a singular, once-and-for-all intervention, but as a continual process of adapting to changing situations and requirements. What, then, will become of Telekom? It is logical to expect that Telekom will respond to the healthy pressures of the marketplace, a new situation for Telekom. It will be stimulated to redouble its efforts and will require freedom for entrepreneurial action. With the growth of market control, it will be possible to reduce administrative controls, especially regarding the management of their own personnel. As a result, Telekom should experience more freedom.

The inflexible salary scale for civil servants conflicts with a market orientation. Especially for management, it should be possible to exceed the limitations of the existing salary scale for public service. Telekom has to be able to attract experienced, dynamic managers from the private sector. The ministry cannot be subordinated to the forces of market competition, yet the enterprise has to be active in a market. The operations of the postal services and of the telecommunications service are taking different paths in their technical development and demand differentiated business concepts. For this reason, separation of the two is imperative.

The Minister would like to establish a third public enterprise for post bank services. The subsidizing of the postal services from the profits drawn from the telecommunications sector should be gradually discontinued. Currently, the postal service gets about 1.5 billion German marks per year from telecommunications profits. In any case, the cross-subsidization should clearly be shown in separate budgets for the two or the three units.

In the future the customer will have a wide choice of equipment, as in the United States. We should have it in a short time; however, the main benefits will be the new services and competition offered by the public enterprise and private companies. That is a large step for us.

Chapter 12

The future of German telecommunications

Karl-Heinz Neumann

On January 1, 1984, the largest enterprise in the world, AT&T, was divided into eight pieces in the largest antitrust settlement in history. On January 1, 1989, the largest enterprise in Europe, the German Bundespost, was divided into three pieces in the largest organizational reform of public enterprises in Germany. These two divestitures do not have many similarities, but the divestitures represent major steps in the worldwide reform process in telecommunications. It is instructive to analyze the reform process in Germany and its probable outcome, and compare it with reform in other countries, specifically European ones.

The political reform package in Germany is larger than that in other western countries with telecommunications policies. Its size is due to the fact that we are trying to take two major steps in our telecommunications structure. The first – and in many countries the only – step is the formulation and implementation of a competitive environment in telecommunications. The step is one of liberalization, not deregulation. The second step is the shaping of a new regulatory structure and an organizational restructuring of the major supplier.

The second major aspect consists of four elements:

- Separating regulatory from business functions in telecommunications;
- Separating postal functions from telecommunications;
- Defining the regulatory models and instruments;
- Shaping the managerial structure of the Bundespost and legislative requisites for better internal efficiencies.

It is essential to separate regulatory from business functions in Germany because those functions are incorporated according to the old-fashioned PTT structure in a federal ministry. And separating postal functions from telecommunications will bring us in line with the major industrialized countries, which now have the two businesses separated. The

United States, for instance, separated the business and regulatory functions from the beginning. In Japan, telecommunications was separated from the postal services in the late 1940s, and it has become organizationally independent from the managerial administration. In Great Britain, the post office was separated from the governmental administration and was organized as a public enterprise in 1969. In these and other countries, telecommunications has been independent and directly regulated.

The industrialized countries not only differ in the speed with which they change their policy and structure, they also differ in the starting points for liberalization. The starting point in Germany is not as bad as often stated abroad. Although the Bundespost is currently the only provider of the transmission network, resale and shared use of voice leased lines are restricted though resale and shared use of data leased lines are relatively free. The Bundespost has a formal monopoly on basic services, but much data communication is transmitted and switched by private leased line networks.

The value-added service market is a competitive market dominated by private suppliers with limited market participation from the Bundespost. In the late 1980s the market volume was estimated to be 8 billion German marks per year. Nevertheless, there are still restrictions against using public network services to offer value-added services, thereby limiting an exhaustion of the market potential.

Concerning the customer premises equipment (CPE) market, we must distinguish between manufacturing and supplying CPE. Manufacturing of CPE in Germany is carried out exclusively by private industry. The Bundespost does not conduct any development or manufacturing activities, although it does supply some CPE with minor market shares. There is a monopoly only on simple main station telephone handsets. It is evident that the status quo of other countries, which started liberalization earlier and are discarding it now, has been less liberal. Nevertheless, the competitive part of Bundespost's activities in telecommunications is less than 10 percent, but the overall Bundespost market share in telecommunications is slightly less than 75 percent. In comparison, the Bell system market share was much higher in the 1970s.

Reform started with a change in government in 1983. When the new government was re-elected in 1983, it declared information and communications as a major reform area. Most of the early activities of the new government concentrated on cabling and therefore media policy. Another activity, centered on information, communications technology, and microelectronics, began in 1984. In 1985, a governmental commission was formed to make recommendations on the future structure of telecommunications. Eberhard Witte's report on the results of this commission's work is included in this volume (Chapter 11).

The governmental commission on telecommunications somehow has been a typical German commission with regard to its structure and mandate. The commission's members should and did reflect vested interests in the telecommunications policy debates and all political parties. It was not a pure expert commission but a typical German pluralized commission, as we call it, of opinions and interests. The mandate was not only to develop a consistent new model for structuring the telecommunications market, but also to discover the opinions of social groups with special interest in that area and to factor these opinions into their recommendations.

Taken together, these aspects did not allow for recommendations based solely on economic considerations. Rather, the main task of the commission was to construct a new social and political consensus in organizing telecommunications. In evaluating the recommendations, therefore, one must take into account these conditions. The progress and impact of the commission's work can best be attributed to the change of thinking between a few years ago and the present. A few years ago, no one would have regarded the proposed model as realistic for political implementation. Today, the model has a good chance of becoming a reality.

What has happened since September 1987, when the commission finished its work – and what will happen in the future? In September 1987, the Minister for Posts and Telecommunications received the mandate to formulate the government's new policy for telecommunications, to come up with a restructuring plan for the Bundespost along the lines recommended by the commission, and to prepare a cabinet decision. This work is now coming to an end. After that, there will be negotiations between the ministries that have responsibilities for this field; besides the Ministry of Posts and Telecommunications, the ministries of economics, finance, and interior are involved.

The organizational elements of the reform called for a new legal structure upon which the Bundespost can base its activities. Therefore, it is planned to replace the current postal administration law with a completely new law that defines the structure of the Bundespost and the responsibilities of governmental authorities in its regulatory and controlling functions. Furthermore, there will be small but important changes in the current telecommunications law. After some experience with a new competitive situation, the government is planning to create a new telecommunications law early in the 1990s. In addition, a governmental document will define the new policy in terms of its reasons, context, and details. This document will include all political decisions on structure and policy that are not reflected in changes of law. Thus, the reform will require parliamentary involvement, which will occur after the cabinet's decision goes into effect. Given the usual time for parliamentary debate, it is possible that the new laws and therefore the new telecommunications structure will be enacted within a year.

The probable outcome of the political debate on telecommunications reform is uncertain. I predict that there will be two major organizational elements of the reform. The first is separation of regulatory and business functions, where the regulatory functions will go to the new Ministry of Postal Services and Telecommunications. It is likely that there will be an organizational separation of postal services, telephones, and postal banking services; so in the future the Bundespost will be an umbrella organization for three different public enterprises.

A network monopoly will exist for the Bundespost in general, but it will be only a transmission monopoly and not a monopoly for public switches. Moreover, the network monopoly may have two major extensions: satellite communications (we want to introduce competition) and mobile communications, where we are considering competition in all three aspects of mobile communications – radio paging, private mobile radio telephones, and public mobile telephone communications.

Competition will be introduced in all kinds of telecommunications and value-added services except for the telephone service. There will be no regulation of private service providers except registration procedures. Free and unrestricted competition will exist in all areas of the CPE market, including the market for telephone answering. The Bundespost will reform its tariffs on telecommunications to effect more cost control for leased lines and switched telephones. Long-distance tariffs will be reduced by the early 1990s to one-third of their current level.

Due to its position as a monopolistic network provider, the Bundespost will be prohibited from having a competitive advantage, but we are considering no structural separation or safeguards in preference for nonstructural safeguards against anti-competitive practices. There will be competition in services by regulatory control of cost allocation and pricing.

The question has been asked, Why will the German telecommunications system in the future not be a totally liberalized and competitive one? For one thing, nowhere in the world market is the telecommunications industry an unrestricted one. Everywhere in the world, telecommunications is a highly regulated market with various degrees of competition in its different segments. Even in countries that have opened up all parts of the market to competition, regulation has increased, not decreased. Therefore, it is incorrect to say that we are observing a move toward deregulation in telecommunications.

Why will we sustain a network and a voice communications monopoly? In answering this, we should consider the four policy options that demonstrate degrees of service competition. The first option is to have unrestricted competition in all kinds of telecommunications and value-added services. The second option is to have unrestricted competition in all services except the telephone service. The third option is to have a monopoly on basic services and competition in value-added services. And the fourth theoretical option is to have a monopoly on basic services and some value-added services.

These policy options were the starting point in many countries for deregulating the service sectors, and they cannot be combined with models of organizing the competitive environment on the network side. From an economic point of view, the most logical arrangement does not have different competitive models for the network and the services side. In both segments of the market, competition should be allowed. Unrestricted competition in the service sector and a continued network monopoly is possible, but it makes no sense. Yet under a regime of unrestricted service competition, including resale and shared use, a network provider has no option but to choose a cost-based pricing strategy for the services provided: There is no opportunity to finance far-reaching social or infrastructural obligations, which is exactly the reverse of network competition. Thus, if unrestricted service competition is politically feasible and desired, there is no reason for any kind of network monopoly. If the political or regulatory process, however, imposes social infrastructural or financial obligations on the telecommunications system, they can be financed only by external subsidies or by restrictions on competition in the service field.

A monopoly in the service market, including telephony or basic services, is not compatible with network competition; however, the telephony monopoly allows for exemptions from the network monopoly. These policy options show that telephony is the last step in opening the telecommunications sector for competition. Hence, telephony monopoly is sustainable only in conjunction with a network monopoly.

In Germany, the future Telekom's telephone services must be a main source for financing social, infrastructural, and financial obligations (e.g., the subsidy for postal services, the subsidy for the general budget, and the financing of far-reaching infrastructural needs). We are in a situation where soon this kind of subsidizing will not be possible or compatible with competition in the service area. On the basis of the current market volume, about one-third of the whole market will be open to competition in Germany; but in a few years this will be more than 50 per cent because the competitive parts of the business have far higher growth rates than the monopoly parts – and the growth rates will accelerate with competition. But one should look not only at this quantitative dimension but also at the more important qualitative dimension. The most innovative and dynamic part of the market will be open to competition, while the monopoly relies on more traditional areas retained with only average growth rates.

In Europe there is a common conception of how to structure telecommunications. Accordingly, a common policy is emerging, with every country reforming and restructuring telecommunications. This movement is pushed and defined by a common authority, the European Commission. Although the European Commission is only partially endowed with the legal power to implement policy, this model will form the benchmark for national models. The German model fits totally with the European model and therefore has a healthy future with respect to the European community.

These considerations may be astonishing to those in the United States, but in Europe we have a dual legal system, and the European one dominates that of the national member states. By 1992 we want to have a bona fide common market, which means that we in Europe have to share ideas rather than try to export our individual national models.

The regulatory model is being criticized in Germany from one side as too liberal, and from another side as not liberal enough. Thus, simple logic would assure us that the model must be a good one! For economists, the arguments for a less liberal market environment are not very serious. Most of these arguments are ideological in nature or are based on economic interests. The inherent characteristic of the German model favors more competition and thus gives hope to an economist. But the model may be too cautious as compared with today's possibilities of competition. Even so, it has a good chance of fitting the economic environment.

We still observe different regulatory models in the western world in telecommunications. Yet all countries are moving in the same direction of organizing telecommunications as an open and competitive market. This process took more than two decades in the United States and is still going on. In Europe, the process, which started later, will need less than a decade, which is partly a function of learning externalities from the United States' experience. I am convinced that sometime in the first half of the 1990s we will make regulatory structures and telecommunications as homogeneous as we had them up to the 1970s. I am also convinced that these structures will be different from those in the 1970s, and that the German regulatory model will fit in with the competitive environment.

Chapter 13

Telecommunications policy in France

Jean-Pierre Chamoux

The French telecommunications system was of extremely low quality until the 1960s. At that time, most provinces had manual telephone exchanges. It was almost impossible for a new subscriber, say a newly married couple, to get a telephone line without being on a waiting list for about two years. There were 8 million lines in the public sector in 1973 with very poor service, and now we have the 'Minitel'.

By 1980 the French network had been upgraded to modern standards, and most users have received the telephone set that they had been expecting for quite a long time. Full, automatic dialing was in operation by 1978, and we now have 25 million main lines in the country. Most trunk lines are fully digital, and about 50 percent of the subscribers can access within a few days or a few weeks a full digital service; this figure will soon be over 90 percent of the network.

The change was clearly drastic. It had been planned by the state with strong involvement of the government, and the decisive decision was made in 1974 when President Giscard d'Estaing determined that modernizing the French telephone network was a national priority; but he also said that this priority should be met without a single penny coming from the budget. So from that day, which in my opinion was the first step in deregulating the system, the people who were in charge of the Telecom network and its modernization had to cope with using just the revenue from the telephone system and by borrowing money on the international market. It happened, and the result has been good enough to pay off the investment, despite the major economic changes we experienced between 1978 and today, including the shifts in inflation rates worldwide and the fluctuations in exchange rates.

The first characteristic of the French network is its remarkable level of digital equipment in front lines and switches. It is one of the most advanced digitalized networks in the world, fully ready for any type of narrow band digital application. ISDN's eventual developments, which were under test in Britain, are based on this high level of digital equipment.

The second characteristic is the flexible French regulatory system, which is not new. Our basic rule in telecommunications was established in 1837, when it was enacted as the legal rule to start the first telegraph, which was an optical telegraph. This regulation allows any communication system to be installed or operated either by the state or by a person authorized by a responsible member of the government. This has supported a competitive market already in two major fields which have been more recently deregulated abroad. One is PBX sales and installation of private networks within private premises, on development grounds, for instance; and the second field is terminal equipment provisions, which have been very liberal in the past twenty-five years, particu- larly with respect to computer systems, modems, and similar devices. This was different from major European countries, and was extended as well to the first telephone sets.

There are also some drawbacks in the system. The telecommunications service, the DGT, is state administered and serves the public. Even though it is extremely satisfactory within the new competitive international environment that we are facing, the profits made by the system, particularly on telephone use, are high enough to be very tempting when the state budget is tight. From 1983 onwards, the treasury has siphoned away large shares of this revenue. The amounts siphoned off in the last few years have been around 20 percent of total revenue, which is much too high to permit sufficient reinvestment.

A second drawback is the pricing structure used by the state administration. This undermines, in my opinion, the competitive edge of our telecommunications system in many sectors where the technical capability of the network is unbeatable. Revision of telephone pricing is underway, but much remains to be done because the system is still bound by the constraints of public service provided by the state. This means that to create a price or a new pricing arrangement requires an official decree.

The third drawback is the relationship to users, whether professional or residential. This relationship has to be fully reviewed to introduce a consumer-driven marketing system in place of the traditional engineering and administrative type of organization that characterizes the telephone story in our country.

Despite these drawbacks, it appears that a significant change in the telecommunications economy will alter our organizational structure, our pricing structure, and also the way the state behaves with respect to the public. In response, we have initiated an experimental method of deregulation by introducing competition in four fields.

The first is mobile communications. The public radio telephone system in France served about 35,000 cars at the end of 1987, and this was far short of demand, somewhere between one-eighth and one-tenth of the total demand according to market research. We decided in 1987 to issue a call for proposals to operate a national radio telephone system, fully cellular in the 450 MHz band, which was the only place where we could eventually have frequencies available for that experiment. The winning consortium was announced as a new operating company that was formed by a water-supply company known under the name Compagnie Generale des Eaux, and its associates. The first units patched to the network are portable systems called NMT (a nordic mobile telecommunications system), and this system is provided on common ground by the Finnish Company NOKIA, and the French Company ALCATEL. The whole country will be covered by 1991, and the system will be fully competitive with the existing system operated by the state. We foresee 120,000 subscribers with the frequency band available, which is small in comparison with what the state (DGT) is using. The DGT will probably serve 150,000 users, which demonstrates the ability of the market system when called on to cope with such problems. This opens a significant breach in the monopoly of the DGT and creates a new radio infrastructure that competes with the existing one. It will operate the system on a completely modern base, including an unregulated pricing system. It will do whatever the market says; it is up to the market to decide.

The second field is radio paging. This, too, had been released to the market and has led to authorization of a French broadcasting company that operates on radio and television bandwidths. Since 1987, they have been selling a system based on the RDS technique. The forecast is that they will take on about 20,000 new subscribers every year, at least for the initial years; our goal is to have 100,000 subscribers by the early 1990s.

The third field is resale of telematic services. This was made possible from a network of leased lines from the DGT, because we have no other provider since we issued a decree in 1987. This whole field was set up in a year. The decree allows private companies of any kind (whether banks, insurance companies, service companies, or whatever), either French or international, to provide a service from networks of leased lines, and to offer any kind of telecommunications service of that sort, provided that certain conditions are met: no voice traffic; and standards will be as far as possible publicly available. In the long run we hope that there might be international standardized protocols. This is set up today as an objective and not as an obligation. Small operators will have only to register, but no prior examination will be asked for and no license is necessary. You simply register and then build up the process just as you like. Large operations, which we have set up first to test this hypothesis, will have to get their license renewed annually. The idea is not to control everything but just to test the first phase and after a few years all controls will be lifted.

The fourth field is cable networks, which had not been fully developed in France. This field had been part of the public monopoly according to a 1982 national plan on cable distribution, which stated ambitious objectives to develop fiber optics. But the new law of telecommunications enacted in 1986 ended the monopoly of the DGT in this sector, opening cable distribution network to private operators. Several utilities companies have invested in the field and we now have five major competitors in this market. The public broadcasting company, as I mentioned, was privatized in 1987 and is now going into that field on a fully competitive basis. Meanwhile, the DGT has consolidated its share of the market at a costly investment. Though they are trying to compete, I think that they will learn from that segment of the market what competition means.

I will conclude by reviewing the thinking behind the newly implemented telecommunications law. In preparing the bill we sought to maintain the infrastructure of the network as a regulated sector of the industry. Included in this infrastructure are the basic lines and the public switches, as would be done in placing a value on what it costs to create an airport, a canal, or a highway. The service sector, aside from residential telephones which, for political reasons, are said to be lent to the user, was considered as competitive by nature and operated by companies that might have nothing to do with the traditional telephone and telex systems. Banks or computer services are possible providers of any kind of service, which includes setting the value of these services, whether they be commercial, financial, or technical.

The enacted law separated telecommunications from postal services, creating France Telecom as a public corporation in charge of network operations and run as a state-owned company. It did not include any privatization of the system because of political opposition especially from public sector unions. France Telecom will keep both the domestic and international monopoly over basic network and voice services, but the law does allow competition in the supply of terminal equipment and value-added services.

Chapter 14

Telecommunications policy in Japan

Tetsuro Tomita

The reform of the Japanese telecommunications policy began in 1948 with the reorganization of the Ministry of Communications into the Ministry of Postal Services and the Ministry of Telecommunications. This bifurcation meant that the telecommunications industry no longer would be burdened with covering the deficits of the postal system.

The second stage of reform involved three laws: the Radio Wave Law, the Broadcasting Law, and the Radio Regulatory Commission Law. All were enacted in 1950. To diversify journalism, the use of radio waves by the private sector was encouraged. The first Japanese private radio broadcaster was licensed in the same year the law was established, and by 1953 private television broadcasters also emerged. In the four decades since, private broadcasters have been vigorously competing amongst themselves and with NHK, the public broadcasting system, which has a completely different source of revenue for its operation.

NHK presently consists of two television, two radio, and one FM nationwide networks, all covering 99 percent of Japan. One hundred and thirty-seven private broadcasters have formed five television networks, one radio network covers 90 percent of Japan, and one FM network covers a slightly smaller area. NHK is now experimenting with the operation of two DBS (Directed Broadcast Satellite) channels. The private sector is planning to increase its one DBS channel to three by the summer of 1990. Experimental distribution by DBS of High Definition Television (HDTV), thought to be the television of the future, is also in process. It is clear that Japanese broadcasting has achieved, both in quantity and quality, the highest level of development. The most important reason for this, bar none, was that the framework of the 1950 law provided the basis for a competitive environment.

The third stage of reform, different from the second, had to do with monopoly of NTT. Three laws enacted in 1953, the Wire Telecommunications Law, the Public Telecommunications Law, and the Nippon Telegraph and Telephone Public Corporation Law, were intended to change the government monopolies to public monopolies. The laws not only denied new entrants to the telecommunications business, but also restricted the establishment of private networks or in-house communication. For example, the microwave circuits necessary for transmission of television programs planned by broadcasters were not approved, and circuit services had to be obtained from NTT in 1953. According to the Wire Broadcasting and Telephone Law of 1957, small-scale telephone networks were approved for agricultural cooperatives, but they did not become telephone operators due to limitations of NTT network connections.

The strictness with which these policies were applied is worth noting. As an example, in the spring of 1959, a Pan Am staff official visited the Ministry of Posts and Telecommunications to request a direct radio channel between Pan Am pilots and dispatchers in order to ease the newly introduced jetliner's operations. At the time I was a junior staff member of the Aeronautical Radio Section of the Radio Regulatory Bureau of the Ministry. I made an intensive effort to establish a non-profit organization like Airlink of the United States to handle such radio circuits for foreign carriers. However, the Ministry's final decision was to nominate the reluctant KDD, the international carrier, as a radio circuit operator in the name of monopoly policy. It was at that moment that I made up my mind that a Telecommunications Business Law was necessary, and that moment marked the beginning of my twenty-six years of personal struggle with telecommunications monopoly.

Another example of the carrying out of the monopoly laws has its setting in Gion, the oldest and most classical center of Geisha houses in Kyoto. In the spring of 1963, the General Secretary of the Gion Association came to my office where I was the chief of the Wire Telecommunications Section of the Regional Radio Regulatory Bureau. The Gion Association has a long history, first being approved several hundred years ago by the government of the Tokugawa Shogun. The General Secretary of the Gion Association wanted to have a privately switched telephone network connecting 280 Geisha houses in order to facilitate the rotation of Geisha girls, and to cope with increasing foreign guests on the occasion of the Tokyo Olympic Games of 1964. I struggled with a very complicated process in order to be able to give the Minister's license to the Gion Association in accordance with the Wire Telecom- munications Law. I finally succeeded, but not until after the Olympic Games. The consequences for the Ministry were severe, however. The National Diet's Communications Committee adopted a resolution accusing the Ministry of violating monopoly policy. I had thought of the Gion network as a PBX over a field rather than within a building, and saw no way in which it could be interpreted to be a violation of monopoly policy. The Gion private telephone network is the first monument to Japanese deregulation. If you go to Kyoto you will see the license decorating the wall of the clearing house in Gion.

At the end of the 1950s, with the proliferation of computers, there was a desire to use the public telephone network, the cheapest method of data transmission. This was allowed only in 1972, however, fourteen years after AT&T instituted services of the Dataphone 50. In general, Japan, during the two decades prior to 1985, lagged about a decade or more behind the United States in the introduction of new services, mainly due to our monopoly policy. Examples include the Open Sky Policy initiated in 1972 in the United States, and followed in Japan with the CS2 in 1983, VAN in the United States in 1973, and VAN in Japan in 1982, the Carterfone case of foreign attachments in the United States in 1968, and movements liberalizing foreign attachments to the phone in Japan in 1972, 1982, and 1985.

Concerning the inevitable 1985 reforms, the four stages of the reform began in 1985 with the replacement of the Public Telecommunications Law by the drastic changes of the Telecommunications Business Law. Japanese monopoly policy in telecommunications obstructed progress. A comparative analysis with the development of the various types of broadcasting made this clear. There was a need to promote innovation in telecommunications through a competitive market. This was the most compelling reason for the enactment of the Telecommunications Business Law.

Along with the enactment of the Business Law, the Public Corporation Law was abolished and the new NTT Law was passed. There was a desire also in NTT for an environment of free corporate administration after the thirty years of excessive control. For example, the yearly budget necessary for business operations required the approval of the National Diet. Therefore, it was thought that there was no alternative to the abandonment of the monopolized market in favor of a competitive market. It was thought that the large deficit, including the ¥30 trillion deficit of Japan National Railways, accumulated by the finance ministry over more than ten years, could be alleviated somewhat by selling NTT shares. In a sense, the largest contributor to the privatization of NTT was the Ministry of Finance.

In the private sector, it is natural that telecommunications equipment producers are directly affected and would welcome liberalization of policy that offered possibilities of large sales in an active market. Companies such as trading houses that had abundant capital and personnel, but lacked business leverage, felt the liberalized policy to be a welcome rain from heaven.

The Ad Hoc Commission on Administrative Reform was a direct promoter of reform, but it cannot receive the entire credit for its success. As mentioned above, there was strong support from all sectors of society and no opposition. There has never been any reform in Japan as widely blessed as this one.

What follows is a synopsis of the 1985 reform. Although the Telecommunications Business Law contains 144 articles, the content of the legislation is straightforward, its crucial point being as follows: Type One businesses, facilities owners, and Type Two businesses, facilities lessors, are distinguished and administered differently. Type One businesses, because of their large investment in equipment, are regulated. In other words, the permission of the Minister of Posts and Telecommunications is necessary for the creation of fees and the initiation of business. For Type Two businesses, the Ministry of Posts and Telecommunications must be notified of the start of business, but there is no control in the form of the fee approval. Notification is obligatory, and therefore a form of administrative regulation, but no administrative office holds the right of rejection and there is no mechanism for controlling entry into the market. Japan's administrative offices can use the information gained through obligatory notification only for the compilation of statistics. Free entry into the Japanese market on the basis of notification can be thought to be completely on a par with the deregulated conditions in other countries. In three years since the institution of the laws, there have been no complaints from business.

The most eloquent proof of eliminated restrictions is that as of November 1989 the number of the new entries, including Type One and Type Two, reached 849. Among those there are twenty-seven Special Type Two businesses, including fifteen international VAN companies, and 767 Type Two. The majority capital of twelve of the companies is foreign. Total revenue of Type Two carriers is estimated at around ¥850 billion.

Type One companies numbered fifty-five, including three that concentrate on specialized local network services. They started long-distance telephone services as of September 1987. There are also two companies specializing in satellite communications, two in international communications, four in local network services, seven in cellular telephone services, and thirty engaged in paging services. In these companies, foreign capital investments can be seen from such sources as Hughes Communications, Motorola, and Merrill Lynch. The revenue of these companies amounted to ¥110 billion in 1988.

The new NTT Law that transformed NTT from a public to a private corporation can also be said to be succeeding in that NTT has reorganized through the establishment of more than 100 affiliated companies for streamlining purposes. Additionally, NTT's data communication division, with annual revenue of around ¥200 billion, became a separate wholly owned subsidiary, and NTT announced that its holdings will be reduced in the near future. However, it is still uncertain whether diversification will have positive effects on NTT's management.

The 1985 reforms have been a great success, but the question remains of how conditions of fair and harmonious market competition are to proceed. In the initial report of the Ad Hoc Commission on Administrative Reform, the final stage of NTT's privatization is set in the manner of the breakup of AT&T. But in case it is not carried out as proposed, the Liberal Democratic Party (LDP), together with the Ministry of Posts and Telecommunications, devised in the fall of 1983 a plan of action to carry out privatization, preserving the integrity of NTT as a single body. An amendment was added to the draft of the new NTT Law to the effect that it must be reviewed in five years.

At present, the process of law is proceeding as scheduled with the entrance of new operators. One wonders, however, how long it will take before newcomers of Type One command 10 per cent or ¥500 billion of NTT's ¥5 trillion market. According to the law, NTT has come to be merely one of many telecommunications business operators. But the condition of the market is like ten or so ants competing with an elephant. Given such a condition, one must ask what administrative measures should be taken so fair competition can be established. The future duties and obligation of the Ministry of Posts and Telecommunications are very large. In case harmony cannot be achieved between the ants and the elephant, a drastic second reform plan, including the possibility of the breakup of NTT, must be prepared. In fact, in October 1989, the Telecommunications Advisory Council of the Ministry of Posts and Telecommunications issued an interim report concerning NTT's management and market conditions. In the report, divestiture is considered, along with other alternatives, as an effective measure for coping with many serious problems NTT presently has; namely, inefficient management, unfair advantages in the market, and so on. The Advisory Council's final report is to contain recommendations of measures the government should take as a result of the review of the NTT Law.

At the Pacific Telecommunications Conference in Hawaii in 1984, I heard Americans use frequently the phrase 'fair competition.' At that time, I was using the concept of 'harmonious competition.' Now I would like to revise this to 'excessive competition.' This phenomenon can be seen in the example of the numerous hardware manufacturers such as NEC, Toshiba, Hitachi, Mitsubishi, Matsushita, and Sony. In addition, there is the situation of seven major television networks competing for ratings daily in an area smaller than California. Such excess competition is responsible for the development and the strength of the Japanese product and of Japanese television programs. In other words, the more competition the better.

Chapter 15

The politics of international telecommunications reform

Jill Hills

Since its beginnings with the telegraph, the telecommunications industry has been closely linked with governments.[1] For many years, despite differences in ownership between AT&T and other posts and telecommunications administrations (PTTs), there was a remarkable unanimity of purpose in governmental telecommunications policies. The old concept of telecommunications was that of a natural monopoly; that is, it was argued that the entry costs in fixed capital investment were economies of scope and scale such that a duplication of facilities would increase unit costs and hence prices to the consumer. The old system involved hidden cross-subsidies from long-distance to local services, from business to residential access, from existing consumers to potential consumers, and from urban to rural areas. Telecommunications policy held within it elements of social policy and also goals belonging more to macroeconomic, employment, industrial, defense, or science policy than the expansion of telecommunications. Hence the old policy bene-fitted similar constituents in all industrialized countries: individual residential consumers, rural areas, trade unions, and telecom-munications equipment manufacturers. Concomitantly it disadvantaged large distributed businesses, urban areas, and potential entrants either to the network operating markets or to the equipment markets.[2]

Many changes have taken place in the telecommunications sector, beginning with the liberalization of equipment in the United States and gathering force over the last five years. Yet no similar cross-national consensus on what market structures should look like or who should benefit has yet emerged.[3] Countries' policies differ on structures and goals, and so my purpose in this essay is to explain policy changes within three industrial countries – the United States, Japan, and Britain.

I maintain that economic interests arise and shift according to the opportunities afforded by new technology and to the position of domestic industry within the world economy. But the ability of economic interests to influence policy depends on their ability to co-opt bureaucratic interests and to establish legitimacy in the eyes of the public through their use of ideology. The ideology itself is a product of long-term historical relations and short-term pushes and pulls of economic interests. In the United States and Britain, ideology relating to the market historically emphasizes the autonomy of the firm, whereas in Japan it stresses the primacy of the state.[4]

Within the telecommunications industry, the picture is one of competing interests within business as well as competing interests in bureaucracies. Bureaucracies have their own private agendas, and at times these state interests may prevail, as currently in Japan. In general, however, shifting coalitions of state and private capital, bolstered by the legitimacy of ideology, are responsible for shifts in policy.[5] Despite differences, in all three countries government regulation of telecommunications is becoming more politicized as losers in the market turn to political activity for compensation and as bureaucrats strive to extend their control.

Several technological developments in telecommunications have produced changes. First, and perhaps of greatest importance, has been the digitalization of switching, which has led to the convergence of traditional telecommunications (voice transmission) with that of computing (data transmission) and video transmission – and to conflicts between the systems of regulation prevalent in the previously discrete industries. The reduction in costs of fixed investment through optic fiber and satellite technology has brought into the market new equipment manufacturers and new operators. At the same time it is now possible for large businesses to construct their own private networks for less than what it would cost for continued usage of PTT long-distance networks. In addition, information provision and other specialized services or niche sectors in the business community have brought new service suppliers into the market.

New facilities providers, new equipment manufacturers, new service suppliers, and large users have invaded a sector that was previously the prerogative of government-backed PTTs. In turn, the new entrants have their own agendas and interests, not necessarily married with those of the incumbents. Alliances have been formed between new and old interests and with elements of the state in order to swing policy in their favor; much of this activity is intended to change governmental rules for the market.

Where competition has been allowed with the PTT, these rules or regulations have been necessary for fear of cross-subsidization between monopoly and competitive services. Much of the experience in this matter came from the pre-divestiture behavior of AT&T.[6] The result of continued regulation to effect liberalization has been that companies depend on bureaucracies for permission to enter markets or to pursue strategies within markets. In general, competition has had the ironic effect of increasing, rather than decreasing, the relation between state and industry.

Despite the usage of the terms deregulation, re-regulation, and privatization to describe the divestiture of AT&T and the entrance of competition into the British and Japanese markets, the initial regulatory frameworks for each were considerably different. Also different were the pressures that brought each about, ranging from large users and potential entrants in the United States who were allied to a political ideology antipathetic to regulation, to the Thatcher government's ideological predisposition to the needs of the city, to pressure from new Japanese capital and foreign entrants who allied themselves to bureaucratic interests in Japan.[7]

In the United States the regulatory framework established by the Federal District Court in 1984 provided for the breakup of AT&T into seven regional operating companies and a long-lines company, on the basis of a market segmentation between regulated monopoly services and unregulated competitive services. The stated intention of this market segmentation was to stop AT&T from using its local service as a bottleneck to competitors. At the time the RBOCs (regional Bell operating companies) and AT&T were split into regulated companies, responsible for network operation (primarily voice), and unregulated ones, responsible for enhanced services. AT&T, allowed to keep its manufacturing and R&D, was split from the major market for its equipment – the local operating companies. Although AT&T was allowed to manufacture, the RBOCs were not. The court did allow the RBOCs to take over AT&T's Yellow Pages and introduced a waiver clause permitting them to return to court to apply for entry into any market in which they would not be dominant. AT&T rates remain regulated through the FCC, while the RBOCs are separated into voice carriage (regulated by the states) and unregulated companies, with market segmentation policed by the court.[8]

The court added to the regulatory framework of the FCC and the individual states a further but autonomous system of regulation. However the FCC still remains responsible under the Federal Communications Act for the provision of universal service at a reasonable price. Other agencies such as the NTIA of the Commerce Department, the State Department, the Office of the Trade Representative, and the Pentagon, as well as Congress, have all become directly or indirectly involved in domestic telecommunications policy.

In Japan the regulatory framework established by the 1984 Telecommunications Business Law freed the equipment market of regulation and split carriers into Type I (facilities providers), Special Type II (national or international leased line service suppliers), and General Type II (dedicated networks). Type I had to be owned by a 70 percent majority of Japanese, and Special Type II could be foreign controlled; both could operate internationally, although it was assumed that international competition with KDD, the sole Japanese international carrier, would come from Type II entities.[9] NTT was to be privatized, but the government continued to hold 30 percent of its shares. Its future organization was to be reviewed in 1990. Obligations of universal service and the retention of R&D were placed on NTT. The only further market segmentation is a ban on the connection of voice-only private networks to the switched network.

Subsequently the Ministry licensed three terrestrial Type I long-distance competitors with NTT and two satellite competitors. Several hundred General Type II service suppliers have also been registered by the Ministry (regulation is lighter than for Type I entities), although less than twenty are thought to be active. In the international market the Ministry has licensed a Type I facilities provider, of which Cable and Wireless of the UK and Pacific Telesis are the major foreign participants and has further licensed a Japanese consortium to provide international service via leased lines. In addition, an agreement with the United States has allowed Type II suppliers to market value-added networks on an international basis, and an amendment to the Business Law to this effect was made in 1987.

The telecommunications law of 1984 gave the Ministry of Posts and Telecommunications a greater role in the regulation of telecommunications. The Ministry of Trade and Industry stays involved through the promotion of R&D projects and because it views the wider area of information technology (of which telecommunications is part) as its rightful territory.[10]

In Britain the liberalization of the equipment market in 1982 was then regulated by the Department of Industry. Its failure to control British Telecom (BT) was the prime reason for the establishment of the Office of Telecommunications (Oftel) to regulate the sector. The Telecommunications Act of 1984 which allowed for the privatization of BT also set up Oftel, under the direction of Bryan Carsberg, an accountancy professor. Under the Act the primary duty of Oftel's director is to exercise his powers relating to the licensing of BT and other operators in order to secure telecommunications services that satisfy all reasonable demands for them; several secondary duties, such as promoting the interests of consumers, promoting R&D, promoting foreign business use of UK telecommunications, and promoting international transit services, are placed on the Director. He exercises power in relation to existing licenses independent of the Ministry, but the Minister continues to have the power to issue new licenses and to have responsibility for international telecommunications.[11]

Market segmentation was originally based on liberalization of the equipment market, a duopoly of voice carriage between BT and Mercury (now wholly owned by Cable and Wireless), and the further liberalization of value-added network (VAN) services. Because of difficulties in defining VANs, however, all data transmission was subsequently liberalized. Simple resale of voice transmission was subsequently liberalized in July 1989. Cellular mobile radio is divided between a BT company and Racal Vodaphone. Oftel is responsible for regulation of the whole sector together with the licensing of cable TV transmission. It is also responsible for consumer complaints and for the provision of information.

BT is regulated by price cap. Its license divided services into those whose tariffs would be regulated by Oftel – a basket of services including monthly access charges, long-distance tariffs over the PSTN, and local calls – and others. BT was obliged not to raise tariffs over that basket of services by more than the Resale Price Index of inflation minus 3 percent, but it could rebalance tariffs within the basket. A further provision limited it to no more than a 2 percent increase per annum in residential access charges.[12] In view of the limited competition offered by Mercury, which has primarily concentrated on major business customers in London and other major cities, Oftel has also moved into the regulation of services not covered by the basket, such as leased lines.

Turning to the American market, in 1968, when the Carterfone decision liberalized the use of equipment in the United States, there was no consideration of the trade implications, which did not become apparent until the maturation of the Japanese market in the early 1980s. Nor were the industrial policy implications of the AT&T divestiture taken into consideration. But with a Schumpeterian analysis one could argue that monopoly profits are necessary to fund innovation, and that the divestiture has exacerbated the present condition of American trade balances and innovation.[13]

The liberalization of the American customer premises equipment market (CPE) that preceded AT&T's divestiture opened it to foreign penetration. The balance of trade went from a surplus in 1981 of $1.5 billion to a $2 billion deficit in 1986, with the largest share of imports coming from Japan and the Asian newly industrializing countries. In response, American companies have taken to manufacturing in lower wage economies such as Singapore and Mexico. The CPE market is now almost lost to American domestic manufacturing production.[14]

In the switching market the divestiture not only released the regional Bell companies from purchasing switches from AT&T's subsidiary, but demanded that they should not discriminate in favor of AT&T. By the late 1980s AT&T had lost its near monopoly, sharing the market instead with Northern Telecom, and competing with foreign manufacturers. AT&T badly needs switching export markets, of which the European is the most important. It has attempted to make that entry through alliances with European firms such as Philips and Olivetti. Although there is no evidence that AT&T is cutting back on R&D, the lack of expansion in its domestic market share without commensurate export markets seems likely to lead to a downgrading of technology.[15]

In general, then, the American telecommunications equipment market is characterized by increasing foreign penetration of investment, a faster increase in imports than exports, an increase in overseas manufacturing by American firms, and a decreasing share of the home market for American companies. Coupled with the competitive fragmentation of the bureaucracy, it is this economic situation together with market fragmentation that has encouraged companies in the use of political rather than market competition.

A major factor in the bureaucratic standoff has been the overlay of an autonomous system of regulation by Judge Harold Greene's court on that already operated by the FCC and the state regulators. Yet, in undermining the authority of the FCC, the court continues a trend begun in the early 1980s. At that time, under the chairmanship of Mark Fowler, the FCC became a body occupied with deregulating the telecommunications and broadcasting markets, thereby bringing it into conflict with

Congress.[16] During the divestiture the issues of faster depreciation and of access costs, as well as the FCC's belief that interexchange carriers should be freed from all such charges, further alienated a Congress concerned to protect individual consumers. Challenges to the FCC by state regulators through the courts have limited even more its operations to inter- rather than intrastate regulation.[17] The FCC's efforts to compensate for the erosion of its base by entering the fields of technical regulation at the national level, and attempting to regulate at the international level, originally foundered, partly because of its hands-off ideology and partly because of bureaucratic competition.

Allied mainly with the old telecommunications sector, represented by AT&T and its divested RBOCs, the FCC has come under pressure from new entrants such as information processing companies and AT&T's long-lines competitor, MCI, from a Congress concerned about rising residential telephone bills, and from the court itself. Judge Greene has made no secret of his belief that the FCC is incapable of regulating the RBOCs. Nor are its major client groups unified. The *Modified Final Judgment* (MFJ), with its emphasis on forbidding RBOCs preferential treatment of AT&T, effectively isolates them from each other, while they remain in the wings as possible competitors to AT&T if the MFJ were lifted.

The perception at the time of the divestiture was that AT&T had the better prospects. The RBOCs were expected to perform as public utilities with a maturing market and high costs, and they immediately exploited fears that they would be uneconomic entities in order to gain concessions from the court and increased tariffs from state regulators. Subsequently, the RBOCs have moved into non-telecommunications businesses as well as pressing to remove market divisions imposed on their activities. Forbidden to manufacture, at first BellCore influenced product manufacture through R&D, but the RBOCs spend little on R&D. For the FCC, one way to solve the trade imbalance would be to allow the RBOCs into manufacturing. In its application to the court it was joined by the NTIA and Congress itself. But the application worsened the situation since Judge Greene determined that R&D also constituted manufacture. Only later was it acknowledged that even if the RBOCs were to manufacture CPE, they would also manufacture abroad.

Other FCC actions related to the trade deficit can be viewed as responding to AT&T's need for overseas markets. During the confrontation with the French government over the penetration of AT&T into the French market, it demanded details of foreign purchases by RBOCs.

Its action trod on the toes of other agencies, as did its review of access charges for enhanced service suppliers.[18] The issue of whether AT&T should be regulated by means of a price cap as in Britain or by rate of return brought the FCC into more conflict with a Congress concerned that the proposals would be to the detriment of the individual consumer.[19] Although the court's autonomy eroded the power of both the FCC and Congress in domestic telecommunications, their competition with each other further weakened their influence. A movement headed by the NTIA in 1988 to remove policymaking from the court came to nothing and was replaced by a demand that the FCC should be placed under the executive branch.[20] The poor rating given to the FCC was also evident in the removal of its power over international telecommunications contained in the revised trade bill of 1988.[21] However, the appointment in 1989 of Alfred Sikes from the NTIA to head the FCC has brought rapprochement between it and Congress, and the establishment of a division within the FCC to oversee international telecommunications.

The burgeoning trade deficit in telecommunications equipment has provided the only unifying theme for policy in a fragmented market and a fragmented bureaucracy. In response, in 1988, Congress enacted a bill that demands reciprocity from countries running a telecommunications deficit with the United States. The bill is therefore primarily concerned with manufacturing and exports. Similarly, a further attempt by the FCC and Congress to legislate the takeover of telecommunications policymaking from the courts, scheduled for 1990, centers on the RBOCs and manufacturing. But Congress has left untouched so far the whole issue of export controls, the relation of controls to export markets of equipment, and the relation of regulation to innovation.[22]

With the bureaucratic standoff continuing, attention has shifted to international policy where the new service suppliers are the dominant economic coalition. These suppliers are a small, unified group intent on increasing their foreign investment. Their contribution to the balance of payments is not large, yet in an alliance with the USTR, Commerce, and State they have appealed to the ideology of free trade to further their aims through the ITU and GATT.[23] Hence, despite the intention that in the United States the manufacture of high technology products should be increased, the implications of current policy developments are of fragmentation, lack of standardization, failure to take advantage of economies of scale and scope, and disintegrating domestic manufacture. Bureaucratic competition has led to a policy vacuum filled by the only unified group in the market.

Turning to the Japanese, we see that the past mercantilist industrial policy has been held up as a model for Western European democracies to emulate. Underlying the models of Japanese policymaking is an inherent proposition that it is a rational one, led by bureaucrats with long-term goals for enhancing the Japanese national interest.[24] Because the Ministry of Trade and Industry (MITI) has always been regarded as the strongest ministry, even when there is conflict, the pattern has been to view that ministry, in conjunction with the Ministry of Finance, as the long-term industrial decisionmaker. Nevertheless, the internationalization of Japanese manufacturing has eroded MITI's power base, and the recent Telecommunications Bill has turned power over telecommunications to the Ministry of Posts.[25]

Under Prime Minister Nakasone, who left office in 1987, the power of bureaucrats was reduced. To circumvent the policy bottleneck of interministerial competition and to coordinate privatization policy proposals across several ministerial areas, he established bodies such as the Ad Hoc Administrative Council, which made recommendations on the privatization of government monopolies such as telecommunications and railways. Since then, the fall from power of Prime Minister Takeshita and the weakening of the ruling Liberal Democratic Party by the Recruit Scandal has left the way open for bureaucrats to compete for power.[26]

In the telecommunications sector, from the early 1980s Japan has depended on exports to the United States for most of its total output. The liberalization of telecommunications equipment has brought in major exporting electronics companies such as Sony, Sharp, and Matsushita. In general, manufacturers who rely on the American market have interests which demand that American pressure for entry to Japanese domestic markets be met. Therefore, American interests have forceful advocates within the domestic arena.

In contrast to the rest of the world, data-processing companies grew out of telecommunications companies, so the convergence of technology between the two manufacturing industries had little salience for market entry. But in the bureaucratic world it sparked a turf war between MITI and the Ministry of Posts and Telecommunications. Hence there are duplicate advisory committees in each ministry, with the same personnel sometimes serving on both. Some issues such as standardization of equipment have occasionally reached an impasse, with both ministries aspiring to leadership. Others, like the entry of a foreign-backed competitor in the international market, have seen an alliance between exporters and MITI. Each issue produces a new alliance.

Just as the worldwide constituency in the telecommunications sector has multiplied, so has that within Japan. If those in this sector could be said previously to talk with a collectivist voice, they do not do so now. NTT itself buys from and competes with the manufacturers. These trends in a loosening of ties between manufacturers and NTT have been furthered by NTT's diffusion of procurement. In turn they have increased NTT's political isolation.

NTT and KDD were the monopoly operators of the telecommunications network until 1985 – the one a public company, the other privatized but under governmental control. Relations between the two entities and MPT have been the opposite of that which might be expected by their formal status, however. Whereas NTT was historically autonomous from the ministry, KDD had very close relations, often headed by retired bureaucrats in the Japanese system of 'amukudari' or descent from heaven.

It seems that in the period following liberalization MPT has exerted far greater control over NTT than either American or British regulators have done to their counterparts. NTT's activities are constrained by the need to apply to the ministry for permission to provide new services, to form new subsidiaries, to alter tariffs, and to authorize its business plans. NTT is limited from entering manufacturing by an undertaking which it gave during the passage of the privatization legislation in 1984. Also, whereas BT has signed agreements with other European PTTs to provide one-stop shopping for large corporations wanting private networks, after liberalization NTT was forbidden to enter the international market in competition with KDD, although KDD was allowed to enter the domestic market.

NTT has been under an obligation to cooperate with its competitors; but as NTT has increased productivity and has introduced many new services, so MPT has found it more difficult to control. The introduction of ISDN in April 1988 illustrates the division of opinion between NTT, seeking profits and targeting mainly business customers, and MPT. The ministry stated that it wished to see NTT's monthly ISDN access charges to business reduced by 60 percent and the cost to individuals reduced by 70 percent. It also called for the related consumer equipment to be reduced in price by 75 percent. So far as it is possible to ascertain, the MPT's desire to see lower access charges is not based on cost or profit criteria. Rather it demonstrates the ministry's political efforts to widen its public support.[27]

What is conspicuously lacking is economic regulation of NTT in terms of clearcut rules. The ministry's political orientation – fueled by its endemic competition for status with MITI – leaves the system of regulation open to abuse. For instance, NTT's request for an increase in its local call tariff held at ¥10 since 1977, has met with demands from MPT that the company make public its costs and profits on its various services. The intention seems to be that the ministry should be absolved from responsibility for any increase. In 1984 MPT stated that it was not in favor of NTT's reducing its tariffs below those of its competitors, and subsequently NTT has been obliged to keep its tariffs about 10 percent higher than theirs in order to allow them to gain market share. Yet NTT had a return on turnover of only 8 percent in 1986, 10 percent in 1987, and 9 percent in the 1988 financial year. Its 10 percent reduction in profits follows the entry of three long-lines competitors and the divestment of its data-processing business to a separate company, and has resulted in a reduction in the value of its shares.

NTT has previously seconded personnel to the MPT, but several of its competitors already have ex-MPT personnel in senior positions. The most recent recipient is Motorola, where several MITI personnel were already in place. In contrast, MPT's bid in 1987 to have its own person replace Dr Shinto as the president of NTT failed, primarily due to the opposition of Dr Shinto himself; in turn, the need for politicians' support may relate to Dr Shinto's involvement in the Recruit Scandal. His resignation from the chairmanship in late 1988 once again opened the door for ministry influence over NTT.[28]

The Telecommunications Business Law passed in 1984 provided for a review of the network's structure after five years. In November 1987 MPT announced that it would undertake this review and in April 1988 received the support of the Telecommunications Council, an advisory body to MPT that is run by the ministry, but endows MPT plans with a seemingly independent legitimacy. Although Prime Minister Takeshita and the LDP were then reported to be unenthusiastic, MPT announced that it would set up an advisory council to consider the breakup of NTT along the lines of the AT&T divestiture. The Council duly reported in 1989 in favor of breaking NTT into regional companies.

The proposal for the divestiture of NTT had originally been made by the Ad Hoc Council on Administrative Reform in 1982, but it was rejected by the LDP, still heavily dependent on rural votes, which feared the costs to rural areas. The proposal is being pursued despite the views of Keidanren (the economic organization) that it is too soon to revise the law. MPT's stated aim is to lower telephone rates and improve service.[29] However, a divested NTT would not only solve the problem of how to control a company that was gradually becoming formidable to regulate, but would also give MPT the opportunity to place its own people at the helm of the ten regional companies. Rather than diminishing MPT control, it would increase it. MITI has opposed the plan. Ironically, while the weakening of the LDP by the Recruit Scandal has opened the opportunity for increased bureaucratic competition between MPT and MITI, the potential electoral implications of divestiture mitigate against its adoption. Currently Japanese telecommunications policymaking is little more than a ritualized game of inter-ministry competition.

Britain is widely seen to have a telecommunications policy similar to that of the United States and to be its ally in the international telecommunications community. In actual fact Britain's liberalization has been far more tightly controlled than that of the United States, and it has gone less far than in either America or Japan. The prime limiting factors have been the government's intention to sell British Telecom's shares and the desire to ensure British Telecom and Mercury's profitability.[30] Regulation of BT demanded by computer manufacturers following BT's liberalization was instituted in terms of a 'light rein.' Thus, in a crucial sense, possible competition has had to meet the test of its potential impact on the duopoly's profitability and on the government's ability to sell other state monopolies. The conflict between this desire and the liberalization of markets has resulted in selloffs, like that of BT, in which little competition has been introduced into the markets and in which the consumer has been left to the mercy of private rather than public monopolies. A failure by Oftel to address these problems for the consumer, except on an individual basis, led to a public backlash in 1987. This public backlash has eventually instigated not only stricter control of BT, but renewed emphasis on liberalization on the part of government.

The previous consensus of limited competition within the domestic market coupled with pressure for liberalization within the rest of Europe has shifted. Whereas previously a coalition of DTI, Cable and Wireless, and large user groups provided the major impetus, and in particular the demands of Cable and Wireless for support in its international strategy for a global network met with government approval, primacy is being given to domestic liberalization once more. Although international policy mirrors that of America, the British are less handicapped by a fragmentation of bureaucracy and competing agency agendas. Oftel does not have the autonomy to introduce competition into the domestic market that might undermine international policy, but the government has shifted domestic policy away from the protection of BT and

protection of domestic manufacture.[31] In so doing it places at risk both
BT's research and development of new technologies and its leading role
in the standardization of equipment within Europe. Yet despite a
growing trade deficit in telecommunications equipment, industrial
policy currently plays no part in telecommunications policy, which has
become entwined in policy toward the mass media.

Foreign, and particularly American, capital is entering Britain in the
telecommunications market, but indirectly through holdings in cable TV
companies. Cable TV has been slow to start in Britain, partly because of
lack of funding but also because Britain has one of the highest rates of
penetration of video recorders.[32] The original intention of market
segmentation has been compromised by the lack of investors. BT has
entered the market for carriage of local franchises and for programming:
It has interests in four of the ten franchises given. Cable TV companies
can compete in telecommunications only if they ally themselves with
either BT or Mercury. Since BT has no interest in competing with itself,
the three companies providing local service are all linked to Mercury.[33]
The White Paper on broadcasting of 1988 suggested, however, that
carriage of cable should be delinked to programming.[34] Coupled with a
loosening of regulations governing foreign investment, the threat of
such a delinkage has had the effect of bringing American companies,
faced with a maturing American market, into the British sector. A
further incentive is the possibility of the breakup of the duopoly on voice
transmission. American investment in cable TV operation now rings
London, and operators are demanding the license to switch voice traffic
among themselves. The effect of these developments would be to
regionalize competition in local service.

Meanwhile, BT would like to extend its license to carry programs on
its terrestrial network, thereby enabling the provision of optic fibers in
the local loop to be an economic possibility.[35] This request has been
rejected by government. Instead, the policy emphasis is on separation of
markets based on technology and BT's exclusion from those markets.
Under current thinking, BT would be excluded from the 'personal
communication network' to be installed in the 1990s as a radio-based
bypass of the local loop; furthermore, it may only participate in a minor
fashion in the 'telepoint' licenses to complement existing public pay
phones, and may only compete in cable TV through separate subsidiaries. In contrast, Cable and Wireless has been promised a license
for the personal communication network. Oftel has been involved in
picking the winners in each contest for licenses.

In terms of public debate the institution of Oftel has effectively depoliticized telecommunications. In the past, Members of Parliament received individual complaints regarding BT's service, but now they go directly to Oftel, which acts as the gatekeeper of generic information on telecommunications. This gatekeeper function and thereby the autonomy of Oftel have been strengthened by the failure of the government or of BT since 1982 to publish telecommunications statistics. Information on costs to the consumer, access, usage, and distribution is poor – a matter that Oftel is planning to rectify.[36]

Oftel itself has come under public criticism, following a strike by BT engineers in 1987 and a decline in the public pay-phone service. Oftel's close linkage to BT and the poor public opinion of BT tarnished Oftel's image as a successful regulator.[37] Oftel's first response was to distance itself from BT. It allowed Mercury to compete for the provision of public pay phones, despite the fact that it would skim a loss-making service. Moreover, Oftel demanded better quality of service from BT.[38]

The incident weakened Oftel's autonomy from political control. Soon after, the right wing of the Conservative Party lobbied Oftel effectively on the issue of the teenage chatlines provided by BT. It was claimed that despite the provision of monitors to prevent an exchange of addresses, teenagers regularly evaded such controls. BT's inability to provide technology that would enable parents to curtail use of the service, and its consequent high bills, led to Oftel's demand for rigorous controls from BT. This made the service so uneconomic that it closed almost overnight.

Although BT did not challenge Oftel in the courts, other countries are now doing so, and doubt remains as to whether the powers given to Oftel were intended to include what amounted to censorship. Since these events Oftel has introduced a heavier price cap of BT. The company may raise prices on a basket of services, which now includes connection charges, by the Resale Price Index minus 4.5 percent.[39] Current attention to the individual consumer's interest, including the appointment of a consultant on consumer affairs, suggests that Oftel is seeking to protect its political legitimacy.

The weakening of Oftel's legitimacy has had a further effect. The potential conflict between Oftel's institutional need for autonomy and government priorities has been solved by the co-option of Oftel into government policymaking. In 1988, the Director General of Oftel became a member of the government policymaking committee on the future communications infrastructure, thereby abrogating his independence.

The combined effect of Oftel's weakening, the events in Hong Kong which affect Cable and Wireless, BT's vulnerability produced by its poor quality of service, the entry of new players into the domestic market, and the convergence of telecommunications with broadcasting (which has a high political saliency to the government) is that further liberalization of the telecommunications market has been placed on the political agenda. The aim of the Department is to introduce competition to BT at the local level, through cable TV, through telepoint and the personal communications network. Despite talk of a third company being allowed entry into the duopoly in 1990, this seems unlikely given Cable and Wireless' needs. However, Oftel's co-option into the policy-making process leaves it no room for an independent assessment of BT's arguments or those of manufacturers.

In summary, I have attempted to explain some of the policy initiatives and differences in structure of the markets and deregulation in the US, Japan, and Britain. Each is subject to the constraints of historically varied government relations with industry and with particular companies. Each is differently affected by economic coalitions arising from technological opportunities. And each displays differing strengths in bureaucratic private agendas.

In the US the introduction of a second autonomous system of regulation through the court has produced additional bureaucratic overlap and in-fighting in a policymaking process that was already fragmented. State regulators, the FCC, and the court each may determine the entry conditions to new markets or the ground rules by which companies can compete within markets. With so many bureaucratic and business interests affected by potential legislation, Congress has been unable to achieve the consensus necessary to regain the leadership in policy.

In these conditions companies have developed political strategies in order to gain market advantage. And as AT&T regains its pre-divestiture market share, so competition becomes increasingly political rather than market oriented. The one unifying factor – concern for the trade deficit – has produced a coalition of bureaucratic and commercial interests strong enough to motivate American actions within GATT and the ITU, yet has not produced a strong enough coalition to alter the domestic conditions that have contributed to the deficit.

In Japan the political weakness of the Liberal Democratic Party has given renewed opportunity for the Ministry of Trade and Industry and the Ministry of Posts to pursue their traditional bureaucratic competition. The loosening of ties between the major manufacturers and NTT and the introduction of new network competitors has tended to isolate the company and allow increased economic coalitions against it. The Recruit Scandal and the involvement of Dr Shinto, NTT's president, who had been the most vociferous defender of the company against bureaucratic control, further weakened it and left the way open for MPT to propose its divestiture into regions. This proposal to establish further political control over the company is unlikely to be successful, not only because of MITI's opposition, but because of the changing electoral circumstances in Japan. Not only would such legislation be unlikely to pass an Upper House where the LDP no longer retains a majority, but would also carry the risk of further electoral damage to the ruling party. Hence current bureaucratic games are likely to be defeated by the realities of electoral politics.

In Britain, the establishment of an independent regulatory agency at first took debate on telecommunications policy out of the political arena. But as public impatience with British Telecom increased, so the legitimacy of Oftel as an independent regulator, separate from BT's interests, came under question. Although prior to the 1987 engineering strike Oftel seemed primarily concerned with BT's profitability, since that time government policy has been redirected toward further liberalization and competition. As a result of regulatory control of market entry, BT is being prevented from competing in new markets, while facing increased competition in its previous domestic markets. The result is likely to be not only a curtailment of its research and development work but also an increase in its investment abroad. In contrast to the US, the government is less concerned with the trade deficit in telecommunications equipment than with the convergence of telecommunications and broadcasting and its policy toward the latter. Although Oftel's sudden conversion to the interests of small consumers and its increased control of BT can be seen as an attempt to re-establish its public legitimacy, its co-option into government undermines its independence and benefits BT's competitors.

The regulations of telecoms in all three countries demonstrate one common factor – the increasing politicization of telecommunications as bureaucracies fight for territory, as they appeal to the general public for legitimacy, and as those who have lost their edge in the market (be it national or international) appeal to government to act on their behalf and alter the rules of the game for their benefit. In 1990, despite formal liberalization and privatization, telecommunications is a market as much if not more dominated by political priorities as it was twenty years ago.

NOTES

1 The research on which this article was based was supported by Economic and Social Research Council grant E0023 2196. The author would like to thank the Electrical Engineering Department at Waseda University, Tokyo, the Communications Policy Program at the Massachusetts Institute of Technology for their hospitality, and all those in each of the countries who agreed to be interviewed.
2 Jill Hills, *Deregulating Telecom: Competition and Control in the USA, Japan and Britain* (London: Frances Pinter, passim, 1986).
3 Robert Bruce, Jeffrey P. Cunard, and Mark D. Director, *From Telecommunications to Electronic Services* (London: Butterworths for IIC, 1986); *The Telecom Mosaic* (London: Butterworths, 1988).
4 Jill Hills, *Information Technology and Industrial Policy* (London: Croom Helm, 1984).
5 I am indebted to Edgar Grande, Mogens Kuhn Pederson, and Rob Van Tulder for clarification of the concept of 'social coalition' at the European Consortium of Political Research, Research Sessions, Mannheim, December 1987.
6 See: Steve Coll, *The Deal of the Century: The Break Up of AT&T* (New York: Simon and Schuster, 1986); Gerald Faulhaber, *Telecommunications in Turmoil* (Cambridge, Mass.: Ballinger, 1987); Peter Temin, *The Fall of the Bell System* (New York: Cambridge University Press, 1987).
7 Kevin Morgan, 'Breaching the Monopoly: Telecommunications and the State in Britain,' University of Sussex, Working Paper Series on Government–Industry Relations, 1987.
8 Jill Hills, 'Issues in Telecommunications Policy: A Review,' in *Oxford Surveys of Information Technology, 1987* (Oxford University Press, 1988); Kevin Morgan and Douglas Pitt, 'Coping with Turbulence,' Paper to Communications Policy Research Conference, Windsor, June 1988.
9 Kokusai Denshin Denwa, 'Development of Japan's Telecommunications Business under the Telecommunications Business Law,' KDD, Tokyo, 1987; Jerry Sevagglio, 'VANs in Japan,' *Telephony*, 212, September 28, 1987, pp. 155–9; Tetsuro Tomita, 'Liberalising Japanese Telecom,' *Intermedia*, 16, No. 2 (1988), pp. 37–9.
10 Kazuya Hirobe, 'Harmonization between National Telecommunications Law and International Telecommunications Law,' Legal Symposium, *Harmonization of Global Telecommunication Systems*, Geneva, ITU, October 21–3, 1987; Jill Hills, 'The Internationalization of Domestic Law and Regulation: US Industrial Policy on a Worldwide Basis,' Paper to Communications Policy Research Conference, Windsor, June 1988.
11 Oftel, *Annual Report, 1983-84*, London, Oftel, 1985, pp. 15–16; Bryan Carsberg, 'Oftel – The Challenge of the Next Five Years,' *Information Technology and Public Policy*, 4, 1 (1986), pp. 1–11; 'Oftel – Its Role and Relationship with British Telecom,' *British Telecommunications Engineering*, 5 (1986), pp. 33–9.
12 Department of Trade and Industry, *Licence Granted by the Secretary of State for Trade and Industry to British Telecommunications under Section 7 of the Telecommunications Act 1984* (London: HMSO, 1984).

13 On the implications of a Schumpeterian analysis see: John Horrigan, 'State Telecommunications Policy,' unpublished paper, July 20, 1988. On the impact of divestiture upon technology see: Michael Borrus, Francois Bar, and Ibraham Warde, *et al.*, *The Impacts of Divestiture and Deregulation: Infrastructural Changes, Manufacturing Transition and Competition in the US Telecommunication Industries* (Berkeley, Calif.: BRIE Working Paper No. 12, 1984); Henry Geller, 'Telecommunications Policy Today: Against Technology,' *Issues in Science and Technology*, 11 (Winter 1986), pp. 30–7; John McDonald, 'Deregulation's Impact on Technology,' *IEEE Communications Magazine*, Vol. 25, 1 (1987), pp. 63–5; Michael Noll, 'The Effects of Divestiture on Telecommunications Research,' *Journal of Communication* (Winter 1987), pp. 73–80. On trade effects: NTIA, *Assessing the Effects of Changing the AT&T Antitrust Consent Decree* (Washington, DC: US Government Printing Office, 1987); US International Trade Commission, *Changes in the US Telecommunications Industry and the Impact on US Telecommunications Trade 1984* (Washington, DC: USITC, 1984).

14 US House of Representatives, Hearing before the Subcommittee on Telecommunications and Finance of the Committee on Energy and Commerce, on H.R. 3: *A Bill to enhance the competitiveness of American industry and for other purposes*, Serial No. 100-4, March 10, 1987 (Washington, DC: US Government Printing Office, 1987).

15 On competition in R&D see: Erich Bloch, 'Managing for Challenging Time: A National Research Strategy,' *Issues in Science and Technology* (Winter 1986), pp. 20–29; George Eades and Richard Nelson, 'Japanese High Technology Policy: What Lessons for the United States,' in Hugh Patrick, editor, with Larry Meissner, *Japan's High Technology Industries: Lessons and Limitations of Industrial Policy* (Seattle and London: University of Washington Press, 1986), pp. 243–71; Jill Hills, 'Techno-Industrial Innovation and State Policies in the United States and Japan,' in U. Hilpert, editor, *State Policies and Techno-Industrial Innovation* (London: Croom Helm, forthcoming); Ken-Ichi Imai, 'Japan's Industrial Policy for High Technology Industry,' in Hugh Patrick, editor, with Larry Meissner, op. cit., pp. 137–70; Christopher Layton, 'The High Tech Triangle,' in Roger Morgan and Caroline Bray, *Partners and Rivals in Western Europe: Britain, France and Germany* (Aldershot, Hants.: Gower, 1986), pp. 184–204; Meheroo Jussawalla, 'The Race for Telecommunication Technology,' *Telecommunication Policy* (September 1987), pp. 297–307.

16 Mark S. Fowler, Albert Halperin, and James D. Schlichting, '"Back to the Future": A Model for Telecommunications,' *Federal Communications Law Journal*, 38 (1986), pp. 146–200.

17 Joseph R. Fogarty and H. Russell Frisby Jr., 'Supreme Court Decision Upends State–Federal Regulatory Balance,' *Telephony*, 211 (July 14, 1986), pp. 102–11.

18 Jonathan David Aronson and Peter F. Cowhey, *When Countries Talk: International Trade in Telecommunications Services* (Cambridge, Mass.: Ballinger, 1988); Stuart Chiron and Lise A. Rehberg, 'Fostering Competition in International Telecommunications,' *Federal Communications Law Journal*, 38 (March 1986), pp. 1–57; Geza Feketekuty, 'Trade Policy

Objectives in Telecommunications,' Legal Symposium, Telecom 87, Geneva, ITU, 1987; NTIA, *Long-Range Goals in International Telecommunications and Information: An Outline for United States Policy*, NTIA Report, Senate Print No. 98-22, Committee on Commerce, Science and Transportation, 98th Congress, 1st Session, 1983.

19 Federal Communications Commission, *In the Matter of Policy and Rules for Dominant Carriers*, CC Docket 87-313 (Washington, DC: FCC, 1987); Mark Cooper, 'Divestiture Plus Four: Take the Money and Run,' *Telematics*, 5, 1 (January 1988), pp. 1–10; *Washington Post*, February 18, 1988.

20 NTIA, *Telecom 2000: Charting a Course for a New Century* (Washington, DC: US Government Printing Office, 1988).

21 'US Telecom Trade Act to Combat Unfair Practices,' *Transnational Data Report* (November 1988), pp. 11–12.

22 Stuart McDonald, 'Stunting the Growth?: Information, Technology and US Export Controls,' Paper to Information Technology and New Economic Growth Opportunities Workshop, Tokyo, September 12–23, 1988.

23 Jill Hills, 'The Domestic Dynamics of International Telecommunications Policy,' *International Data Report* (March 1989).

24 For similar arguments see: John Zysman and Laura Tyson, *American Industry in International Competition: Government Policies and Corporate Strategies* (Ithaca and London: Cornell University Press, 1983).

25 On the conflict between MITI and MPT see: Chalmers Johnson, *MITI, MPT and the Telecom Wars* (Berkeley, CA.: BRIE Working Paper No. 21, 1987); Jill Hills, *Deregulating Telecoms* (1986), op. cit., pp. 100–157. For another view see: Kas Kalba, 'Opening Japan's Telecommunications Market,' *Journal of Communication* (Winter 1988), pp. 96–106. On regional diffusion of technology see: Sheridan Tatsuno, *The Technopolis Strategy: Japan, High Technology and the Twenty-first Century* (New York: Prentice Hall, 1986).

26 *Japan Economic Journal* (January 14, 1989).

27 On ISDN in Japan see: Megumi Komiya, 'Integrated Services Digital Networks in the US and Japan: A Comparative Analysis of National Telecommunications Policies,' Paper to Pacific Telecommunications Council, Hawaii, 1986; Koichi Asatani, 'ISDN Technologies and Implementation in Japan,' Paper to America's Telecom 88, Brazil, 1988.

28 *Japan Economic Journal* (December 24, 1988).

29 *Japan Economic Journal* (April 2, 1988).

30 Karen Newman, *Selling of British Telecom* (London and New York: Holt, Rinehart and Winston, 1986).

31 Oftel, *BT's Procurement of Digital Exchanges* (London: Oftel, 1985); James Foreman-Peck, 'Competition and Performance in the UK Telecommunications Industry,' *Telecommunications Policy* (September 9, 1985), pp. 215–29; David Leakey, 'A European Strategy for Equipment Procurement,' in Nicholas Garnham, editor, *Telecommunications: National Policies in an International Context* (London: Polytechnic of Central London, 1986), pp. 221–38; Edward Sciberras and B.D. Payne, *UK Telecommunications Subscriber Equipment Industry* (London: Technical Change Centre, 1986).

32 For the background to cable TV policy in Britain see: William H. Dutton, 'The Politics of Cable Television in Britain: Policy as the Outcome of an Ecology of Games,' Paper to American Political Science Association, Chicago, 1987; Ralph Negrine, 'Cable Television in Great Britain,' in Ralph Negrine, editor, *Cable Television and the Future of Broadcasting* (London: Croom Helm, 1985), pp. 103–33.

33 Ian Vallance, 'Keynote Address,' in Nicholas Garnham, editor, *Telecommunications: National Policies in an International Context* (London: Polytechnic of Central London, 1986), pp. 1–12; Bill Wigglesworth, 'Prospects for Competition,' *Information Technology and Public Policy*, 6, 3 (1988), pp. 209–10.

34 Home Office, *Broadcasting in the 90's: Competition, Choice and Quality – The Government Plans for Broadcasting Legislation* (London: HMSO, 1988).

35 Department of Trade and Industry, *Evolution of the UK Communications Infrastructure* (London: HMSO, 1988).

36 Oftel, *Review of British Telecom's Tariff Changes* (London: Oftel, 1986); Oftel, *Quality of Telecommunications Services* (London: Oftel, 1986); Oftel, *Telephone Service in 1988* (London: Oftel, 1988).

37 BT Union Committee, *A Fault on the Line: Report on the First Two Years of Privatised British Telecom* (London: BTUC, 1986); Jill Hills, 'Universal Service and the Liberalisation of Telecoms,' *Telecommunications Policy* (June, forthcoming); Consumers Association Ltd, 'BT – Still Out of Order,' *Which* (June 1988), pp. 266–81.

38 Oftel, *British Telecom's Service at Public Call Boxes* (London: Oftel, 1987).

39 Oftel, *British Telecom's Contract Terms and Conditions* (London: Oftel, 1988); Oftel, *The Control of British Telecom's Prices* (London: Oftel, 1988a); Nicholas Hartley and Peter Culham, 'Telecommunications Prices under Monopoly and Competition,' *Oxford Review of Economic Policy*, 4, 2 (1989), pp. 1–19.

Chapter 16

The struggle for control within the telecommunications networks

Marvin A. Sirbu

My topic centers on the question: Who will control the networks of the future? If we look at who provides telecommunications network services in the United States today, we see that as a result of divestiture we have interexchange carriers and local exchange carriers, but, increasingly, the large corporation is becoming an operator of networks and a provider of network services, stimulated as long ago as 1959 by the *Above 890* decision and by the Specialized Common Carrier decision. Large corporations have been building networks that separate from the carriers the transmission of large amounts of traffic.

What is meant by a large corporate network? Perhaps the largest private network, not really a corporate one, is the federal government network, the 'FTS' or Federal Telecommunications Systems. Started in 1962, it is one of the oldest private networks.

General Motors is currently completing a network that will link all of its many companies and locations and support 250,000 telephones. That makes it considerably larger than many of the 1400 independent telephone companies. Boeing in Washington has a private network with some 70,000 stations and several switches that are central office class. Indeed, many universities have converted to a central office class switch.

Why do we care about the large corporate users and why is it important to focus on this trend of their building networks? First, large users account for a substantial fraction of carrier traffic in revenues. In some areas, 25 or 30 percent of the revenues of the local operating company are accounted for by 1 or 2 percent of the businesses. As they leave the network by building their own systems, the carriers, especially the local exchange carriers, could be seriously threatened.

Second, large users are learning to wield political power, which will change the politics of regulation. In recent years, we have witnessed the

International Communications Association, an organization of 600 large corporate users, form a public policy committee to intervene in state regulatory cases; and the Ad Hoc Telecommunications Committee, also an organization with large manufacturers with private networks, now intervenes in regulatory proceedings. Hence we have additional stake-holders and players in the regulatory process.

Most large networks continue to use transmission facilities supplied by the carriers, but in the future the value added to a network and the profits will be derived from the control of the network, not in the simple carriage of bits. Having this kind of control over a network presents a major change in the way telecommunications service is provided.

There are several reasons why private networks have developed. Perhaps the principal one is the tariff policy. For many years the fixed costs of non-traffic sensitive plants, particularly the local loop from the telephone central office to the customers' parents, have been tradi-tionally recovered not through a fixed charge but through a usage sensitive tax on long-distance service. That tax, paid originally through separations and settlements, is now paid more explicitly through access charges – the carrier common line charges. The tax means that if you are a large user of long distance you will pay an amount much higher than the actual cost of the local access facility.

If you could build an alternative facility or design a network in which you do not have to pay the tax, you will have ample financial incentive to do so. For many years, private lines, which provide service at a fixed price, independent of volume, served as a way to avoid the usage sensitive tax.

To make use of a private line for more than connection between two points, you had to add switching. And so we saw the growth of large networks like FTS or the GM network, in which switching, owned by customers, combined with private lines leased from carriers to provide a switched network service at substantial savings.

A second reason for the growth of private networks has been the perceived unresponsiveness of the carriers. Shortly after divestiture, the lag time to get facilities from the carriers grew, in some cases to 12 and even 24 months. If you built your own network, with your own switching and even your own transmission, the process was under your control and hence you could maneuver more quickly.

In a data-dominated world, rather than merely a voice world, new kinds of capabilities have been needed by users. They want to build their own integrated digital network and have multiple services, what we might call an 'isdn,' but in lower case to distinguish it from the upper case ISDN represented by the worldwide carrier plan for integrated services digital network. The advantage of building such a private network is that it provides the ability to control one's own destiny. The original motivation for the FTS was that during the Cuban Missile Crisis, telephone calling to Florida grew to such enormous proportions that government calls could not get through. President Kennedy decided that the government needed its own network that could control the allocation of resources so priority calls could get through.

The ability to control the network, to allocate resources, to develop new services, to change, to do something as simple as reassign a telephone number to someone who has moved his or her office – that kind of control is part of what corporations have been buying in order to build their own private networks. Such integrated and advanced services are perhaps best characterized by a quote from Thomas O'Toole, Director of Corporate Digital Networks for Westinghouse. In an article describing the Westinghouse network he said, 'The definition of the Westinghouse Network is very similar to the definition of upper case ISDN. We are providing the Westinghouse users an ISDN type of service because that is what they require. This network supports crucial business applications and we simply could not wait for ISDN to come along and fulfill the need.' Users would like to have one entity responsible for the network end to end. In a divested environment, it is not possible to find a carrier who can be responsible end to end; you can do it yourself. That, too, has been a motivation for taking control and building large user networks.

Consider the theory of markets and hierarchies developed by economist Oliver Williamson. He noted that in trying to understand what circumstances will prompt people to procure services in an open market rather than to take them into their own organization and produce them in a vertically integrated way, we must take into account the amount of uncertainty in the marketplace and the degree to which specific kinds of investments have to be made. As certainly as divestiture has become a part of the telecommunications industry, so the amount of uncertainty has grown enormously.

In looking at the kinds of investments users want, we find that custom networks are ones that provide specific services necessary to the strategic objectives of their business – the airlines with their reservation systems, American Hospital Supply with its order entry system, the securities firms with their stock trading systems. As the investments become larger, and the uncertainty remains correspondingly large, the tendency, according to Williamson, is to bring the operations inhouse, rather than trying to procure them from the market. From this we conclude that an important trend of the next decade is likely to be large users trying to take control of the networks.

I mentioned that the value added in networks is in control. From one perspective, if you were a seller of services, transmission or switching, providing the user with the control he wants may be a way to sell him the bare transmission and the switching services. If you provide better network management, you will sell the switch that provides it, and the hardware sale goes along with the selling of the control capacity.

The process of control, however, has many elements. For one, it is the management of the network, which means managing the network's configuration and solving problems if something goes wrong. Another part is service definition control, that is, a kind of control that enables one to recombine elements to define new services. As a network becomes more like a large computer, users want to be able to program it and write software for it, thereby changing the kind of functionality that the network provides. Users also want cost control, and buying fixed-price lease lines, switching assets, or transmission assets has been a way of isolating them from the uncertainties of tariff policy. At the same time, control is not uniquely identified with ownership.

Control has three dimensions to it. One dimension is that of ownership of switching resources. You can buy your own private branch exchange or you can buy switching resources by the call, as you do with the public switched network. Alternatively you can contract for switching resources, as with Centrex, and pay a fixed price without usage measure.

Another dimension is transmission. You can own transmission resources by putting in a microwave system, your own fiber optics. You can lease them at a fixed price, contract them for unlimited usage, or buy them by the call, with package switch and circuit switch services.

The third dimension of control may be thought of as depth. What is particularly important is that carriers have recognized that control is something the end user wants. In the past, the only way to gain control was to buy the equipment. For example, you could buy the terminal that tells the switch what phone number you want assigned to which office. What the carriers are doing now is providing end users with terminals that sit on the end users' telecommunications manager's desk, allowing him or her to program the central office switch to rearrange telephone handsets, to provide overflow-calling or call-forwarding services, or what have you. In other words, while retaining responsibility for operational control and performance and problem management, they have given account control and configuration control to the end user.

Control, then, is not necessarily inherent in the ownership of the facilities.

In examining emerging competition in the network, we have to consider the perspective of equipment vendors, local exchange carriers, and interexchange carriers: How do they want to supply the end user with control; how do they want to view what is supplied by the other players in this structurally separated business? The equipment vendor's view of how the network should look is that the vendor's equipment will sit on the customers' premises, the private branch exchange. All control of the network will be supplied by customer-owned and equipment-vendor-supplied switches. Local exchange carriers and interexchange carriers will be reduced to providing pipes (transparent bit pipes that interconnect the switches). All of it is controlled by equipment on the customers' premises, which makes the user completely responsible for network management with tools provided by the vendors.

The local exchange carrier, by contrast, would like to see the control provided by the central office switch that sits within the local exchange carriers' network. The premise's equipment is reduced to the provision of handsets, with all of the network management residing in the central office switch. But again, the interexchange carrier is reduced to providing the bit pipe, so all of the value added is being supplied by the local exchange carrier.

The interexchange carrier would like to reduce the local exchange carrier to the provider of a bit pipe with no intelligence. The interexchange carrier wants to manage the network from the center, with common channel signaling and software defined network service. Perhaps there would be a PBX at the customer's premises, but a minimally functional one, with most of the network management in the centralized network rather than in the end equipment – or perhaps even supplying Centrex from the interexchange carrier's point of presence. We have seen over the last several years that AT&T has reprogrammed its Class 4 offices so they are capable of providing Centrex services.

What all this means is that three perspectives contend with each other in shaping ideas of how to organize a network. In every case, each of three players is trying to be the one who captures the market for control of the customer's network. That provides the point of contact for the customer for performance resource allocation and configuration management, and often in switching. The strategies of the players in the current environment are to maximize their opportunities to realize each of these scenarios.

For example, for the interexchange carrier, they need to hinder the ability of the LECs to do that. They can try to do so by resisting their efforts to enlarge the scope of services they can provide, such as by developing T-1 links and other links between the interexchange carrier and the customer's premises. This encourages bypass in order to adjust tariffs, as with the Megacom tariff of AT&T, which makes it attractive to bypass the LECs and gain additional flexibility in customized services to offer end users. For example, AT&T had been in a dispute over wanting to offer a specialized service to DuPont where they would put a custom multiplexer in their premises. They were constrained from doing so because under current rules they are required to announce and publicize all of the interfaces by which they interface with customers. The product they want to buy is from NET Corporation, and NET is not interested in having the interfaces of the product made public. Hence, AT&T wants to be out from under such disclosure requirements so they can engage in more customized service provisions.

From a regulatory perspective, the regional Bell operating companies have perhaps the most difficult situation. In order to make a network management work for them, they must be able to at least resell the long-distance services provided by interexchange carriers, if not actually become long-distance facility base carriers, so they have the authority to do least-cost routing on behalf of the customer to manage its network. They also want to gain control over the network's switch vendors. But to reprogram the switch to provide new services, the Bell operating companies have to go to AT&T or Northern Telecom who supply the switch and hence be dependent on them. The Bell operating companies clearly do not want to be dependent, particularly on AT&T, and so their current strategy is to design what they call the Intelligent Network II, which is a generic device that executes call processing primitives, collects the number dialed, connects two lines, and interacts through a signaling channel to a computer called a service control point. This computer, the service control point, has all of the logic for accomplishing a particular service. For instance, if you want a service that routes after three rings to your secretary's number or a voice mail system, the instructions to do that are in the service control point. The switch simply reports to the service control point computer that three rings have gone by and the service control point implements the appropriate logic.

The important part is that the service control point takes the control function of the switching system and extracts it to a place where the operating company has more access to it, can write software more easily, and can develop services more rapidly. Interestingly enough, under Open Network Architecture, the same access may become available to the end user, and so we may see the end user programming a computer that controls the switch. The carrier switch to provide the same services and the value added of that computer and the programs that support it – which are not at all insignificant – then go to competitive suppliers and not necessarily to the Bell operating companies.

Indeed, an example of this is Digital Equipment Corporation, which proposed what they call the computer integrated telephony concept. The idea is that the integration of voice and data services do not have to be carried over the same pipe. I can carry my data over my local area network and my telephone service over a pair of telephone wires. What is important is that I facilitate functional integration by being able to communicate between my data-processing system and the telephone switch; so I can have an incoming telephone number key into my data-processing system and tell me whose customer record to bring up on the screen; or I can have my rolodex on my screen invoke the telephone switch to dial a certain number. Digital Equipment's concept is that a standard interface, what they call the CIT or computer integrated telephony interface, would be defined by switch manufacturers and carriers, and all parties in the data-processing industry would have the ability to access, through that interface, telephone switching resources whether public or private.

What all this leads to is the notion that the control of networks is becoming separated from the physical facilities of switching and transmission, and the diversity and the competitive area is in control. That is where the new services need to be innovated and developed more rapidly.

What are the implications for future regulatory policy? In his book *The Geodesic Network*, Peter Huber argued that transmission costs are becoming higher than switching costs, or rather that switching costs are dropping more rapidly. As a result, the correct design of a network is not a star, which is the configuration when you want to economize on switching, but a geodesic network in which you use much more switching at many more different points.

There are problems with that argument, not the least of which is that with the decline in fiber optics cost, transmission costs today may be declining faster than switching costs. Second, and perhaps more important, switching and transmission costs are declining more rapidly than the costs of software and of management. Therefore, economies of scale lie in pure transmission – at least in the production of switches.

The software that controls switching holds great promise for effecting enormous economies of scale. In developing a standardized generic switch having a specific set of built-in primitives, one might spend perhaps a billion dollars. Moreover, putting together combinations of primitives to form new services is a highly differentiated business. It is one where being small, responsive to customers, and having strategic heterogeneity are essential. We may well envision a situation in which numerous players provide software and control, and a much smaller number of players provide switching and transmission.

Where control is going to reside, whether on the customer's premises or on the carrier's premises, is harder to determine. There is certainly a trend toward centralization of control. Even in private networks, the telecom manager of the corporation tries to concentrate in one location at corporate headquarters all of the software that manages the whole network. In the same sense, AT&T and the regional operating companies are trying to bring into one service control point the software that controls all of their switches. The tendency is to centralize in order to avoid having to update software at every location. You can only do it at one place. If you have to do maintenance on that software, it is where the programmers are. Nevertheless, once software has been built, it is certainly easy to replicate and distribute.

From all this we see that future competition in the networking business extends far beyond the familiar competition between carriers. It is also between carriers and large end users. The competitive battleground has switched from competition over who will provide the simple transmission part of networking services to competition for signaling and control. Yet the signaling and control business is highly differentiated, highly uncertain; the kinds of services that people will want and what the markets for them will be are not very well known. Rate-of-return regulation is based on the premise that one is selling a standardized service with economy of scale, and therefore one must be prevented from pricing the service at monopoly prices.

This assumption breaks down totally for a new service that involves risky innovation. The risk is not that the innovation will be priced too high, but that it might be priced too low and lose money, and the loss will be laid off on other ratepayers. A question that deserves careful consideration is how to set up a situation where carriers have proper incentives to take risks that will be borne by the appropriate parties – by users of new services or shareholders of the carriers – not necessarily by consumers of existing services?

Do the present rules provide a level playing field in this battle for control? At present the regional operating companies are very much disadvantaged by information restrictions and by software restrictions. AT&T as well is disadvantaged by the restrictions on what they can do in information services. The entry of new players creates new problems of coordination. I referred earlier to the fact that many corporations are setting up their own integrated services digital networks that do not correspond to any international standard. It is quite possible that the existence of those networks will derail the creation of a standardized ISDN. Why buy one if you already have one? It is likely that we will end up not with a single international or even national network, where everyone can communicate by using standardized protocols, but with a cacophony, as in the computer business of private systems connected at great cost on the margin, one with each other, and the overall level of conductivity is greatly reduced.

As to who will support the standards for interconnection, the strongest force for standardization is currently the operating companies, precisely because they do not engage in manufacturing. It is in their interest to have the manufacturers standardize the equipment so they can buy it on commodity terms instead of being locked into a single supplier. If we allow them into the manufacturing business, the incentive for standardization may greatly diminish. As a consequence, this will lead to an acceleration of a trend already happening in which large users have incompatible network standards. This separation of control from transport and switching creates opportunities and risks for users and carriers. It is certainly one that we should pay close attention to in looking at the future of telecommunications.

Chapter 17

The future of the telecommunications marketplace

Peter F. Cowhey

What interests me is the international framework in which divestiture is taking place. The second stage in the game that began with the unraveling of telecommunications regulations in the United States has two components that relate to world markets. One is that United States domestic regulation and trade policy for telecommunications will have to be further internationalized in light of experiments and changes in the rest of the world. Inasmuch as Americans are sometimes proud to declare that deregulation has marched from the United States overseas, others' experiments with how to adapt that form of competition to their own circumstances are going to come marching back into the United States with important consequences.

The other component of this second stage is common to all countries: All the experiments with varying degrees of competition in communications and information services pose a fundamental problem of how to organize the world market. In organizing a broader framework for the world market, we will find ourselves subject to yet another round of experimentation with national regulation and changing national frameworks for communications and information policy.

Consider first the topic of bringing back home the regulatory experiment; this can be done by reviewing the process of adaptation and trying to come up with a list of what will happen to the United States in the future. Due to the nature of our political system and industrial structure, regulation happened here earlier than elsewhere. But the coalition for reform looks roughly the same in every country. International change represents a further stage of evolution of that coalition, but, aside from country by country peculiarities, a common denominator extends across the world.

The coalition is comprised of extremely large users of telecommunications systems, as Marvin Sirbu has indicated. A typical rule of thumb is that about 5 percent of the users of national telecommunications systems constitute about half the long-distance demand in the country. Thus, a small, highly organizable set of players has the ability to act politically once the stakes are large enough.

The second group of players is the new electronics companies, especially firms that have moved to the forefront or the influential second tier of the industry since the days of the innovations in microelectronics. Those firms have a less well-established relationship with traditional telephone companies and less privileged supply relations. In general, the firms have been an impetus for reform because they want to break the privileged access between the only telephone companies and their privileged old electronic firm suppliers.

A third set of players is the service firms, many of whom find it indistinguishable between their use of the system and the provision of new services. They now stand as halfway houses, both buyers and sellers, in the system.

The international coalition is evolving as all of them become more highly internationalized as firms, and as they themselves work out their policies in a world undergoing a shift at a broader level. That broader shift could be considered from many angles, but I will mention only a few of them.

Although the United States remains the preeminent economic and political nation on average in the world, there has been a significant redistribution of international strength. It is a rule of thumb in international political economy that the free trade system has greater problems as the dominant world economy declines. Yet, at the same time, a large percentage of world trade is receptive to new impetuses for liberalization, such as the efforts to open up telecommunications markets. Even though the United States' power is declining and there are rising problems for the management of the international trade system as a whole, the reform coalition and other elements in the globalization of the world economy are leading to new efforts to experiment with the regulatory framework that has guided our traditionally closed markets.

I believe that in the future we should not expect that the choices for the world will be between free trade and the collapse into a 1930s style protectionism. Instead there will be an effort to create new forms of selective liberalization tied to much more conscientious efforts to monitor and enforce international liberalization arrangements. In other words, trust will matter less and verification more in future international trade arrangements. That will have important implications for all of us.

The character of domestic political coalitions in regard to domestic regulatory bargains matters more in this game because domestic regulators will have a greater hand in trade politics. The implications for the United States are important. Yet a reform coalition and shifts in international power are not sufficient to explain the situation. Politicians, after all, do not respond only to interest groups: They respond to voters; they respond to a sense of the public interest; they respond to their own ambitions in Washington as significant leaders.

Politicians, not just in the United States but elsewhere in the industrial democracies, have strategic problems with communications systems. First, I know of no country, including the United States, experimenting with competition in communications that has abandoned in full the politics of cross-subsidies in the communications system. Every country, no matter how it is experimenting, remains committed in some way to cross-subsidies for household service; and they remain committed to major equipment suppliers for the communications network in its various forms. In addition, they are committed in many countries (much less in the United States than elsewhere but still even here) to some form of indirect subsidy for labor in those industries. This means that no matter what we say about the competition of markets, politicians will carefully weigh how cross-subsidies will be continued – perhaps at a diminished level, but nonetheless continued.

Congressman Edward Markey (D-Mass.), for example, opposes deregulation for deregulation's sake and wants a fully documented analysis of any change. This opposition establishes the legislative branch's rights to make certain claims about the payoffs from the deregulation process, in addition to asking sound questions about whether the policy proposals themselves are in order.

Moreover, a common theme across countries is that politicians are looking for ways of denying accountability as they introduce change. One of the lessons that politicians have drawn from our experience is that it is extremely dangerous to deal with the basic telephone system too outrightly. Potential complaints by consumers and other messy surprises might arise; and so we are discovering a variety of regulatory experiments that are difficult for the average household voter to decipher. Hide change, if you would, or put it at arm's length by various devices.

Almost every country continues to have a national champion, or champions, in the communications industry. The word 'champion' often brings to mind the image of a single, dominant, national firm that will lead us into the world market. Yet the new champion may be a plurality of firms. In such a highly uncertain and changing industry, however, politicians will scrutinize prominent firms in world markets and ask how they are doing. The same will hold for national markets. The US Congress would hardly permit a complete collapse of competition in the long-distance communications market even if for some reason it would happen as a result of market forces. How many people would allow the theory of potentially contestable markets to carry the day as a form of discipline for AT&T? In some form or other the regulatory system would be tampered with to ensure that there are alternative long-distance carriers, and Congress will probably continue to watch certain bellwether firms (e.g., value-added industries like EDS or General Electric's information services) and see how they are doing. We will find continued constraints on competition in order to guarantee that at least some of our national champions are succeeding. Long-term constraints to the political concerns of working politicians will probably emerge as limitations on the marketplace.

A distinction between the United States and other countries is that the power of administrative bureaucracies in the United States is less on average than in other countries. When we deregulate, the assumption is that one should take away power from the administrative bureaucracy; if you want to change the rules of the game, institute new legislation or take it to the courts. In other countries, deregulation means making it possible for the executive bureaucracy to waive its powers temporarily. For example, many rules for the liberalization of value-added services and information services in other countries stipulate that competition is permissible but that extensive administrative oversight remains. Within that contingency for extensive administrative oversight lie potential trade barriers.

This situation creates difficulties for the United States that are not easily handled in the domestic marketplace. Few firms would accept the idea that the FCC will have unspecified powers of administrative discretion over deciding the fate of the information services market at home. But if the FCC cannot do so owing to our national administrative tradition, it means that the decision will get lodged someplace else in the international market. Where we lodge it and how we lodge it will be major questions for the United States.

Given a variety of national experiments with regulation and deregulation, how do we find a common international framework? One possibility is a continuation of the old international cartel for telecommunications services that is intergovernmentally sanctioned for the

International Telecommunications Union. I do not think that this is a viable possibility, however – even a slightly modified version of the cartel with minor liberalization.

What the United States prefers, of course, is the free trade system. We argue that services are like any manufactured good or raw material: They are potentially commodities, and as commodities they can be subject to the free trade rules instituted for the GATT, the world's trading organization. The United States has decided that for reasons of political expedience with respect to the GATT we will concentrate on enhanced services – value-added and information services only. But within that we are going to try to bring as much of the essence of free trade as possible. The United States, in bringing the free trade rubric to telecommunications and information services, is altering the meaning of the free trade rules themselves. Although we use the rhetoric of free trade rules, many substantive principles will change if we follow this route.

I will name just three principles that will change. First, the United States contends that free trade in communication services should operate as a guaranteed right of foreign investment, something that the GATT has never been able to do in any other group and service. Second, there will be organized rights for large users; that is, we vest large users in the international domain with minimum rights as users, a concept that lies totally outside the traditional domain of the GATT. Third, domestic regulations should be significantly internationalized; that is, that there is a presumption that the domestic regulatory system is subject to systematic oversight by the international community and will have to yield to minimum international obligations. In the long term this concept has important consequences for our federal system as well as for our conventional notions of regulation.

Even if we regard free trade as a beginning point, there is a serious concern that it may not be the end point. There are several alternatives. One follows from Marvin Sirbu's notion that large users seek end-to-end networks and yet current systems do not allow them to have that. To the extent that we have a large user community, it presents the prospect that we may eventually encounter a more massive restructuring of international communications systems than we have imagined thus far.

Consider, for example, a communications system that moves in the direction of the international airline industry, where the thrust is to establish about 15 to 20 major global carriers in the world. Imagine that in the communications system we change to a system dominated by a group of global communications companies, and those companies have their rights organized quite differently from how we view trade. Besides enhanced services, for instance, they could trade voice services. But instead of allowing them to serve everywhere, they would be like the airline market which serves only international gateways picking up and landing traffic in the major business centers of their international users. Furthermore, imagine that the bargaining among governments constitutes a swapping of gateway rights for the rights of the number of carriers allowed to enter the market, much as it is in the airline industry. This kind of arrangement would allow for the combination of voice and data for large services in interesting and innovative ways and permit the sort of oversight of markets that politicians are looking for.

Another alternative is the possibility of new forms of international corporate alliances. For example, AT&T, KDD, and British Telecom are experimenting with the idea of an integrated global service where you can order from any one company services in all three countries with a uniform billing and pricing system. This arrangement constitutes a degree of consolidation and coordination of separate, quasi-dominant carriers that would be unheard of in the past, but may be possible in this market. Because governments are going to control entry, these firms have an incentive to stick together.

A final possibility is when governments say that we recognize the system is much more unstable than in the past, but we still want to retain controls over it. The way we will do that is to grant, on a preferential basis, entry to consortia representing all vested interests. Note, for example, that in Japan, many of the new common carriers represent a consortium of large service firms, large users, and firms in the new electronics equipment business. By an indirect process the new communication carriers in Japan have internalized much of the bargaining that we see in the coalition for reform in other countries. That, too, could be internationalized as the model. Although it is not clear which direction we will take, the United States will find that its regulatory and trade system will be significantly altered by the effort to find a common framework for the communication system of the world.

Chapter 18

TV technology and government policy

Rhonda J. Crane

LESSONS FROM TECHNOLOGY PAST

In the 1960s, when color television was on the verge of becoming a reality, the United States failed to establish its technological system as the world standard. An unusual sequence of events changed what should have been a technical decision into one dominated by international politics and flawed American responses. What should have led to an American victory instead led to a defeat. America lost not only dominance of its technology as the single worldwide standard, but it also lost control of its domestic industry.[1]

Today, as discussions are again revolving around the future of television, the same issues are being rehashed in debate over whether the United States should develop an advanced television technology. It is *déjà vu*, except that this time the world players are much more sophisticated, the stakes are multi-fold greater, and the technologies involved are infinitely more complex.

Most important of all, the consequences of failing to succeed in establishing an advanced television technology extend far beyond the effect on the television industry. Impacts extend to broader areas of the economy and defense. US leadership in technology, as well as in future sales of American products and services in several industries, may shrivel.[2]

THE COLOR TV WAR

Following the Second World War, some thought that the United States aggravated its allies by flaunting its technological superiority, expecting Europeans submissively to adopt US technology. In *The American Challenge* (1967), Jean-Jacques Sérvan-Schreiber argued that unless European countries integrated their economies more effectively, Europe would become a subsidiary of the United States.[3] For the French, economic and technological dependence upon the United States portended a threat to national survival and political independence. This led to a French policy during and since President de Gaulle to invest in large-scale technological developments meant to represent the glory and prestige and independence of France.

These projects have been heavily funded, and referred to as 'National Champions.' SECAM (Sequential with Memory) color television, the Concorde, the first tidal power plant, the largest solar energy furnace, Minitel – to cite just a few – have all been an outgrowth of the same policy.[4]

From failure to develop an indigenous computer industry, the French had learned that development of an industry depended upon owning patents, harnessing industrial capability to manufacture products, and invoking political, economic, and technical control to protect them. Protection of the industry was the key factor, and with SECAM, standards could be utilized as protectionist non-tariff barriers. Though based to a large extent on the American color television standard (NTSC – National Television Systems Committee), SECAM was French-owned.[5]

The SECAM patent offered the French all the requisite conditions to develop a domestic color television industry. The goal was to win international approval for SECAM as the European standard in order to obtain revenues from license and royalty rights, and create an export market for French manufactured goods and technical assistance. SECAM was marketed as technically superior, as the 'European versus American solution,' France as Europe's 'David' against America's 'Goliath.' NTSC was ridiculed as standing for 'never twice the same color,' and of 'horse and buggy' vintage.[6]

While the French were meticulously waging a political campaign to get their system adopted as the European standard, the American effort was plagued by adversarial government–industry relations over the alleged sensitivity of the video recording head (VTR), hindering the promotion and sale of the US technology.

The VTR export controversy which blocked RCA's ability to export the NTSC system, at first seemed to concern whether the VTRs could detect low-flying aircraft. However, documents that were later declassified showed that the primary objection had been based on a mistaken notion that the Department of Defense had funded the development of the VTRs.[7]

American companies were permitted to sell the system, but export restrictions were placed on the video recording head. Under such conditions, what incentive was there for another nation to invest in only part of a system, and possibly not have recording capabilities? Indeed, this was perceived as further reason not to become dependent on US technology, lest it be wrested away. Eventually what happened was that the West Germans developed a third system, PAL (Phase Alternation by Line), incompatible with SECAM and NTSC, but heavily based on SECAM patents.

At the 1965 meeting of the CCIR in Vienna, which was held to determine a single worldwide standard, Europe could not agree on one standard. Though on the eve of the CCIR vote the US government reversed its position, permitting the sale of the NTSC system with the controversial VTR, the decision came too late. France had launched a bold strategy, making a surprise deal with the Russians, a strategy designed to guarantee an export market and prevent PAL from becoming the only European standard. It succeeded: The votes of the CCIR were split.

Ultimately three different systems (and their offshoots) divided the world along political and cultural alignments: France, the Francophone countries (mostly Third World, French-speaking), the Soviet Union, and the East European Bloc on one axis, adopted the SECAM system; West Germany allied with the rest of Western Europe opted for PAL; NTSC stayed in place in Canada, Mexico, Japan, and, of course, the United States.[8]

So, what should have been a technical decision – the choice of a single worldwide color television standard – became one dominated by international politics and inadequate American responses. What should have been a resounding victory for American interests, with a flagship technology, became an exercise in futility as US government interests undermined US corporate interests, and effectively destroyed the broader national interest.

Why is this important? The choice of an advanced television system presents the US government with the capability to rectify past mistakes, open new markets for US industry, and secure a technology base for the future, or follow a course which may be detrimental for the economy and national security.

ADVANCED TV AND THE ELECTRONICS REVOLUTION

The world is poised on the threshold of a dramatic revolution in electronics. What was too costly or impractical in the past will soon become inexpensive and feasible. Technologies will be available which may radically alter industries dependent on or related to these developments. Like a food-chain, there is linkage between what is commonly known as advanced television and multiple other industries.[9]

ATV or advanced television, of which HDTV or high definition television is one form, is the focal point for a combination of these developments. Though consumer-oriented products such as TV sets will provide incredibly detailed images, the television aspects of the electronics are only a small part of the whole: it is crucial to envision the long-term and far-reaching implications of such technologies.

Traditional TV is a relatively 'dumb' medium: turn the knobs and select predetermined programs. New electronics could transform that traditional TV into an interactive central processing unit, with scope and potential for change limited only by the boundaries of our minds and wallets.[10] The software will enable people to use this unit for multiple purposes beyond mere entertainment. The new electronics which will constitute the guts of ATV will be unlike anything that is available today for they will contain more and more information on smaller and smaller elements. The forms will be flatter, the functions faster. In turn, the changes will have implications for other industries.

At stake is not just 'TV' but the very infrastructure of the economy, every industry dependent on or using the new electronics, every industry turning to 'smart' products. Pretty pictures may make great viewing, but it is the internal guts of the new technology that count – politically as well as economically.

There are divergent views associated with this issue. Some charge that the convergence of television and computers have one requirement: The signals must be digital, which means optimally they require a fiber optics network. So the argument is made, 'forget about HDTV, it's already outmoded,'[11] or that 'if HDTV were not a dog, industry would develop it,' meaning, of course, without any assistance from the government.[12] Others ask whether it makes any sense to spend vast sums of money on developing HDTV if the system will be changed in 10–15 years and a better system will emerge?[13] Still others protest whatever way the government chooses to allocate funds: There is always some more socially important cause.[14] Such critics have targeted efforts to buttress America's technological base as unworthy. Why bother to help industry?

There are many reasons to bother. Electronics today is evolving so rapidly, that failure to keep abreast with those developments make it impossible to move into the next generation: In some instances the next generation of technology is dependent on what already exists. That is, it may not be possible to leapfrog ahead, particularly in advanced computers, without first using the existing technology to get there.

A mass market for a national video-equipment industry is essential to preserve a national technology base in defense electronics and a leading position in manufacturing for the information age.[15] Some counter that ATV might account for 'less than 5 percent of total US chip demand in the year 2000.'[16] But estimating the size of the market for ATV is so filled with shortcomings that such figures have little or no validity and should be regarded with utmost skepticism. The fact remains, that in order to build a viable ATV industry and all the other industries contingent on it, the US is going to need a massive and reliable supply of chips and electronic components.

It is necessary to bother about being in the ATV industry now as opposed to waiting for 10 or 15 years, to be in a competitive position, and to be advanced enough to manufacture for that next generation. Most important of all, there are products and services which will flow during that time which will have further benefits and lead to other new developments that otherwise might not be possible.

What critics would suggest is akin to saying that flying should have ended with the Wright Brothers, because better flying systems would emerge in time, leaving no need to bother with anything else until. . . space shuttles were invented, because these would be technologically superior. Would the development of the space shuttle have been possible without the generations of flying machines and experiences preceding its development? How can the benefits for world commerce created by the ability to commute great distances in short time periods be measured?

As for industry seeking government partnership, well, certain types of technologies are not 'dogs' but rather 'superstars,' whose value to the economy is vital, affecting the infrastructure of society, and whose development requires extraordinary research and development assistance. Hence the 'reluctance' to go it alone.

DEFINING THE MARKET POTENTIAL

ATV is more than just television receivers, studio equipment, and program development. In early efforts to capture the economic impacts, Larry Darby suggested that different markets have different growth rates. Projecting various scenarios over a twelve-year period *for just two product lines*, TV receivers and VCRs, his gross estimates were $70 to $150 billion.[17]

Engaging in estimating the potential market for certain product lines provides some 'hard data' to analyze. But it is essential to recognize some of the shortcomings of this approach: Many unanalyzed product lines may be more heavily affected in the future and may not be identified; processes and services which are likely to be affected are ignored, as well as the millions or billions of dollars these may generate or save through cost-reductions; future applications and spin-off industries are not factored into the equation.

Clearly there are industries used in manufacturing or producing for ATV (optics, glass, graphics, film, tape, VCRs, etc.) that will be affected. A short list must also include digital signal generation and transmission, data storage and processing (the importance of which many witnessed first-hand in the enhancement of photographs retrieved from Voyager II), digital interactive video, computers, software development, flat-screen and display technologies, microelectronics, semiconductors, and the like. A recent report from the National Tele-communications and Information Administration (NTIA) noted that:

> Despite this consumer-product orientation, the non-entertainment applications of ATV-related technologies outside the home are likely to be both substantial and quite diverse. . . . High resolution video imaging technologies are coming into increasing use in both the public and private sectors, including, for example, computer work stations, satellite photography, remote sensing and monitoring, command and control displays, surveillance and security, medical diagnostics, and numerous others.[18]

A Congressional Research Service study also found a diverse market for ATV-related applications in the defense industry:

> For its broad range of video applications in battle management, training and simulation, and intelligence analysis, DoD needs high-definition, low-cost, dynamic multimedia displays for presentation of motion video, real-time graphics, maps and photographs. Such technology is used in fighter airplane cockpits, command centers, training simulators, and analysis groups. . . .[19]

From publishing personal magazines to manufacturing design, the gamut of capabilities is almost endless; at present the many possibilities are a matter of conjecture. One might imagine the home of the future where the ATV set will be the entertainment center, produce daily personal newspapers and personalized television programs and advertisements, conduct all business interactions between the home and external locations, monitor the health and well-being of all residents – linking them with medical centers, respond to specific queries for purchasing items viewed in programs, and even superimpose those items in screens of pictures of one's home. Or, one might compare the situation with that of the space program, where the problem of feeding astronauts in space led to countless innovations in the development of the freeze-dried food industry and all the packaging and processing employed to create it.

And there is the view from abroad. How do others estimate the market potential?

STRATEGIC IMPORTANCE OF ATV TO OTHER NATIONS

Competitors overseas are already spending hundreds of millions of dollars on research. Recognizing the strategic importance of ATV to industrial, technological, and scientific survival, a European consortium of seventeen countries is investing over $200 million annually in joint government–industry HDTV ventures.

The European Consortium, known as EUREKA '95, is divided into ten project groups with project leaders neatly divided up between the participating countries and industry strengths, as listed in Table 18.1.

Table 18.1 Project groups and leaders in EUREKA '95

Project groups	Leaders
(1) Fundamentals picture and sound	CCETT
(2) Production – standards and conversion	THOMSON
(3) Studio equipment	BOSCH
(4) Transmission	IBA
(5) HD-MAC encoding/decoding	PHILIPS
(6) Display standard and up-conversions	BBC
(7) Receivers	THORN EM
(8) Carriers	PHILIPS
(9) Programme material	RAI
(10) Bit rate reduction	THOMSON

Perhaps the European position is best expressed in the publication, *The Road To High Definition TV*: '. . . EUREKA is Europe's Answer to Star Wars. . . .'[20] No laggards, the Japanese pioneered ATV research and have been honing their version of ATV (MUSE) for the past twenty years. Estimates of joint government–industry investment to date total $300–$700 million. Japan is clearly not looking at ATV simply as a replacement for an aging TV technology. Quoting a Japanese front-page editorial, Richard Elkus, Chairman of the Prometrix Corporation noted in testimony before the Subcommittee on Telecommunications and Finance of the House Committee on Energy and Commerce: 'One of the key commercial technologies of the 1990s will be High Definition Television (HDTV). . . . Manufacturers of the new equipment will be in a position to move into various broad areas of microelectronics and telecommunications. . . .'[21]

Europeans and Japanese are pouring resources into the development of ATV systems; they share the view that the technology is critical to the future, not just for consumer toys. Both have developed technologies aimed at the US market. As television systems, they operate on different standards, which at this time are not compatible. Programs broadcast on one system cannot be received on sets manufactured for another – for now. One of the lessons that history has taught us is that technology can rise to almost any challenge and make feasible the seemingly impossible.

Can the United States afford politically to become dependent on another nation's standard, another nation's technology? Should the United States, as the French did, view dependence on another nation's technology as a threat to independence and national survival? Are there political risks inherent in relying on another nation's technology?

THE POLITICAL DANGERS OF DEPENDENCE ON FOREIGN TECHNOLOGY

In a recent publication translated from Japanese as *The Japan That Can Say 'No': The New U.S.–Japan Relations*, Shintaro Ishihara discusses the ability of a technologically superior nation to influence the course of action of a technologically inferior nation, specifically, Japan's power to control the United States military through American dependency on Japanese technology and industrial production:

> In short, without using new-generation computer chips made in Japan, the U.S. Department of Defense cannot guarantee the

precision of its nuclear weapons. If Japan told Washington it would no longer sell computer chips to the United States, the Pentagon would be totally helpless. Furthermore, the global military imbalance would be completely upset if Japan decided to sell its computer chips to the Soviet Union instead of the United States.[22]

While this may represent an extreme and questionable view, the author makes clear that when vital technologies are owned and controlled by foreign powers, nations dependent upon those technologies can become dependent upon the foreign powers controlling them:

> History shows that technology creates civilization and determines the scale and level of its economic and industrial development. Eastern Europe and the Soviet Union want state-of-the-art technology and financial aid to make them productive. What country can provide them? Only Japan.[23]

When a nation becomes dependent on another nation's technology, national independence is jeopardized. As a nation becomes dependent on another for vital technology, independence in other spheres – political, economic, and defense – is at risk. The balance of power shifts to the technologically superior nation. It is Jean-Jacques Sérvan-Schreiber's nightmare redux:[24]

> The United States does indeed have cause for concern, if not hysteria. The one megabyte chip used in computer memory banks . . . this vital component is made only in Japan. Japanese manufacturers almost completely control the market.[25]

In Japan, the relationship between government and industry is a partnership, where government benefits from taxes on business profits. Thus, if business does well, government does well. In the United States, that relationship is adversarial. As the American bail-out for Chrysler showed, that need not be the case. When the company did well, the government made a healthy return on its investment, and Chrysler made a healthy return to the market. Yet, the US is the only nation among advanced industrialized countries that does not have a Department of Industry responsible for industrial policy.

Is the development of a strong indigenous technological base the solution? Is this a question of investing in superstar technologies, of 'picking winners and losers,' or is there something more at stake?

SUPERTECHNOLOGIES AND THE CASE FOR
GOVERNMENT ACTION

ATV can best be defined as a 'supertechnology,' a new generation of
technologies which are exceptionally complex and which affect an
economy's infrastructure. Supertechnologies profoundly alter multiple
industries, and make them dependent on one another. Development
requires extraordinary outlays of capital, investment on a scale beyond
the financial scope of a single company. A supertechnology is perceived
as so critical to the national interest that other governments will invest
heavily in it; and its development will make industries using pre-
existing technology obsolete or uncompetitive.

Though many in Congress and the Administration recognize the
implications if the United States is not a world player in ATV, the
impetus to assist US industry in getting a firm foothold has not
materialized. Funds are in short supply. Politicians are fearful of being
labeled 'Uncle Sugar,' and the issue is down-played as 'high-tech
pork-barrel.'[26] Yet, according to Robert Cohen of the Economic Policy
Institute:

> The U.S. could face an annual trade deficit of more than $225 billion
> in electronics and lose more than two million jobs a year by 2010 if
> it fails to develop strong HDTV (ATV) and flat-screen industries
> . . . As a result of this trade deficit the U.S. would lose 792,000 jobs
> in these four (ATV receivers, VCRs, personal computers, and semi-
> conductors) closely linked industries.[27]

Efforts which would seek to establish government–industry cooperation
are labeled 'industrial policy,' and by virtue of this rubric, considered
anathema. Though the US government protects various economic
sectors through price and other supports, there is a notion that the US
government should not provide an equivalent type of support for ATV,
as that provided by other governments. This focus clouds the critical
issue: Should there be a policy to keep America technologically
competitive, economically viable, and secure in its defense?

In the past, losing an industry usually meant losing just that industry,
though ripple effects were felt elsewhere. As a wealthy, healthy nation,
America could withstand the loss of an industry, when the rest of the
economy was vigorous. But, over time, industry after industry has been
lost, and as a result, the US industrial base has been severely weakened.
Moreover, losing an industry based on a supertechnology means the
effects may devastate multiple sectors of the economy. Without a

coordinated strategy there is no control over orchestrating such effects. Left to develop such technologies on their own, companies will likely concentrate on what is feasible and affordable and fits with corporate objectives. These are not necessarily national objectives. That is why it is essential to have a national strategy for supertechnologies and for ATV: Competitiveness must be assured not only in those industries threatened by other nations' actions – in trade, special aid, and the like – but in new fields, where emerging supertechnologies have an inordinate influence on the economy and standard of living, and on the future of the political system.

CONCLUSION

ATV is a supertechnology representing a unique opportunity to rebuild the US industrial base. The potential market for ATV-related industries appears huge. Foreign governments and industries regard it as strategic to their national interests, and this is reflected in the enormous resources committed to its development. In contrast, though it is as vital to America's future, political will is lacking to spark government–industry cooperation, and without it, industry alone may be unable to afford the costs of development, or may focus on specific corporate objectives, not national objectives.

What may be at risk is America's political independence, defense, and economic health. There is a trend developing which, if left unchecked, could turn the US into a subsidiary of other nations, technologically dependent and politically no longer the master of its own fate. Like the Meiji Restoration in Japan, where the privileged class of samurai gave up their power, cut their special hairstyles, and tossed out their swords, it would be a bloodless revolution.

NOTES

1 Rhonda J. Crane, 'Making America Competitive: High Definition TV,' *The Chicago Tribune*, October 3, 1988, Op-Ed, p. 13.
2 ibid.
3 Jean-Jacques Sérvan-Schreiber, *The American Challenge* (New York: Atheneum, 1968).
4 Nicholas Vichney, 'Les Nouvelles Cathedrales,' *Le Monde*, November 5, 6, 7, 1974.
5 Rhonda J. Crane. 'Communication Standards and the Politics of Protectionism,' *Telecommunications Policy* (December 1978), 2, 4, pp. 267–81.

6 Rhonda J. Crane, *The Politics of International Standards: France and the Color TV War* (Norwood, New Jersey: ABLEX, 1979).
7 ibid., pp. 62–70. It was an avoidable and costly mistake leading to the eventual loss of the color television industry.
8 ibid., pp. 72–7.
9 Rhonda J. Crane, 'Staying Competitive in TV's "New Age",' *TV Technology*, January 1989, Guest Editorial, p. 5.
10 ibid.
11 George Gilder, 'Forget HDTV, It's Already Outmoded,' *The New York Times*, May 29, 1989, F2.
12 ibid.
13 Stephen Effros, President of an independent cable operators association, quoted by Evelyn Richards, 'Doubting the Focus on HDTV,' *The Washington Post*, May 21, 1989, H1.
14 Langdon Winner, 'Who Needs HDTV?,' *Technology Review* (May–June 1989) 92, p. 20.
15 David Hack, 'High-Definition Television,' *CRS Review*, June 1989, p. 13.
16 Kenneth Flamm, quoted by Evelyn Richards, *op. cit.*
17 Larry Darby, 'Economic Potential of Advanced Television Products,' *Report to the National Telecommunications and Information Administration*, Department of Commerce, April 1988.
18 National Telecommunications and Information Administration, Department of Commerce, *Advanced Television, Related Technologies, and the National Interest*, March 1989, p. 6.
19 David Hack, Congressional Research Service, CRS Issue Brief, *High Definition Television*, May 25, 1989, Library of Congress.
20 *The Road To High Definition Television*, Booklet based on the status report, High Definition Television System, Eureka Project EU 95 HDTV, March 1987.
21 Richard Elkus, Chairman, Prometrix Corporation in testimony before the Subcommittee on Telecommunications and Finance of the House Committee on Energy and Commerce (Edward Markey, D-MA., Chairman) September 7, 1988, 'Advanced Television and the U.S. Electronics Industry.'
22 Shintaro Ishihara, *The Japan That Can Say No: The New U.S.–Japan Relations* (New York: Simon & Schuster, 1991), p. 21.
23 ibid., p. 105.
24 Rhonda J. Crane, 'Advanced Television: An American Challenge,' *The Boston Globe*, November 8, 1988, p. 46.
25 Ishihara, *op. cit.*, p. 22.
26 Peter Passell, 'The Uneasy Case for Subsidy of High Technology Efforts,' *The New York Times*, August 11, 1989. Also see Robert Samuelson, 'HDTV: High Tech Pork Barrel,' *Washington Post*, May 17, 1989.
27 Robert Cohen, 'The Consequences of Failing to Develop a Strong HDTV Industry in the U.S.,' *Briefing paper*, Economic Policy Institute.

Chapter 19

Negotiating the world information economy

Geza Feketekuty

The world is in the midst of a new economic revolution equivalent in scope to the industrial revolution of the eighteenth century. The strategic resource in this new economy is information. The strategic infrastructure is the telecommunications system. And the strategic territorial unit for organizing production is the world.

In the industrial revolution, the harnessing of energy for production made it possible to expand exponentially the physical power available for manufacturing. The application of human labor in the manufacturing process was reinforced by machinery driven by the water mill and the steam engine. The simultaneous application of the new energy technology to land and sea transportation created the larger markets necessary for achieving economies of scale in manufacturing. Together, the factory and the steam locomotive created the industrial nation states of the nineteenth and early twentieth century.

Over the last few decades, the harnessing of the electron for information processing tasks has made it possible to expand exponentially the information processing capacity available for the production of goods and services. The application of the human mind to production tasks could now be reinforced by computers that can make millions of calculations per second; store, sort, analyze, compare, and retrieve billions of bits of information instantaneously; control whole factories; evaluate alternative designs or scenarios within minutes; and safely guide airplanes, ships, and trains to their destination.

The simultaneous connection of the computer to the telecommunications network created the global enterprise and the global market. Today, global enterprises use computers and telecommunications to combine inputs from around the world in the production of global goods and services. The marriage of computers and telecommunications is thus creating the global village of the twenty-first century, in which everyone is linked by electronic information flows.

The fiber optic cables, microwave transmitters, communication satellites, and computers that make up the modern-day telecommunications network serve as the electronic highways for a new global information economy, driven by the creation, processing, and electronic distribution of information. This new global information economy increasingly controls the production and distribution of the goods and services produced around the world.

The new global electronic highways do several things. They make it possible for global computer manufacturers to produce the same computer parts in many different locations, and to implement the design changes in facilities around the world. They enable global construction companies to assemble equipment, materials, engineers, skilled workers, and managers from around the world at the right time at the right place. They allow global professional services firms to establish project teams made up of management consultants, computer programmers, engineers, and lawyers located in many countries. They permit global manufacturing enterprises to coordinate production and assembly in a dozen countries. They make it possible for global enterprises to coordinate research efforts carried out simultaneously in several laboratories, and to channel the results into coherently designed products.

They enable the information and entertainment industry to reach a global audience from central locations. They permit the creation of truly global electronic markets in which buyers and sellers from around the world trade twenty-four hours a day. In this global electronic market, world prices reflect changes in supply and demand conditions anywhere in the world. Policies that affect the operation of the telecommunications system inevitably influence the global flow of information and thus global trade of goods and services. More than ever before, telecommunications policy can affect the location of jobs and the competitive position of firms.

Telecommunications policies influence international trade in two fundamental ways. First, they can affect the operating costs of global enterprises that use telecommunications services to distribute information-based services or to coordinate global production and marketing activities. Telecom policies will change the competitive position of firms to the extent that they affect the cost of transmitting information, the kind and form of information that can be transmitted, the accuracy and reliability of the transmission, the confidentiality of information, and the capacity of the network through which it is transmitted. Second, telecommunications policies can affect market access where the provision of certain services is open to domestic but not international competition. Telecom policies can determine what can be sold in competition with the monopoly, the conditions in which such services can be provided outside the monopoly, the terms on which the monopoly can compete in the provision of services that fall outside the scope of its monopoly, and how much foreign providers can supply such services.

The technological advances in computer and telecommunications technologies that have given birth to a new economic revolution have also given birth to a revolution in the regulation of telecommunications. Before the marriage of telecommunications and computer technologies, telecommunications was based on a network of copper cables that connected universally black telephone receivers. Since one set of copper cables could meet everyone's needs, it made economic sense to create national monopolies that could provide all the telephone services required within a geographic region. These companies also could jointly provide telephone service between geographic regions by inter-connecting their networks. Little differentiation in the services being offered was either necessary or desirable, and under the concept of universal service everyone was charged the same price.

With the integration of computers into the telecommunications system, telecommunications is no longer an undifferentiated service. Computers make it possible to offer a variety of telecommunications services to different users. They also enable large users to achieve extraordinary economies of scale in their utilization of the telecommunications infrastructure. Finally, since the computers can be attached anywhere in the network, it has become technologically and economically feasible to supply such services competitively from different geographic locations – sometimes across national frontiers.

Government regulations that were designed for an earlier era of undifferentiated telephone service are today often constraints on the provision of the highly differentiated telecom services made possible by computer technology, including coding the telecom signal, switching the signal through alternative routes to maximize requirements, distributing and storing messages, specialized billing arrangements, and customized communications software packages that control the user/supplier interface for certain subscribers.

No single enterprise can supply all the services desired by individual business users, or even households. Since the computers that can generate these diversified services can be connected to the network at any point and need not be provided by the same enterprise that supplies transmission facilities, telecom regulations based on a monopoly model often unnecessarily limit competition in the provision of computer-based telecommunications services. These services do not have the same characteristics of a natural monopoly as does the provision of transmission facilities. Fundamental changes in transmission technologies, such as microwave transmitters and communications satellites, have also eroded the natural monopoly characteristics of transmission services, but the scope for international competition is, at this time, less clear.

Government officials responsible for regulating telecommunications have responded to the changes in technology. Making regulatory changes is difficult, however, because it involves tradeoffs between the maintenance of long-standing social objectives and new economic opportunities. The tradeoffs are not only between abstract notions of the public good, but between the economic interests of different groups, between households and large business users, between traditional local suppliers of services and new long-distance suppliers, between the employees of the traditional communications monopolies and new competitive suppliers.

Within a national context, the economic tradeoffs between policy objectives and different social groups are worked out in legislative and judicial proceedings and in regulatory processes. In the international arena, these economic tradeoffs become trade issues because they affect the commercial interests of different countries, and trade negotiations are the primary tool used by governments to reconcile conflicts in commercial interests. My objective in this article, then, is to spell out the trade policy dimension of the telecommunications debate, to put it into a broader public policy context, and to examine how current multilateral negotiations on trade in services might deal with these issues.

The objective of trade policy and negotiations is twofold: To establish rules that are mutually advantageous and to expand opportunities for trade by dismantling government barriers to trade. Trade officials recognize the legitimacy and sovereign right of individual countries to apply regulations in order to achieve domestic social objectives. At the same time, the aim of trade negotiations is to eliminate or alter trade-restrictive measures that are inessential for legitimate domestic objectives.

International trade agreements can take one of two forms: Either to establish principles, rules, and procedures for determining which government measures should be prohibited, or to change existing policy measures. When negotiating agreements, trade officials act as intermediaries between business interests and regulatory authorities. Their objectives are to reduce barriers, to establish fair and mutually beneficial rules for trade among commercial enterprises operating in a market economy, and to establish principles and procedures that minimize how much domestic regulations distort trade.

The GATT rules for multilateral trade assume that trade based on market competition is fair and mutually advantageous, and that government intervention in commercial transactions should be kept within agreed limits. The GATT system gives competing enterprises from different countries considerable freedom to make commercial transactions within the framework established in trade agreements.

In summary, the strength of a trade policy approach is in its emphasis on mutual commercial advantage, competition on a market-oriented basis, and removal of obstacles to mutually beneficial trade. Trade officials thus have a dual role in the government: To guard the country's commercial interest and to guard a system of trade rules that permit competition among enterprises from different countries.

Before the technological revolution in telecommunications blurred the distinction between regulated telecommunications services (usually provided by a monopoly) and unregulated computer services (usually provided by competitive firms) the question of market access and fair competition for foreign suppliers would have been considered a non-issue, and trade officials would have been summarily dismissed had they raised the question of market access to regulated telecommunications services, which were reserved for the monopoly. The integration of computer and telecommunications has blurred the lines of distinction between regulated, non-competitive services and non-regulated, competitive ones. Regulatory changes have opened up computer-based telecommunications activities to competition in many countries, and this has created differences in the level of market access for telecommunications services. At the same time, the monopoly suppliers of non-competitive services have been allowed to provide competitive telecommunications services in competition with their customers, thereby raising questions of fair competition.

In a similar sense, before the revolution in computer technology opened up new applications in telecommunications, the issue of user access to telecommunications services and equipment would have been considered largely a non-issue. All that was available to business users was the basic telephone service and the universal black telephone receiver which the monopoly provided. On rare occasions the telephone company, under the influence of local business people, might drag its feet in providing a new foreign company with telephone service; but under the concept of universal service these occasions were limited.

The connection of computers to telecommunications networks has tremendously increased the usefulness of telecommunications for managing a global business and delivering services to customers. The problem is that many of these business applications are highly custom- ized and the monopoly suppliers of services could not provide all the products needed. Moreover, businesses found that they could reduce costs and increase the performance of the network by connecting their computers to leased telephone lines rather than paying the telephone company for the transmission of individual message units.

We can thus summarize the reasons for the new trade policy dimension to telecommunications issues as follows. The emergence of domestic competition has opened up the possibility of trade and the need for a trade policy. International competition among commercial enter- prises from different countries must be based on commonly accepted rules provided by trade agreements. The need for rules has become particularly apparent in light of regulatory differences among countries, which create differences in market opportunities.

The increasingly varied application of computer and telecommuni- cations technology to the operation of international businesses and to international trade in services has added another trade dimension to telecommunications policy. Manufacturing and services businesses are using international telecommunications facilities to coordinate the activities of production units located in different countries and to centralize many managerial and administrative functions. The telecom- munications system has also become the foundation for international trade in information-related services: data processing and databases, computer-based telecommunications, finance, entertainment, and professional.

One can gain insights to the role of trade negotiations in forming telecommunications policies by considering the results of a recent survey on the trade dimension in telecommunications. Russ Pipe, the publisher of the *Transborder Data Reporter*, conducted the survey and reported his findings in the November 1989 issue of that periodical. A questionnaire was sent to 502 individuals residing in 48 countries; recipients were selected on the basis of their involvement in telecom or trade policy and their professional responsibilities in international organizations, national governments, businesses, higher education, research, journalism, and consultancy. A total of 197 responded, a little less than half from Europe, 35 percent from North America, 15 percent from Japan, and a smattering from other parts of the world. About 80 percent of the respondents agreed that enhanced and value-added services were tradeable and therefore subject to trade negotiations. What is more remarkable is that 45 percent agreed that basic telephony was tradeable.

Tradeability was seen as related to the nature of information flows. Approximately 90 percent thought that on-line commercial information processing and retrieval services should be viewed as trade issues, as compared with 76 percent who thought that EDI systems which communicate with customers and suppliers should be so viewed, 62 percent who thought that closed user groups such as SWIFT and SITA should be so viewed, and 50 percent who thought that intracorporate networks should be so viewed. About 60 percent regarded telecom primarily as an intermediate service that supports aviation, banking, insurance, or other services.

Participants in the survey were asked to consider the relative importance of several objectives of trade agreements covering telecom services. Some 75 percent from the telecom and trade policy area saw the ability of users to acquire new services where they do business as the most important objective. Other objectives having almost the same importance were selling telecom services in foreign markets on an equitable basis, accelerating the deregulation of telecom services, and expanding world trade.

The results of the survey were quite remarkable as an indication of a shift in opinion on the trade dimension in telecommunications. Of course, that trade dimension, as made clear elsewhere in this article, goes far beyond the issue of whether telecom services are tradeable across borders, and in some ways tradeability in this narrow sense of the word is beside the point. The large positive response in the survey to the question of the 'tradeability' of telecom services needs to be interpreted broadly as recognition of the growing international competition in the provision of many telecom services rather than a conclusion that locally consumed telecom services are being provided across national borders from other countries.

The key issues from a trade point of view are market access and fair competition. Market access issues focus on the ability of foreign enterprises to sell services in a country's market on the basis of market considerations; that is, the right of foreign providers to sell to domestic users purely on the basis of production costs. Fair competition (or fair trade) issues focus on the terms of competition between foreign and domestic suppliers, or more specifically on whether foreign suppliers will be competing with domestic suppliers purely on the basis of market considerations or whether the domestic government has established regulations or programs that favor the domestic supplier.

Telecom regulations raise issues of market access and fair competition with respect to the provision of computer-based telecommunications services and the access of business users to services and equipment. Trade policy concerns in telecommunications more specifically center on the ability of providers of computer-based telecommunications services to sell such services competitively and equitably in foreign markets, and the ability of foreign users of telecommunications services to acquire services and equipment in a country where they want to do business on a competitive and non-discriminatory basis.

Market access issues with respect to the provision of computer-based telecommunications services arise principally in connection with domestic regulations that prohibit competition in the provision of certain services, or regulations that prohibit or limit foreign providers from supplying these services. As a rule, market access issues do not arise with respect to the provision of basic telecommunications services (i.e., services involving the provision of transmission facilities) since the economic rationale for the exclusive provision of these services is still widely accepted.

Computer-based telecommunications services are often referred to as value-added or enhanced telecommunications services, though these terms have come into use in the course of national regulatory decisions and often are given a much narrower definition than implied by the term 'computer-based telecommunications services,' which is used in this essay. In fact, much of the current trade debate over market access concerns the definition of value-added or enhanced telecommunications services in different countries.

Other market access issues with respect to suppliers of competitive computer-based telecommunications services concern mandatory standards that unjustifiably discriminate against technical specifications used by foreign providers of telecommunications equipment or services. What is unjustifiable in this connection? Any standard that establishes narrow technical parameters when broader ones would equally well accomplish a desired social objective.

Arguments over standards in telecommunications have revolved around some of the following issues: Whether equipment attached to the public telecommunications network should meet only a harm-to-the-network standard or whether they should meet a higher quality of service to the customer standard established by the telecom authorities; whether communications protocols, which interconnect publicly accessible networks, and software interfaces, which allow different computer programs to talk to each other, should adhere to mandatory standards, or whether each user should be able to use whatever protocols or software interfaces that best meet the user's need. Since the issues in the debates over standards are highly complex and technical, the debate over standards often focuses on the procedures that should be followed in the setting of standards and who should have a right to participate in setting standards.

Other market access issues relate to the purchasing practices of telecom monopolies. Such monopolies often maintain a close relation to favored domestic suppliers of service inputs to the exclusion of competitive foreign suppliers. Since the monopolies are not under competitive pressure to minimize costs, they are not under any economic pressure to consider foreign bidders, while at the same time they might be under considerable political pressure to purchase from local suppliers.

Fair competition issues with respect to foreign suppliers of competitive telecommunications services usually revolve around the terms under which the monopoly suppliers of non-competitive services are also allowed to provide competitive services. At issue are the ability of the monopoly to subsidize the sale of competitive services with profits obtained from the sale of non-competitive services and the ability of the monopoly supplier to deny a competitor access to the telecommunications network on a non-discriminatory basis. That is, the basic issues are cross-subsidization and monopoly power. The aim of trade officials is to assure an arms-length relationship between competitive foreign suppliers and a domestic monopoly where they are allowed to compete with each other. The same trade policy considerations also call for an institutional separation of the regulatory authority from the telecommunications monopoly. After all, if an entity is able to regulate and compete with other suppliers of computer-based telecommunications services, the temptation to use regulations to disadvantage the competition will be difficult to resist.

The principal user-oriented trade issues in telecommunications concern the acquisition and use of equipment and services by foreign firms to meet their global communications needs. At this most general level, the issue seems non-controversial. The controversies arise when a foreign enterprise wants to acquire its own equipment from the most competitive source in the world rather than being forced to buy or lease equipment provided by the telecom monopoly. In a similar manner, controversy is generated when a foreign firm wants to lease private circuits to meet its communications needs on high volume routes rather than being forced to use the public network for all its communications needs.

The technical regulatory issues that arise in the context of these user-oriented debates include: Disputes over the right of private business users to purchase equipment from any supplier and to attach such equipment to the public network; to lease private lines; to establish a private network by linking together leased lines, privately owned lines within the premises of a firm, and privately controlled computer switching facilities; to interconnect private networks with other private networks or public networks.

A parallel set of issues arises over limitations placed by the regulatory authorities on the use of private networks. The question is whether private networks can be used to establish communications links within a single firm, to establish communications links between a firm and its customers or suppliers, to establish communications links within a closed user group (i.e., a group of users – such as SWIFT, an interbank settlement network or SITA, an air reservation network – that have a common need to exchange data for a particular purpose), to share communications facilities with other firms in the same geographic location for the purpose of obtaining better economies of scale, to resell part of the capacity of the private network to other users.

From the firm's point of view, the private acquisition of equipment and communications circuits can substantially reduce its communications costs and substantially increase its control over the technical performance characteristics of critical portions of the communications network. By controlling the flow of data or messages through its terminal equipment, computers, and circuits that constitute a communications network, an enterprise can maximize desired features such as security and reliability of transmission, the capacity and bandwidth of the network, and compatibility of the network with the company's computer software systems. By interconnecting its private network with other private networks a firm can reduce the cost and improve the quality of its communications links with suppliers, dealers, and major customers. By interconnecting its private network with the public network a firm can give widely dispersed customers or suppliers access to data banks connected to the private network.

A bank that wants to give large depositors the ability to manage cash balances held in branches around the world can offer this service at a reasonable price only if the corporate treasurer can dial into the bank and access its internal network of leased lines that connect the bank's computers around the world. In a similar way, database providers that maintain different databases in computers spread over a wide geographic area can offer subscribers access to these databases at a reasonable price only if the customer can access the internal network of leased lines that connect together the firm's computers.

From the point of view of the local authorities, the acquisition of private circuits by individual enterprises leads to lower revenues and reduces the control of the telecommunications monopoly over the most rapidly growing portions of the communications network. Leasing private lines to businesses is less remunerative than charging businesses for individual toll calls. Moreover, allowing firms to connect their leased lines to the public network enhances the chances that the private network will be used for long-distance telephone calls, a service only the monopoly is authorized to provide in most countries. Finally, the introduction of private networks and equipment reduces the ability of the telecom monopoly to set uniform standards of quality and compatibility for the whole system, and creates a risk that private equipment or software could harm the public network.

The issues, then, concern income and control for the business user and the telecom monopoly, and the resolution of the conflicts requires public policy tradeoffs between economic efficiency and traditional regulatory concerns. These issues are not unique to foreign firms; domestic firms have the same problems in the domestic regulatory context.

Differences in the pace and direction of reform in individual countries have resulted in major differences in national regulatory practices. Why should trade officials concern themselves with these differences? Because what the regulations permit can effectively limit market access for internationally traded information services and competitively disadvantage global firms that have adopted the new computer and telecommunications technology to manage their international activities more efficiently.

Trade policy concerns in telecommunications tend to focus on competition and the terms of competition. These issues cannot be resolved through trade policy considerations alone; domestic regulatory concerns must be given equal weight. As previously mentioned, however, changes in technology have altered the economic conditions that supported a purely monopolistic market structure in telecommunications. The economic rationale for competition, at least in computer-based telecommunications services, is now much stronger and the argument for maintaining a monopoly structure for all services that might be loosely classified as telecom services is much weaker.

The rationale for competition in the provision of telecommunications services, as in the provision of other goods and services, is to spur suppliers to produce the services consumers want at the least cost. The results of a lack of competition in telecommunications have been all too visible: lack of consumer choice, high prices, limited innovation.

Two key reasons are usually given in support of a monopoly structure in telecommunications: First, the provision of telecommunications services is a natural monopoly; second, the provision of telecommunications services is a public good. Installing the cables, microwave transmitters, and switches that constitute the communications grid is a capital intensive activity that involves significant economics of scale. For most households and businesses, a single telephone cable provides all the telecommunications capacity that is needed, and so having more than one network to serve households and a majority of businesses seems wasteful. This is the natural monopoly argument that underlies the traditional communications monopoly.

General public availability of communication services results in advantages to a community over and above the advantages that individual households and businesses derive from having access to the telecommunications system. It leads to more frequent communications among citizens, and therefore assures a better informed and more harmonious citizenry. It enables many people to reach many employees, voters, and neighbors who might otherwise not have a phone. It also allows these individuals to notify authorities promptly of any natural disasters, accidents, and other emergencies that can affect the public. In short, the argument is that telecommunications is a public good that deserves to be subsidized.

The need for a subsidy does not in itself provide a rationale for a monopoly structure. The link to the monopoly is provided by the ability of a monopoly to subsidize universal access to local telephone service by charging households less than the cost of the production and distribution of local services and by charging them more for long-distance services, which are considered by many to have less compelling social value. In a similar sense, the monopoly can charge businesses the same rates as households, even though the higher volume of telecommunications traffic generated by business leads to higher capacity utilization rates and therefore lower costs for the same services to businesses.

These arguments were generally accepted until recently, and telecommunications was largely the province of national monopolies. This has changed, partly because a revolution in telecommunications and exponential growth in the telecommunications traffic generated by businesses has made it less of a natural monopoly. At the same time the disadvantages of a monopoly structure in relation to lost economic opportunities has become much more pronounced than in the past.

As I have stated already, the provision of computer-based telecommunications services does not require the same massive investments as the provision of transmission services, and the market is large enough in most countries to support many suppliers of these services. The new services therefore do not have the same characteristics of a natural monopoly as the transmission services.

Advances in microelectronics have also changed the economics with respect to satellite-based long-distance communications. Technological advances have reduced the capital cost of installing earth stations for satellite transmissions to the point where even individual companies can afford to establish their own satellite telecommunications networks, and indeed find it cheaper to do so than to pay the rates charged by the public companies. At the same time that it has become cheaper to build satellite networks, the volume of traffic has expanded to the point where the market can easily support competitive systems in heavily used segments of the market, thereby further undermining the natural monopoly argument. Technological change has thus even eroded the argument that the provision of transmission services is necessarily a natural monopoly.

The natural monopoly argument can still be made with respect to the local network that serves individual households and smaller businesses, and this leads to the key question whether the expansion and operation of the local network should be subsidized through the preservation of a monopoly structure for computer-based telecommunications services, for the long-distance network, and for the intracorporate and inter-corporate network. Those who favor the continuation of a monopoly structure answer this question in the affirmative. Those who support competition either argue that no subsidies are necessary or that there are other ways of subsidizing the local network, such as direct government subsidies and access charges imposed on anyone who accesses the local network from a long-distance network or private network. Those who support competition also point to the growing costs of a monopoly structure in the form of lost economic opportunities.

The disadvantage of a monopoly structure is that it tends to reduce the variety of telecommunications services available to users and makes it too expensive to introduce many new services. It also increases the production costs of national enterprises and reduces their competitive position in international markets. The technological explosion in electronics (computer chips), materials (fiber optic cables), and space transportation (communication satellites) has vastly increased the opportunities for innovation in telecommunications with respect to the provision of a much wider range of services and with respect to the installation of more efficient hardware and software. No matter how well run a monopoly is, it is bound to resist change.

Economic growth in the most advanced economies today is tied to innovation in telecommunications. This is because many of the productivity improvements in manufacturing and services today depend on the installation of new computer systems that tie together widely dispersed production and marketing facilities. Moreover, many of the most innovative new products in services involve the electronic distribution of information-based services through value-added networks. In both areas, progress depends on adapting the new technologies to fit the requirements of these systems and on reducing communication costs. It is impossible for any organization such as a telecommunications monopoly to develop all the necessary technology even if it had incentives to do so.

Technological advances, then, have led to the multiplication of potential channels for transmitting telecommunications signals (copper cable, fiber optic cable, satellite, microwave), for switching signals (electromechanical switches versus advanced computer switches), and for transforming a client's message into an electronic signal (phones, fax machines, modems). This has made it possible to offer varied services by linking together different facilities and equipment. The range of these services is so broad that a single organization no longer can be expected to meet all the specialized customer needs.

One of the traditional objectives of domestic regulations in telecommunications has been to assure businesses and households equitable access to services provided by the telecommunications monopoly. In many countries this objective has been encompassed by the term 'universal service.' Other regulations have dealt with such issues as the price the monopoly was allowed to charge for services and the monopoly's right to set standards and to control the equipment that could be attached to the network.

Countries that have moved to permit competition in some telecommunications services have found it desirable to introduce new regulations designed to assure fair competition between the monopoly supplier of telecommunications services and non-monopoly suppliers of telecommunications services open to competition. These regulatory changes are reviewed here because they have relevant counterparts in the new trade rules that have to be written to govern competition between monopolies and foreign suppliers of telecommunications services open to competition.

Countries that have decided to allow competition in segments of the domestic network have found it desirable, and indeed necessary, to separate the regulation of telecommunications activities from the management and operation of the national telecommunications monopoly. In the United States the two functions have always been separated because AT&T was a private company. Even in the United States, however, AT&T established all the regulations concerning the operation of the network and controlled all the equipment that could be attached to the network. In most other countries, where the national telecommunications monopoly was part of a government ministry, the monopoly itself wrote all the regulations.

With the establishment of competition in some segments of the telecommunications system it no longer could be assumed that the managers of the monopoly could act as neutral and objective arbiters of regulations with respect to the provision of services subject to competition. It therefore became necessary to create new regulatory agencies that could establish evenhanded regulations. One of the priority objectives of regulatory authorities in these situations is to ensure that newly established enterprises that seek to compete with the telecom monopoly are not overwhelmed by the monopoly before they have a chance to establish themselves. There is, moreover, a continuing need to ensure that a monopoly supplier of transmission services does not cross-subsidize its competitive activities from profits generated by monopoly activities, and that it does not use its position as the exclusive supplier of certain transmission facilities to disadvantage competitors dependent on such facilities.

Another priority regulatory objective in a competitive environment is to ensure the coherent development and implementation of standards by independent suppliers of telecom services and equipment, thus ensuring the interconnectability of separately managed networks. So long as the monopoly had exclusive control over the whole telecommunications system, it could set the standards for all network and terminal equipment and services. In the context of a competitive environment, standard setting has to be open to all suppliers. Moreover, given the more differentiated needs of users as a result of the diversification of technology, many regulatory authorities have recognized that standard setting should be open to all suppliers as well as users.

Another regulatory concern, in light of the rapid growth of private networks, has been the so-called bypass issue. The rapid growth of private data networks has reduced the potential revenue of the telecom monopoly. The reasons for this are twofold: The leasing of lines is less remunerative than the provision of tolled services and the unauthorized use of private data networks for long-distance telephone calls leads to a loss of telephone traffic, which in most countries remains the exclusive preserve of the telecom monopoly. These concerns about bypass have made many regulatory authorities reluctant to widen the authorized use of private networks, or to allow the interconnection of private networks with the public network. These restrictions on private networks have led to major trade disputes in recent years.

The argument between telecom authorities and enterprises over the use and interconnection of private networks appears to require a tradeoff between two competing, equally legitimate public policy objectives. One objective is the ability of the telecom monopoly to support universal phone service and the other is to promote economic growth through the innovative application of the new telecom technologies by business enterprises. To avoid making this tradeoff explicitly, many telecom authorities have adopted a case-by-case approach, making concessions to individual enterprises or user groups where the economic arguments or political pressures proved difficult to resist, but maintaining the restrictions for everyone else. This strategy discriminates against smaller enterprises or groups that do not have the clout to obtain special treatment, and it raises questions of equity and economic efficiency.

There is only one satisfactory way out of the dilemma created by the bypass issue, but it requires modifying two strongly held regulatory concepts in telecommunications: Cross-subsidization of local phone service to households and full control of the telecom monopoly over the switching of the public network. Traditional regulatory philosophy called for uniform pricing of telecom services, regardless of cost, as part of the concept of universal service. Thus, households have been required to pay less than the fully allocated cost for local telephone service, and large business enterprises have paid substantially more for telephone service than warranted by the large economies of scale involved in high density and long-distance traffic.

The large and growing gap between the charges imposed by the telecom monopoly for the use of the public network and the cost of establishing a private network has made use of the public network unattractive to many businesses. As noted earlier, another major reason why businesses have established private networks is that it gives them greater control over the switching of traffic, and hence greater control over the quality of the circuits used to transmit vital business information.

The economic pressures generated by the bypass issue have convinced many regulatory authorities and telecom monopolies that it is in their interest to move to cost-based pricing and to give users more control over the switching of data packets and messages. Thus, alternative means of subsidizing the local network, such as local access charges, are being developed to make it possible for the telecom monopolies to lower their toll charges for public switched communications traffic. Efforts are also under way in Europe and the United States to give business users of the public switched network greater control over switching, thus reducing the need for private networks. In the United States more control over switching will be made possible by ONA (Open Network Architecture) and in Europe by ONP (Open Network Provision).

The rationale for international competition in computer-based tele-communications services is the same as the rationale for domestic competition – to provide consumers with a wider range of services at a lower cost and thereby stimulate economic growth. As I mentioned in the beginning of this essay, innovation in telecommunications has become one of the principal engines of growth and the application of the new technology to international telecommunications has led to inter-national specialization in the production of goods and services. A liberalization of international competition will stimulate a further expansion of trade and investment and increase global economic growth.

The rationale for trade rules for international competition in tele-communications is the same as the rationale for domestic regulations for domestic competition – to define the scope of competition and to establish equitable ground rules for competition. In particular, such rules must deal with potential competition between monopoly suppliers of transmission services and competitive suppliers of computer-based telecommunications services.

To date, most trade negotiations on telecommunications issues have been conducted on a bilateral basis. These bilateral trade agreements can provide insights to the scope and content of a future multilateral trade agreement. Negotiations currently under way in the GATT on an international agreement on trade in services are expected to lead to the negotiation of a telecommunications annex. Such an annex would elaborate on the application of the agreement to telecommunications services.

In 1986 trade ministers launched multilateral trade negotiations called the Uruguay Round. These negotiations, scheduled to conclude at the end of 1990, cover fifteen broad areas, including trade in services. At the time they launched the Uruguay Round, ministers set forth key objectives for the negotiations in a document called the Uruguay Declaration. With respect to trade in services, ministers agreed that:

> negotiations in this area shall aim to establish a multilateral framework of principles and rules for trade in services, including elaboration of possible disciplines for individual sectors, with a view to expansion of such trade under conditions of transparency and progressive liberalization and as a means of promoting economic growth of all trading partners and the development of developing countries. Such a framework shall respect the policy objectives of national laws and regulations applying to services and shall take into account the work of relevant international organizations.

The Uruguay Declaration thus establishes three levels of objectives for the negotiations on trade in services. At the operational level, the Declaration states that the negotiations should seek to develop principles and rules for trade in services generally, and that this framework for trade in services should be supplemented by rules that would apply to specific sectors.

This conclusion resolved a major debate over the feasibility and desirability of negotiating trade issues in services as diverse as telecommunications, banking, insurance, professional services, data processing, and transportation, within a common framework. Some argued that each services sector raises unique issues that have nothing in common with other sectors, and that it made no sense to negotiate such issues under the common heading of 'trade in services.' Others argued that many of the principles and rules of the GATT could be applied to trade in services, and that a framework of principles and rules would be more likely to succeed in achieving a broad liberalization of trade in services than would a sector-by-sector approach.

The language in the Uruguay Declaration supports the traditional trade policy view that across-the-board rules are needed to advance the liberalization of trade barriers. At the same time, the Uruguay Declaration recognizes that sectoral differences are more fundamental in services than in goods, and that effective negotiations ultimately have to get down to a sector-by-sector level.

A framework approach puts the emphasis on general economic principles that are difficult to oppose in the abstract. And, once agreed, they can provide a basis for challenging restrictive arrangements that serve narrow sectoral needs and interests. A purely sectoral approach, though, emphasizes what is different about each sector and the unique characteristics in each sector that justify the status quo. A purely sectoral focus would have made it much more difficult to bring out the broader economic reasons why a liberalization of policies would further the public interest. Thus the decision to negotiate a framework first was tied to the broader liberalization objective.

After setting out the operational objectives of the negotiations, the Declaration goes on to state that the purpose of negotiations is to achieve an 'expansion of such trade under conditions of transparency and progressive liberalization. . . .' With this language, the Declaration not only makes it clear that the primary focus of the negotiations should be the expansion of trade in services, but it also lays out a path for pursuing that objective: Establish transparency in policy measures that restrict trade in services and liberalize measures that restrict trade in services. This language resolved the dispute over whether it was appropriate to expand trade in services through liberalization.

Alternative objectives that could have been adopted include an equitable or fair distribution of market shares in world trade in services, the harmonization of national regulations affecting trade in services, and the resolution of regulatory conflicts whenever traded services are subject to overlapping jurisdiction of national regulators.

The statement on objectives also establishes the negotiations 'as a means of promoting economic growth of all trading partners and the development of developing countries.' This language reminds negotiators that the ultimate purpose of their efforts should be to promote economic growth and development. It should also be read as a statement by ministers that liberalization of trade in services and development of a framework of rules for trade in services can advance economic growth, including developing countries.

In the course of the debate over the inclusion of services, the fear was often expressed that a GATT framework agreement on trade in services could undermine national regulatory objectives. The Declaration addresses these concerns by stating that 'such a framework shall respect the policy objectives of national laws and regulations applying to services.' This language spells out the obvious – that any trade arguments on services will have to leave countries enough flexibility to pursue domestic regulatory objectives.

By focusing on the objectives of national laws and regulations rather than the laws and regulations themselves, the language of the Declaration leaves open the possibility that the liberalization of trade might require changes in the way national laws and regulations implement policy objectives. This is a distinction that has become well established in the GATT with respect to the application of technical and regulatory standards to internationally traded goods. The Standards Code, negotiated in the Tokyo Round of Multilateral Trade Negotiations (1973–1979), gives countries the right to pursue national regulatory objectives but requires they pursue them in a manner that minimizes distortions of trade.

Another concern often voiced in the debate over services was that GATT negotiations could conflict with international agreements negotiated in sectoral organizations such as the International Telecommunications Union (ITU). In recognition of this concern the language of the Declaration provides that a framework agreement 'shall take into account the work of relevant international organizations.'

The negotiations will have to address the relation between a trade agreement in services and agreements in telecommunications. Here, too, GATT agreements negotiated in previous rounds of negotiations can serve as useful models. In the area of standards, for example, governments had to define complementary responsibilities for the GATT and the International Standards Organization (ISO). While the challenge to define a division of responsibilities may be greater in services than it was in goods, the language in the Uruguay Declaration is based on the proposition that such a division of responsibilities can and should be worked out.

For the first two years of the negotiations, the negotiating group on services (GNS) focused on the first part of their mandate, namely the development of a multilateral framework of principles and rules for trade in services. This led to a tentative agreement, at a meeting in Montreal in December 1989, on the key elements of a future multilateral framework for trade in services. The meeting brought together ministers for a Midterm Review. The text of the agreement on services does not have the legal precision of a binding agreement and does not contain all the elements of the eventual framework agreement, but it covers most important principles and concepts likely to be incorporated in the framework agreement on trade in services.

The key principles adopted at Montreal include:

- Transparency – full publication of 'all laws, regulations and administrative guidelines relating to services trade.'
- Progressive liberalization – establishes the objective of a progressive reduction of 'the adverse effects of all laws, regulations and administrative guidelines' on trade in services in order 'to provide effective market access.'
- Market access – links achievement of market access to a choice of the preferred mode of delivery (e.g., cross-border delivery of information services through the telecom network, cross-border movements by either a supplier or consumer of services, establishment of production or distribution facilities in the importing country).
- National treatment – foreign services or service providers granted market access under the provisions of the framework agreement on trade in services would be accorded 'treatment no less favorable than that accorded domestic services or services providers . . . in respect to all laws, regulations and administrative practices.'
- Regulation – recognizes the right of countries to introduce regulations for the achievement of national policy objectives, provided such regulations are consistent with the liberalization commitments under the framework.
- Increasing participation of developing countries – addresses the developmental objective of developing countries, including the provision of effective market access for services that can be produced by developing countries.

Most of these principles are derived from general economic or political principles associated with good government. The transparency principle, for example, is based on the notion that one cannot expect producers of services to participate in productive economic activities if they do not know the rules of the game. The national treatment principle states that a commitment to grant foreign providers market access in a certain services activity needs to be buttressed by a commitment to treat domestic and foreign suppliers the same way when applying regulations aimed at domestic regulatory objectives. If the objective of a regulation is to protect a domestic industry from foreign competition rather than to achieve a domestic regulatory objective, then the regulation should be treated as a protective trade measure rather than as a domestic regulatory measure.

Other principles such as right of establishment and labor mobility, which were only indirectly addressed in the Montreal text, deal with how foreign service providers can gain effective market access. Trade in services often requires the establishment of a business facility in the importing country, and the right of establishment would therefore provide a legal basis for securing an essential means for gaining market access. Trade in services in other cases requires travel by professional experts or managers to the importing country, and the right to labor mobility would provide the legal basis for achieving market access in these cases. Adoption of these principles would not prevent governments from creating rules for establishment or labor mobility, but it would explicitly make such rules a legitimate subject of negotiation.

One of the issues that remains unresolved concerns how much the adoption of a multilateral framework will lead to an initial set of binding commitments (i.e., the extent to which the agreed principles are to be applied to regulatory measures affecting international transactions in specific services). The United States has taken the position that the principles in the multilateral framework should bind signatories to all policy measures taken in covered sectors, except insofar as a country chooses to except or reserve a policy measure from the application of the discipline. All exceptions or reservations would subsequently become subject to negotiation as part of a mutual reduction of barriers to trade. Other countries have argued that the principles in the multilateral framework agreement should be treated as objectives, and that they should become binding only insofar as a country agrees to bind specific policy instruments in individual sectors in future negotiations. In either scenario, the creation of the multilateral framework would be followed by negotiations on policy measures.

The text adopted in Montreal also spelled out how the negotiations would proceed over the next two years. It was agreed that the negotiations would turn to a consideration of individual sectors. Since individual sectors in services have many unique characteristics, the general principles will have to be fine-tuned and supplemented for some sectors to make them operationally meaningful. Where such refinements or additions are found to be desirable or necessary, they are likely to be incorporated in sectoral annotations or annexes that would become an integral part of the multilateral framework agreement. Telecommunications is one of the most likely sectors to be covered by such an annex.

Policy measures that affect international transactions in telecommunications, data processing, electronic information services, and related activities will be central to the negotiations on trade in services. Most likely, the full range of services covered by these industries will be treated as a single sector for purposes of carrying out any sectoral reviews and the subsequent negotiation of sectoral annotations. Since the negotiators in Geneva have not gone beyond collecting factual data in individual sectors, it is not possible to be specific about the content of a sectoral annex on telecommunications. Since recent trade agreements on services have included provisions on telecommunications, however, a review of these agreements can shed some light.

The US and Canadian agreement has provided a particularly useful precedent that is likely to influence the negotiation of any telecommunications and information services annex. In many respects it goes beyond what could be negotiated now multilaterally, but many of the principles incorporated in the US and Canadian agreement are likely to be incorporated in a telecommunications annex negotiated in the Uruguay Round.

The telecommunications provisions in the US and Canadian Trade Agreement call for three things. First is non-discriminatory access to, and use of, telecommunications transport services, including: The lease of local and long-distance telephone services; full period flat rate private line service; dedicated intercity voice channels; and public data services for the movement of information including intracorporate communications; the sharing and reselling of telecommunications services; and the purchase or lease of terminal equipment. Second is the maintenance of access for the provision of enhanced telecommunications services through the use of the network and computer services within and across borders of both parties. Third is the assurance that monopolies which also offer enhanced service on a competitive basis do not benefit from unreasonable cross-subsidization or other anti-competitive practices from their related monopoly service activities. Appropriate safeguards such as separate accounting records, sufficient structural separations, and disclosure will be put in place.

In constructing a telecommunications annex to the framework agreement, trade negotiators will need to take account of realities that will influence the telecommunications environment. Telecommunications will be subjected to revolutionary changes in technology and regulation for some time to come. Given the prospect for continuing change, trade negotiators will need to avoid formulating long-term trade agreements on the basis of regulatory terminology currently in fashion. Instead, trade agreements will need to focus on basic principles. Trade agreements will also need to address the process that is followed in making regulatory decisions, with the aim of ensuring that all those with an interest are included in the process.

Another reality is that the pace of regulatory change will differ from country to country and cannot be squeezed into a uniform schedule. Some countries will move faster in opening up telecommunications activities to competition; others will move more slowly. The trade rules that are adopted should accommodate these differences, while at the same time recognizing that differences in regulation create differential rights and obligations. Moreover, for the foreseeable future some telecommunications activities will be reserved for monopolies in a majority of countries, while other telecommunications activities will be open to competition. This calls for generic rules to ensure that competitive or supplier–customer relations between the monopoly suppliers of telecom services and competitive suppliers of related services are fair and market oriented.

Another factor is that telecommunications is becoming an important component in the delivery of services. This has led many vendors to incorporate the telecommunications component in the sale of the services product. Telecom services are thus often part of the package when acquiring services such as electronic information, electronic banking, electronic shopping, and electronic insurance. The same development can be expected to surface with maintenance activities associated with the sale of manufactured products. Trade agreements will have to include principles to help ensure that regulatory decisions in telecommunications do not adversely affect the competitive position of suppliers of non-telecommunications goods and services, while at the same time avoiding a situation where regulators responsible for these non-telecommunications activities get wrapped up in the regulation of telecommunications activities.

Yet another reality is that issues related to standards will be an important area of overlap between regulatory concerns in telecommunications and commercial concerns about the impact of regulatory decisions on trade. Interconnectivity will be a major regulatory concern in the provision of many telecommunications related goods and services, yet the imposition of standards that are too closely tied to certain technologies can be a deterrent to economic innovation and growth. It may be useful to develop guidelines as to when voluntary standards will provide adequate means for ensuring interconnectivity, as against compulsory standards, and to develop an understanding of the procedures followed in setting standards in order to ensure the broadest involvement of all parties with a stake in the development of those standards.

The major objective of a telecommunications annex to the framework agreement on trade in services will be to elaborate the principles and procedures in the framework with respect to telecommunications services. The annex would address the application of the framework principles to the trade interests of three groups: Foreign providers of telecom services that have been opened up to competition according to the progressive liberalization schedule; foreign enterprises that want to use the telecom network to distribute information services such as database or electronic banking; foreign enterprises that use the telecommunications network to transfer data to other facilities of the firm, to outside suppliers, and to customers. The principles of the annex would be binding on all countries that decide to adhere to the framework agreement, though each country could enter a reservation in its liberalization schedule with respect to the application of these principles to specific measures or services.

By drawing on the agreement reached at Montreal with respect to the key principles to be included in the framework agreement and by pulling together the major conclusions of the analysis provided throughout this essay, one could set out some elements of a telecommunications annex. One is *transparency*. The annex could amplify the transparency requirement by extending it to internal regulations and guidelines of telecom monopolies, including accounting procedures designed to separate monopoly business from competitive business, procurement rules, and cost accounting associated with services offered to the public.

Another element of a telecommunications annex is *progressive liberalization*. The annex could tie progressive liberalization of competition (by domestic and foreign enterprises, including liberalized rules for the use of private networks) to phased regulatory reform that could differ from country to country. Each country would be required to agree to a schedule for reforms, depending on its own requirements and legislative procedures. At the same time the agreed schedules would have to result in balanced rights and obligations. Provision could also be made for periodic review and renegotiation of the progressive liberalization schedule. In light of the rapid pace of change in telecommunications technology and regulations, there may have to be more frequent negotiations in telecommunications than in other sectors – for instance, an annual or semi-annual review and negotiating schedule.

The annex could address, in some detail, what *market access* entails in telecommunications. In particular, the annex could address issues such as the right of establishment and the right of non-establishment. Under the right of establishment foreign providers of competitive services covered by the progressive liberalization schedule would have the right to establish local facilities required to produce or distribute the covered services. Under the right of non-establishment, foreign providers of covered services would be allowed to provide services across the border from a foreign location via the telecommunications network, without having to establish local facilities in the importing country.

The annex could spell out the application of the *national treatment* principle to telecom regulations, as they affect the commercial interests of both foreign users and foreign providers of telecommunications services. The annex would extend the national treatment obligations to the actions of regulatory authorities and telecom monopolies. Application of the national treatment principle to the telecom services offered by the monopoly would be linked to a so-called access to the network principle.

The annex could address *access to and use of public network services*. More specifically, the annex could: Guarantee access to services provided exclusively by the telecom monopoly (or monopolies) on reasonable terms and conditions, and to the extent possible, on a cost-justified basis; establish the right to acquire leased lines from the monopoly providers of transmission facilities for the purpose of establishing private, switched networks; permit the interconnection of private networks with other private networks or the public switched network; allow the switching of private networks by foreign firms or by any third parties chosen by the foreign user; allow the acquisition and attachment of equipment to the public network, provided it does not harm the network or users of the network; allow foreign enterprises to use proprietary protocols and communications software, in accordance with their needs and those of their customers; allow foreign firms to process, store, and transfer data across national borders so long as they abide by regulations designed to protect privacy, intellectual property, public safety, and national security.

The annex could establish the legitimacy of *regulation* aimed at the achievement of enumerated objectives, while affirming a commitment to avoid unnecessary distortions with respect to trade in telecommunications network services and the use of the network as a channel for intracorporate and intercorporate data flows.

With regard to *monopoly* considerations, the annex could establish an arm's length relation between the sale of monopoly services and the sale of competitive services by any telecom monopoly. Telecom monopolies would be specifically prohibited from cross-subsidizing competitive activities from the profits generated by the provision of monopoly services. Monopolies would also be required to offer all exclusive telecommunications services on a non-discriminatory basis to all potential customers, including foreign competitors, and to offer these services under the same terms, conditions, and rates available to themselves when they use these services in their competitive businesses.

The annex could provide for an open process of setting *standards* by giving foreign providers of competitive telecom services and foreign users of the telecom network an opportunity to participate in the process. The annex could also establish the principle that standards should be mandatory only to the extent that is necessary for the operation of a public network or for overriding public interest considerations.

The annex will need to deal with the concerns of *developing countries* such as their access to global networks and their need for additional time to meet the liberalization objective.

The annex would also need to spell out the application of *non-discrimination* in telecommunications. Generally, the agreement would guarantee all signatories non-discriminatory treatment with respect to services covered by the agreement. Monopolies would not have automatic rights in foreign markets to services for which they have exclusive rights in their own market, but each country would be allowed to establish ground rules for the participation of foreign monopolies in their market. Each country would also have the right to negotiate preferential agreements with other countries with respect to competition in telecommunications services not covered by the progressive liberalization schedule. Third countries would be given the right to join such agreements on the same terms and conditions.

It is worthwhile, in concluding this essay, to reflect on the impact that GATT's trade negotiations on telecommunications issues have had on the global information industry. First, and foremost, the discussions have constituted a global consciousness-raising effort regarding the trade dimension of information and telecommunications services, and the trade impact of regulatory actions in these areas. Trade officials, and more broadly officials with economic management responsibilities, have been drawn into domestic debates over the future course of regulations affecting these and other service industries. This has made regulatory officials more aware of the broader economic impact of regulatory decisions, and the need to avoid the negative impact of excessively detailed or restrictive regulation on economic innovation and growth.

Many American businessmen deeply involved in these negotiations consider this first impact of the negotiations the most important result in the near term. The new technologies in themselves open up vast new areas for trade in services that are not currently regulated, and so long as the negotiations can slow down the introduction of new regulations that could restrict the introduction of new services, much will already have been accomplished. Beyond this, the involvement of trade officials has helped focus and accelerate the reform of telecom regulations in line with the new technologies.

The GATT negotiations have legitimized the deliberations on policy issues related to international transactions in information and tele-communications services, as well as other services, by trade officials. This represents a revolution in bureaucratic assumptions with regard to policymaking in services. It has moved key regulatory decisions in countries like Japan, Germany, and even the United States toward a pro-market position. While the involvement of US trade policymakers in foreign regulatory decisions in telecommunications is well known, less is known publicly about how US trade officials interact in domestic regulatory decisions.

Finally, the GATT discussions have made it legitimate to address issues related to international transactions on services in bilateral free trade agreements like those between the United States and Canada, the United States and Israel, Australia and New Zealand, and within the European Community. Negotiations on these agreements have paved important new ground with respect to the information and telecom-munications industries. They have reinforced an emerging consensus that telecommunications services should be open to competition and subject to international trade rules. They have also reinforced the view that the impact of telecom regulations on the international delivery of information services is a legitimate subject of trade negotiations.

BIBLIOGRAPHY

Aronson, Jonathan D. (1984) 'Computer, Data Processing, and Communication Services,' in Robert M. Stern (ed.), *Trade and Investment in Service Industries: US–Canadian Bilateral and Multilateral Perspectives.* Toronto: University of Toronto Press, for the Ontario Economic Council.

Aronson, Jonathan D. and Peter F. Cowhey (1984) *Trade in Services: A Case for*

Open Markets. Washington, DC: American Enterprise Institute for Public Policy Research.

Aronson, Jonathan D. and Peter F. Cowhey (1988) *When Countries Talk: International Trade in Telecommunications Services.* Cambridge, MA: Ballinger, for the American Enterprise Institute, Washington, DC.

Bar, Francois and Michael Borrus (1987) 'From Public Access to Private Connections: Network Policy and National Advantage.' Paper presented at the Fifteenth Telecommunications Policy Research Conference, Airlie House, VA., Sept. 27–30, 1987.

Bressand, Albert (1988) 'Computer Reservation Systems: Networks Shaping Markets.' Unpublished paper, Promethe Institute, Paris.

Bruce, Robert R., Jeffrey P. Cunard, and Mark D. Director (1986) *From Telecommunications to Electronic Services.* London: Butterworth for International Institute of Communications.

Bruce, Robert R., Jeffrey P. Cunard, and Mark D. Director (1988) *The Telecom Mosaic.* London: Butterworth for the International Institute of Communications.

Bruce, Robert R. (1988) 'Telecommunications: The Need for a Policy Framework,' in *Keeping Pace: U.S. Policies and Global Economic Change*, edited by John Yochelson. Cambridge, MA: Ballinger, for the Center for Strategic and International Studies.

Business Week (1988) 'Enterprise Networking: Key to Your Company's Future.' Special Supplement, April 11, 1988.

Commission of the European Communities (1987) 'Green Paper on the Development of the Common Market for Telecommunications Services and Equipment.' Brussels.

Crawford, Morris H. (1988) 'EC 1992: The Making of a Common Market in Telecommunications.' Program on Information Resources Policy, Center for Information Policy Research, Harvard University, Cambridge, MA.

Dizard, Wilson P. and Lesley D. Turner (1987) 'Telecommunications and the U.S.–Canada Free Trade Talks.' Paper published by the International Communications Project of the Center for Strategic and International Studies, Washington, DC (mimeo).

Dunn, Donald A. and Octavio Sampaio (1988) 'Pricing Interchange Access,' Center for Economic Policy Research, Stanford University (mimeo).

The Economist (1985) 'The World on the Line,' Nov. 23, 1985.

Feketekuty, Geza and Jonathan Aronson (1984) 'Meeting the Challenges of the World Information Economy,' *The World Economy* 7, pp. 63–86.

Feketekuty, Geza (1987) 'Trade Policy Objectives in Telecommunications.' Paper published by the International Telecommunications Union in connection with the Legal Symposium of Telecom 87, a conference organized by the International Telecommunications Union in Geneva, Switzerland in October, 1987.

Feketekuty, Geza (1988) 'Telecommunications and Trade: Implications for GATT and ITU,' in *Transnational Data Report*, May.

Feketekuty, Geza (1988) *International Trade in Services: An Overview and Blueprint for Negotiations.* Cambridge, MA: Ballinger.

Feketekuty, Geza (1989) 'International Network Competition in Telecommunications,' in *Electronic Highways for World Trade; Issues in Telecommunications and Data Services*. (Edited by Peter Robinson, Karl Sauvant, and Vishwas P. Govitrikar as part of the Atwater Series on the World Information Economy.) Boulder, Colorado Westview Press for the Atwater Institute, Montreal, Canada.

Forester, Tom (ed.) (1985) *The Information Technology Revolution*. Cambridge, MA: MIT Press.

GATT (1989) 'Trade in Telecommunications Services.' Restricted Background Paper prepared by the Secretariat for the Group of Negotiations on Services.

Gilhooly, Dennis (1988) 'Commercial Common Carriers: Too Little, Too Late?'. Paper presented at the IIC Telecommunications Forum, held in Brussels, Belgium, July 14–15, 1988.

Gilhooly, Dennis (1988) 'Unlocking the Network: Can Open Network Provision Create Real Competition in Services?' *Communications Week International*, July 1988.

International Telecommunications Union (1988) 'ITU–GATT Consultations on Trade in Services and Telecommunications.' An unpublished paper prepared by ITU staff for consultations with the Group for Negotiations on Services, which is carrying out negotiation on trade in services within the umbrella of the Uruguay Round of Multilateral Trade Negotiations.

Jussawalla, Meheroo (1987) 'The Information Revolution and its Impact on the World Economy.' Paper prepared for the international seminar, Toward an International Service and Information Economy: A New Challenge for the Third World, sponsored by the Friedrich Ebert Foundation, mimeo, publication forthcoming.

Jussawalla, Meheroo and Chee-Wah Cheah (1987) *The Calculus of International Communications*. Littleton, CO: Libraries Unlimited.

Komatsuzaki, Seisuke (1988) 'A Summary of Questionnaire Survey on Deregulation/Regulation Situations in Telecommunications Services Area in 33 Countries.' Unpublished paper prepared by a research group at the Research Institute of Telecom Policies and Economics, Tokyo, Japan.

Mestmaecker, E.-J. (1987) 'Toward a New Regime for International Telecommunications.' Paper presented to the Legal Symposium, Part III, 5th World Telecommunications Forum, Geneva, Switzerland, October 21–3 , 1987.

Noam, Eli M. (1987) 'The Public Telecommunications Network: A Concept in Transition.' *Journal of Communication* 37, 1, Winter 1987.

Organization for Economic Cooperation and Development (1979) 'The Usage of International Data Networks in Europe.' Study prepared by Logica Limited, London for the Information, Computer, Communications Policy Committee, Paris.

Organization for Economic Cooperation and Development (1980) Policy Implications of Data Network Developments in the OECD Area. Papers presented at a working session of the Information, Computer, Communications Policy Committee, Paris.

Organization for Economic Cooperation and Development (1983) 'Transborder Data Flows in International Enterprises' (DSTI/ICCP/82.23). A report issued by the Information, Computer, Communications Policy Subcommittee of the Industry, Science and Technology Committee.

Organization for Economic Cooperation and Development (1983) *Telecommunications: Pressures and Policies for Change*. Paris.

Organization for Economic Cooperation and Development (1985) 'Trade in ICC Services: The Impact of Changing Market Structures in Telecommunications Services on Equipment Trade.' ICCP (85) 14. Paris.

Organization for Economic Cooperation and Development (1987) *Elements of a Conceptual Framework for Trade in Services*. Paris.

Organization for Economic Cooperation and Development (1988) 'Telecommunications Network-Based Services: Implications for Telecommunications Policy' (ICCP/87.5). Paper prepared by the Secretariat for the Committee for Information, Computer and Communications Policy.

Organization for Economic Cooperation and Development (1988) 'Trade in Telecommunications Network-Based Services' DSTI/ICCP/TISP/88-2. Paris.

Pipe, Russ (1987) 'The Ultimate Bypass.' August 1, 1987 issue of *Datamation*.

Pipe, Russ (1988) 'ITU–GATT Relations: How Tradeable are Telecom Services?' November, 1988 issue of *Transnational Data Report* XI, 9.

Pipe, Russ (1989) 'Telecommunications Services: Considerations for Developing Countries in Uruguay Round Negotiations.' Study prepared for the UN Conference on Trade and Development, Geneva (Project INT/88/020-1104).

Quinn, James Brian (1988) 'Services Technology and Manufacturing: Cornerstones of the U.S. Economy,' in *Managing Innovation: Cases from the Services Industries*, edited by Bruce R. Guile and James Brian Quinn, Washington, DC: National Academy Press.

Raavendran, Laina 'What is Trade in Telecommunications Services?: Are We Asking the Right Questions?'. Unpublished Paper by author who is associated with the ITU in Geneva.

Rada, Juan F. (1987) 'Information Technology and Services,' in Orlo Giarini (ed.) *The Emerging Service Economy*. Oxford: Pergamon Press for the Services World Forum, Geneva.

Rein, Bert W., Danny E. Adams, Carl Frank, Bruce McDonald, and Robert E. Nielson (1985) 'Implementation of a U.S. "Free Entry" Initiative for Transatlantic Satellite Facilities: Problems, Pitfalls, and Possibilities.' *The Georgetown Journal of International Law and Economics* 18, 3, 1985.

Robinson, Peter (1987) 'An International Policy Framework for Trade in Services and Data Services: The Current Debate in International Organizations.' Paper prepared for an International Seminar, Toward an International Service and Information Economy: A New Challenge for the Third World, sponsored by the Friedrich Ebert Foundation.

Roseman, Daniel (1988) 'Towards a New International Framework for Telecommunications and Information Services: Issues and Prospects.' Unpublished paper prepared for the Institute for Research on Public Policy, Ottawa, Canada.

Rubin, Michael Rosers (1986) 'US Information Economy Matures.' *Transnational Data and Communication Report*. June 1986 issue.

Sauvant, Karl P. (1986) *International Transactions in Services: The Politics of Transborder Data Flows*. The Atwater Series on The World Information Economy No. 1, Boulder: The Westview Press for the Atwater Institute.

Services Policy Advisory Committee to the U.S. Trade Representative (1987) *Telecommunications and Information Services in the Trade in Services Negotiations: An Industry View.* Washington, DC: Office of the US Trade Representative.

Snow, Marcellus S. and Meheroo Jussawalla (1986) *Telecommunications Economics and International Regulatory Policy: Annotated Bibliography.* New York: Greenwood Press.

Epilogue: Communications policy in crisis

W. Russell Neuman

One effect of the explosive growth of new communications technologies over the past twenty years has been a rather dramatic disruption of established business practices in the industry. Technological change has also made obsolete the 1934 Communications Act which established the Federal Communications Commission (FCC) and the basic principles of telecommunications and spectrum regulation in the United States. Communications lawyers and lobbyists are delighted, and very busy. Scholars in the field of communications policy relish the opportunity to witness and analyze history in the making.

But others are not so pleased. The FCC and communications subcommittees in the Senate and House are frustrated by the hectic rush to put out regulatory fires without the time to put the technological, regulatory, and social needs in perspective and develop an integrated legislative response. Industry executives are nearly paralyzed because the regulatory uncertainty makes long-term planning very difficult. At the same time, both European and Asian nations are redoubling efforts and investment in communications technologies at home and, where it is not expressly forbidden, buying a controlling interest in strategic chunks of the American communications infrastructure.

To understand the crisis and the current needs for communications policy research, it may be helpful briefly to review a timeline of technological innovations in communications. The fundamental technology of high speed printing was perfected in the early 1830s and the corresponding business practices and economics of the newspaper, magazine, and book industries have been relatively stable for the last century and a half. After a wild period of competitive telephony, the basic technological and regulatory architecture of the American telephone system was crystalized by the Kingsbury Commitment of 1912 and the near-monopoly of AT&T. Radio broadcasting was initiated in the early 1920s and television broadcasting in the late 1940s under a principle of minimal regulatory constraint and licensed access to the spectrum by a mixture of commercial and educational entities. Once established, each of these industries defined a unique and fundamentally non-competing marketplace for its services. The technology in each case was mature and stable. Because of limited entry of competitors due to a reinforcing mixture of regulatory, spectrum, and scale-economy factors, these industries grew to be quite profitable with returns on investment well above the overall industrial average.

THE INDUSTRIAL CRISIS

By the 1970s, the growth of cable TV, satellite communication, and high-speed computing began to disrupt the existing structure. The first effect of these new technologies was to begin to break down the long-standing barriers to competitive entry within industry sectors. New companies aggressively sought regulatory approval to connect with the existing telephone network and to compete with it first for specialized services and shortly thereafter for traditional long-distance carriage. Cable companies got their start by simply carrying over-the-air TV signals to neighboring communities unable to receive regular broadcasts because of distance or geography. But in the late 1970s they discovered that they could receive national programming by satellite and compete virtually head-to-head with over-the-air broadcasting. The second level effect was a gradual blurring of the boundaries between what were previously non-competitive industries. At the moment, for example, the telephone industry is aggressively pursuing regulatory approval to carry television programming and compete directly with cable and broadcast television.

   Firms have adopted a variety of strategies for coping with the new competitive threats and opportunities. Some have turned to government and lobbied for protection from competition. Some have opted for the traditional strategy of buying out competitors and pursuing significant vertical and/or horizontal integration. Others have invested in developing a competitive advantage through proprietary technology. Still others have adopted a wait-and-see or mixed strategy. Each industrial sector – broadcasting, publishing, and telecommunications – is still thriving and quite profitable. But it is increasingly recognized that in ten to twenty years these industries will be transformed and integrated into a single all-electronic, all-digital broadband network, in effect, an 'information fabric' for the switched delivery of voice, text, high resolution graphics, and high resolution video. These changes will also draw a significant portion of the computer industry into the fray.

INTERNATIONAL ISSUES

As part of the general trend toward an integrated global economy, advanced communications is a focal point of international economic competition and strategic trade disputes. For example, trade in services including telecommunications services were once the focus of the Uruguay Round of GATT multilateral trade liberalization negotiations. The foreign policy and social impact of global communication is also substantial. Given the fast-paced integration of Germany and the European Community and the fragmentation of the Soviet bloc, US participation and goals in international organizations must be reassessed. The roles in the global information economy of various international organizations as well as regional standards agencies (not to mention global/multinational/local corporations and private standards alliances) are all being questioned. Getting the international communications policymaking process right for the 1990s is a significant challenge and would certainly benefit from independent academic research on these critical issues.

THE KEY COMMUNICATIONS POLICY ISSUES FOR THE 1990s

The following are some of the key underlying communications policy issues that dominate the 1990s. This list, by its nature, can be neither exhaustive nor very well developed. My purpose is only to outline some of the most pressing problems with an eye to how research in these areas could enhance our ability to take advantage of what the new technologies might offer. The list is for the United States but, as we have seen in this volume, the issues have a way of quickly crossing national boundaries. In a real sense this is a world agenda, reflecting common problems.

Deregulation

The Kingsbury Commitment self-destructed on January 1, 1984. Legally, this was a modification of a 1950s antitrust judgment against AT&T. But in reality, it was the most dramatic of about a dozen changes in the technical and regulatory architecture of the American telephone network made over the span of two decades. The parallel deregulation of broadcasting is more complex and less dramatic but equally important. The justification for regulation in both cases was the natural monopoly (and limited spectrum) character of the dominant technologies. New competing delivery systems and the need for interconnection, made 'free market competition' a newly viable alternative to constraints of traditional bureaucratic regulatory structures. The difficulty is that we now have a fast-evolving network architecture and no architect. Furthermore, many elements of the network, such as the local exchange carriers and cable providers, effectively are still local monopolies which will require some regulatory oversight. It is critically important that independent, carefully conducted academic research on the costs and benefits of alternative regulatory strategies be made available to industry and government.

Spectrum regulation

The more efficient use of the spectrum, the effective use of higher frequencies within the electromagnetic spectrum, and the refinement of electronic and optical cable technologies may mean that the era of spectrum scarcity has passed. But that does not translate into a complete free-for-all of unregulated spectrum use. The flexible and efficient allocation of spectrum at a time when many new services are being proposed and old ones being reorganized will require a major effort of technologically sophisticated policy research.

Rate regulation

Because monopoly provision of communications services will no doubt be with us for some time, advanced procedures such as 'price-cap' regulatory structures will need to be explored and researched, so that the monopoly components of the communications architecture can keep up with the fast pace of technological advance in the non-regulated sectors.

Content regulation

There was a time, some years ago, when several prominent scholars speculated that content regulation would no longer be necessary because enhanced technology and new competition would make the need for such delicate matters as the FCC's Fairness and Equal Time Doctrines a thing of the past. We have moved, however, in quite the opposite direction. With enhanced information and entertainment services in telecommunications, state and federal regulators are forced to confront content limitations in telephony and other media. Because of continued problems of competition and monopoly control in the domain of broadcasting and electronic publishing, we find that content regulation is still a very active and important area. It is complicated further now by issues of intellectual property protection. In each case, policy research requires a thorough understanding of the changing character of the electronic storage, switching, and transmission technologies.

Equity issues

There is growing concern that if we are not careful, the fast pace of technological change in the information and communications industries may leave a large stratum of our society isolated from the electronic flow of information. The principles of universal service, information access, and an open marketplace of ideas may be lost in the complexities of inter-industry negotiations. It is an especially appropriate research focus for academic work.

Privacy and security issues

The pervasiveness of electronic communications and the interoperability of digital networks raise new questions about the balance of citizen privacy concerns and an efficient, convenient, and secure network for communications and economic transactions. The capacity of advanced systems to encrypt successfully electronic data transmissions will probably solve part of the problem. More difficult policy questions will concern rights of access to the accumulating economic databases, which are a by-product of electronic transactions, and protections against misuse.

Education and training

In an integrated global economy characterized by a continuous communications flow and capital mobility, the relative skill level (and motivation) of workers becomes a paramount determinant of economic performance. The quality of life and standard of living is also of course affected by education and job satisfaction. Communication and information technologies and services may enhance the quality and extend the availability of educational services. But numerous policy issues must be addressed to realize these possibilities.

Industrial rivalries

The pattern of recent years has been for interested corporations and industry associations to fund economic and policy research in an effort to win a favorable regulatory ruling or to win a debate in a technical standards forum. That will and should continue. But the need for independent, academically grounded research of significant scale and scope should provide additional and non-adversarial input into the technology policy and standards negotiations processes.

Free markets versus core infrastructure

One view, most often expressed by economists, is that the development of new communications technologies and services is best left to the private sector without any involvement of government agencies in an attempt to 'pick winners' or determine an 'industrial policy.' It is an important argument and has characterized the American policy in this area for many years.

The difficulty is that the free market ideology applies most appropriately to competitive commodity markets. The nature of the integrated network and the increasing importance of generic digital imaging and communications technologies requires a fundamental rethinking of these issues. The electronic network is the core infrastructure of the information economy. The natural concern of the government with the postal and transportation infrastructure as necessary to commerce becomes increasingly appropriately applied to communications. There were few objections when the 1934 Communications Act restricted the foreign ownership of the American broadcasting and telecommunications infrastructure. How these principles should be applied to the newly evolving technologies is a difficult question.

THE CHANGING FUNCTIONS OF COMMUNICATIONS MEDIA

The transition from separate industries of telecommunications, computing, broadcasting, and publishing into an integrated digital network will need to draw on more than the fields of policy, economics, and technologically focused research. This transition is not like the shift from black and white to color broadcasting in which the basic functions and social role of television remained unchanging while the technology advanced. In this case, how the media will be used for home shopping, two-way and interactive video communications, computer intensive education, distance education, as well as the human complexities of networked MIS and CAD-CAM in the commercial world, present very difficult problems for human factors and psychologically grounded research. Videophone and videotex are examples of very promising technologies which ran into insurmountable human factors and marketing problems. What is needed is more than narrowly focused, proprietary, product testing. The industry could benefit greatly from a significant scale, academic, public research program on the human factors and human use issues of advanced imaging and communications systems.

INTERNATIONAL CONCERNS

Finally, I note that each of the above issues is intertwined with questions of national economic productivity, equitable trade relationships, and the global balance of power. If current trends continue, the United States and some other established industrial economies may well find themselves in the position of an underdeveloped colony, exporting raw materials and importing manufactured ones. Advanced electronics and communications clearly will affect economic competitiveness and international trade. The content of international communication including, for example, telephone conversations, Hollywood films, television news, and business and consumer information services, may also affect the emerging global networked society. Questions of international scope represent an important element of a coordinated research effort in advanced communications technology and policy.

This volume draws together the perspectives and experience of a mixture of academic researchers and industry experts. There is a shared sense of crisis and of opportunity. It is fitting, perhaps, that we conclude with an agenda for further research.

Glossary

ADAPSO	Was the Association of Data Processing Service Organizations. This American-based group recently changed its name to the Computer Software and Services Industry Association
ATV	Advanced television
Bell Operating Companies	The local service networks once part of the overall Bell (AT&T) system but independent after 1984. Also known as Regional Bell Operating Companies (RBOCs) and Regional Holding Companies (RHCs)
Bell System	AT&T before the divestiture decision
BT	British Telecom
CCIR	International Radio Consultative Committee
CPE	Customer premises equipment
DBS	Direct broadcast satellite
DTI	Department of Trade and Industry (of the United Kingdom)
FCC	Federal Communications Commission, a federal level regulatory agency in the United States
FTS	The Federal Telecommunications System, the United States government's private telephone network
ISDN	Integrated Services Digital Network
ITA	International Trade Administration, a component agency of the United States Department of Commerce

LATA	Local Access Transport Area. The local exchange can consist of one or more LATAs
LEC	Local exchange carrier
MFJ	Modified Final Judgment, the ruling in 1982 of the Federal District Court for the District of Columbia that required the breakup of the Bell System in the United States. The modification was to a previous antitrust judgment (1954) involving the Bell System
MITI	Ministry of International Trade and Industry, the Japanese government ministry in charge of economic promotion activities
NTIA	National Telecommunications and Information Administration, a component agency of the United States Department of Commerce
Oftel	The Office of Telecommunications, a British government regulatory agency
ONA	Open Network Architecture, which would give communications service providers equal access interconnections with the basic telephone network
PBX	Private branch exchange
POTS	Plain old telephone service
P&T	Post and Telecommunications Authority
PTT	Post, Telegraph and Telecommunications Authority
RBOCs	Regional Bell Operating Companies – the Bells
RHCs	Regional Holding Companies – the Bells once again
VAN	Value-added network
Yellow Pages	The local commercial, as opposed to the residential, telephone listing in the United States and Great Britain. It has the potential of producing a large source of revenue due to the fact that it contains paid advertisements

Index